Praise for Always Another Country

'Sisonke Msimang's *Always Another Country* is my favourite kind of memoir, so lyrical and dreamlike that it reads like a novel. It's an artful meditation on exile and return, womanhood and motherhood unfolding against the backdrop of post-apartheid South African politics'

TAIYE SELASI, author of *New York Times* bestseller *Ghana Must Go*

'Sisonke Msimang kindles a new fire in our store of memoir, a fire that will warm and singe and sear for a long, long while'

NJABULO S. NDEBELE, author of *Fools and Other Stories* and *The Cry of Winnie Mandela*

'If you read Sisonke Msimang's memoir you go on a brave and intimate journey with her. Msimang delivers a deep call for fierce courage in the face of hypocrisy and, no matter where we come from or where we go, compassion in the face of our shared humanity'

YEWANDE OMOTOSO, author of *Bom Boy* and *The Woman Next Door*

'Brutally and uncompromisingly honest, Sisonke's beautifully crafted storytelling enriches the already extraordinary pool of young African women writers of our time'

GRAÇA MACHEL

'A lyrical and admirably subtle exploration of how elusive our place in the world is: a reader's delight'

EUSEBIUS MCKAISER, author of *Run, Racist, Run*

'Like many exiles, Msimang has a yearning for stability, and her energetic and emotive narration add intimacy and poignancy to her recollections. An irresistible read'

Farmer's Weekly

'Msimang animates each locale with the kind of deft precision that make the cities, towns and countries characters unto themselves. Msimang's debut memoir is triumphant mostly because it is beautiful and honest'
The Con Magazine

'Sisonke Msimang's book has joined the chorus of black women who have used memoir and autobiography to tell their stories in order to defy the erasure of their lives and significance. If you appreciate the dance between memory, fiction, history and nostalgia (with a dash of vulnerability for good measure), *Always Another Country* is highly recommended'
ATHAMBILE MASOLA, *Mail & Guardian*

'The story is riveting and keeps you wanting to dip back in for more. The use of language is a formidable force to be reckoned with – sentences are skillfully, beautifully con-structed and I often found myself going back to be lost in pull of the words'
Nasty Women

'Filled with love, hope, uncertainty, and dreams, Msimang takes us on a journey through Zambia, Kenya, Canada, the USA, to South Africa in the 1990s. The book is a tribute to her parents whose love for each other and their family glows through the pages'
Writers Write

Always
Another
Country

Sisonke Msimang

Always Another Country

A Memoir of Exile and Home

WORLD EDITIONS
New York, London, Amsterdam

Published in the USA in 2018 by World Editions LLC, New York
Published in the UK in 2018 by World Editions LTD, London

World Editions
New York/London/Amsterdam

Printed by Sheridan, Chelsea, MI, USA

This book is memoir. Some names and identifying details have been
changed to protect the privacy of individuals. Some events have been
compressed and of course the dialogue I quote as verbatim could not
possibly have transpired exactly as I have committed it to the page.
Still, I have done my best to ensure this book represents the truth as
I know it.

British Library Cataloguing-in-Publication Data
A catalogue record for this book is available on request from the
British Library.

ISBN 978-1-64286-000-9

First published in South Africa in 2017 by Jonathan Ball Publishers

Twitter: @WorldEdBooks
Facebook: WorldEditionsInternationalPublishing
www.worldeditions.org

For Mummy

Contents

Prologue

THESE STORIES BEGIN with the tale of a young man. One winter's morning in 1962, in anger and exhausted by the condition of being black, he joins an illegal army. The following year, he slips out of the country. The year after this, his leader Nelson Mandela is captured and tried for sabotage. In that trial, Mandela faces a life sentence but his bravery does not flag. Instead he rises to the occasion and utters the famous words 'I am the first accused,' and the world taken note as it watches an African man stand firm in the face of almost-certain death.

By the time Mandela appears before the judge to answer to sabotage charges in 1963 – by the time he has said he is prepared to die for the struggle against white domination – the young man who will one day be my father has fled the country and has already been in Russia for a year, learning how to shoot a gun and decipher Morse code. Like other recruits, he leaves without saying goodbye to his parents or his cousins or his best friend. He wakes up, after months of careful and near-solitary planning, and disappears into the mist. A decade later, he is in Lusaka. After leaving the Patrice Lumumba Friendship University in Moscow, he goes to Tanzania where he works alongside other comrades to establish a military base. He travels to Guinea-Bissau and stands alongside Amílcar Cabral's forces staring down the Portuguese on the frontlines. By the time he reaches Lusaka, the man is no longer so young and has seen friends die.

He meets a pretty young Swazi woman who is pursuing her studies. That woman becomes his wife and, eventually, my mother. She loves him, although she is ambivalent about his revolution. She is smart enough to mistrust wolves in revolutionary clothing but wise enough only to air her scepticism in private.

Together Mummy and Baba travel the world. My sisters and I are born in the 1970s, when my parents live in Zambia, where the African National Congress (ANC) has its headquarters. From there we move to Kenya, and then to Canada, then back to Kenya and after that there is a brief stint in Ethiopia. Eventually, after Nelson Mandela is released from prison in 1990, we come home.

My sisters and I are freedom's children, born into the ANC and nurtured within a revolutionary community whose sole purpose is to fight apartheid. We are raised on a diet of communist propaganda and schooled in radical Africanist discourse, in the shadows of our father's hope and our mother's practicality.

On the playground we cradle imaginary AK-47s in our skinny arms and, instead of Cops and Robbers, we play Capitalists and Cadres. When we skip rope, we call out the names of our heroes to a staccato beat punctuated by our jumps: 'Govan Mbeki,' hop, skip, 'Walter Sisulu,' skip, hop:

'One!' Jump.
'Day!' Jump.
'We!' Jump.
'Will!' Jump.
'All!' Jump.
'Be!' Jump.
'Freeeeee!'

South Africa is now free and those of us who care about the country are coming to see that the dream of freedom was a sort of home for us. It was a castle we built in the air and inside its walls every one of us was a hero. When we first returned from exile the castle stayed firmly in our mind's eye. We told ourselves we were special and we sought to build a Rainbow Nation. We knew South Africa was a complicated and brutal place and not just a country for dreamers, but this did not stop us from dreaming.

Today, South Africa is politically adrift. Many of us – the ones who went into exile, the ones who were imprisoned, the ones who lost loved ones to the bullets of the white minority regime – are unsure about our place in the country, and uncertain of South Africa's role in the world. People used to point to South Africa to demonstrate that good can triumph over evil. We used to be proud of ourselves. Today, suffering and poverty – once noble – are not only commonplace (they have always been), but acceptable. We no longer rage against them. We have come to look past the pain of black people because it is now blacks who are in charge. The wretchedness of apartheid is ostensibly over, so the suffering of blacks, under the rule of other blacks, is somehow less sinister – which does not change the fact of its horror.

So, here we are: Nelson Mandela is dead and so are Walter Sisulu and Govan Mbeki. Lillian Ngoyi and Ruth First and Fatima Meer and Neville Alexander and Dennis Brutus and a whole raft of great women and men who stood for and embodied a more just humanity are all gone. In their place is a new country, one that is ordinary and disappointing even as it has its moments of startling and shiny brilliance.

The South Africa I had imagined as a child was a place of triumph, a crucible out of which a more dignified humanity would emerge. My parents were freedom fighters, so they cast our journeys around the world as part of a necessary sacrifice. Our suffering was noble. South Africa would one day be great because the indignities meted out to us were teaching us to abhor injustice, in order to inoculate us against inequality.

And yet here we stand in a South Africa that is free but not just. For me, this is perhaps the most difficult fact of all to accept. It is hard to say, but I am coming to understand that perhaps it is true – that heroism is impossible to sustain during ordinary times. When the guns died down and the smoke cleared we discovered we were not exceptional. All along, we had been only human. This may be a message I have been fighting my whole life. I have always been a believer and the thing that I have believed in more than anything else has been the South Africans' ability to triumph over apartheid. I have not had much of a faith in God, but I have been guided by a belief in humanity – in the leadership of the

ANC, in my parents, in the collective of South Africans of all races to be better than their circumstances dictated. I believed in all these things until apartheid ended and, if I am to be honest, even though the past two decades have been disappointing in many ways, I am grateful that my wide-eyed wonder has been tested. For what is life if we live it only in a dreamlike state, believing what we are told and not knowing what is there in plain sight for us to see? In South Africa, the past twenty years have taught me that some people are complicated, that they will disappoint you and that you will love them still. It has taught me that some people are unrepentant and will never be sorry and that there is a place for them here, too, because history tells us grace is more important than righteousness; that uneasy peace is better than war.

In spite of what it stole from me – many of the securities usually associated with home, my ability to speak my mother tongue, access to aunts and cousins and nephews and neighbours whom I may have been able to call friends – exile was my parents' greatest gift. Still, reft of a physical place in this world I could call home, exile made me love the idea of South Africa. I was bottle-fed the dream: that South Africa was not simply about non-racialism and equality, it was about something much more profound. When you are a child who grows up in exile as I did, when you are a refugee or a migrant, or someone whose path is not straightforward, you quickly learn that belonging is conjunctive: you will only survive if you master the words 'if,' 'and,' 'but,' 'either' and 'both'. You learn that you will be fine for as long as you believe in the collective, your tribe. Trusting them, and knowing they have your best interests at heart, is crucial for survival.

You belong and you stay close that you may live. I grew up believing in heroes, so the past decade of watching the moral decline of the political party to which I owe much of who I am has been hard. My idols have been smashed and I have been bewildered and often deeply wounded by their conduct. I have asked myself whether I was wrong to have believed in them in the first place. I have wondered whether it was all a lie. I have chastised myself. Perhaps I was simply a foolish child.

If I were given five minutes with my younger self – that little girl who cried every time it was time to leave for another country – I would hold her tight and not say a word. I would just be still and have her feel my beating heart, a thud to echo her own. I would do this in the hopes that the solidity of who I am today may serve as some sort of reassurance, a silent message that, no matter the outcome, she would survive and be stronger and happier than she might think as she stood at the threshold of each new country.

This – I think – is all she would need: a message so she may know the road is long, the answers incomplete and the truth fractured and, yes, still worth every tear and scrape, every bruise and stitch. I would hold her in her woundedness and her pretending and in her striving and her need, and hope she might learn on her own and without too much heartbreak what I know now, which is that her own instincts will be her best comfort and, time and again, her heart her will be her saviour.

This book is both personal and political – it is about how I was made by the liberation struggle and how I was broken by its protagonists and how, like all of us trying to find our way in South Africa, I am piecing myself back together so that never again will I feel I need a hero. I've written this book because too few of us – women, refugees, South Africans, black people, queers – believe in our instincts enough to know that our hearts will be our saviours.

Burley Court

WHEN I WAS LITTLE, we stayed in a series of flats. First it was Burley Court, then some apartments near the University Teaching Hospital and then a small complex in a neighbourhood called Woodlands. The one imprinted on my mind is Burley Court – perhaps because it was the biggest, perhaps because it was the one Mummy spoke of the most. Burley Court was just off Church Road, which was a busy street close to the centre of Lusaka. The residents of Burley Court were part of a new generation of urban Africans who were not concerned with what whites thought of them. Each block smelled like *kapenta* fish and frying meat. As you walked past open doors and windows you could hear the tinny sounds of Thomas Mapfumo's 'Matiregerera Mambo' or the elegant chords of Letta Mbulu's 'There's Music in the Air'.

Like most kids in newly independent Zambia, I was born free and so carried myself like a child who had every reason to believe she was at the centre of the universe. Our parents also conducted themselves with an unmistakable air of self-assurance. They behaved as though the ground beneath their feet was theirs and the sun in the sky had risen purely for their benefit; as though the trees were green simply to please them. They laboured under the merry illusion that the Copperbelt three hundred kilometres north of Lusaka would power their gleaming futures forever more. They believed they would have the kind of wealth that generations before them had been unable to attain, shackled as they had been to a colonial yoke. They thought – naively, with hindsight – that their own children might become doctors and lawyers and mining magnates. They were innocents, you see. Though they were grown men and women at Independence, their liberation had come in the heady times before the price of copper plummeted, before the plunging currency brought them to their knees and made them beg for reprieve. When I was little the adults in my life were still buoyed by the idea that they had found their place in the sun.

Each morning the men who were breadwinners in our flats left for their government jobs. Their wives waved them off because they were almost middle class and had been persuaded to believe in the curious colonial set-up in which women stayed home and took care of the children and behaved as though this precluded them from other forms of economic labour. Housebound – but assisted by poorly paid housegirls – they turned to idle gossip and raucous laughter. They shelled peanuts and tightened their *chitenges* and prepared meals fit for their husbands, who were little kings in their own homes. The men for whom these women preened and clucked returned at dusk, striding with great purpose towards their families, making their way to tables laden with *nsima* and meat stews, to smiling wives whose middles were slowly broadening as they settled into city living, and children brimming with book learning and shiny with achievement.

Mummy talked about Burley Court with such rich memories – about how, every afternoon, once their homework was done, the Burley Court children ran up and down the polished concrete stairwells of Building One or Building Three. In her recollection, we were a rowdy crew of polyglots who screamed in Nyanja and Bemba and saved English for the best insults. Terrence, a beanpole of a kid with a Zambianised British accent, was the most eloquent of us all. He would fire off jokes veiled as insults that were halfway threats to whomever happened to catch his eye.

'You! Your legs are so thin. Eh! Please eat so that I can beat you nicely and not worry about breaking you! Isn't it that every night when your mother calls you upstairs for food she just pretending? How can you be eating and still staying so thin-thin like this?' Terrence himself was long and bony with skin that looked as though it had never been near a jar of Vaseline, let alone lotion, yet somehow he had the market cornered on skinny jokes.

I was not as brave as Terrence. I understood perfectly well that I was an easy target. I spoke Nyanja – though not as fluently as the rest because I was not Zambian. This meant that, although I had all the hallmarks and memories of an insider, I wasn't one. I could not afford to make the same kinds of jokes. I tended towards the middle of the pack because I knew I was vulnerable. The wrong joke about the wrong child, and the pack could turn against me. Laughter can dry up quickly when you are a child: one minute you are making the gang howl, and the next you are in tears because someone has called you a refugee.

I had to choose how I would distinguish myself and I knew that it had to be safe.

So, I never joined Terrence in his attacks and I never laughed too heartily. I was simply one of the pack – playing hopscotch on the bumpy pavement in front of the steps of Building One in the evenings as twilight settled on the city and cars whizzed past. No one would have thought to look twice at me, nor at my little toddling sisters. We were children like all others; our skinny arms flew and our brown legs kicked high into the air. It was the same, evening after evening: we jumped and landed, threw the stones further and faster, desperate to get in one last skip before we were called inside.

◆ ◆ ◆

There were three of us. I was the first. Then came Mandlesilo, born in 1977 when I was already three, and then Zengeziwe, who followed in 1979. As a child, Mandla was stubborn in the way that middle children must be if they are to survive childhood emotionally intact. She was quiet in a manner more thoughtful than it was shy. She also cried easily – a trait that has followed her into adulthood and which has a great deal to do with the fact that she is the kindest and most sensitive among us. Wedged between an overbearing older sister and a younger sibling who never met a show she couldn't steal,

Mandla was our conscience, the moral ballast that kept us out of trouble simply by virtue of her own principles. Zeng and I would happily have hidden our crimes from our parents, but Mandla wouldn't let us. She preferred that we not sin in the first place.

Zeng was a crowd-pleaser and remains one today. She was the kind of baby who woke up singing and then gurgled her way through the day, a sweet manipulator whose every sin you forgave because she was too brazen and too gorgeous to resist. This has been her enduring trait. She makes you laugh until your belly aches, even as you know you ought to be weeping with the knowledge that she is not as happy as she seems and is far more complex than she would have the world believe.

As children we were moon-faced and medium brown with plaited hair and ashy knees. We were observant and thus preternaturally sarcastic. We wisecracked our way through breakfast and joked through lunch and told hilarious stories as we played in the dimming light. And because the world was not yet cruel we were innocent in a way that softened our repartee.

Bath time was special. In the tub, Mummy often teased us about our dirty fingernails and scraped knees, about our blistered palms and our chapped feet. She would run a wet cloth over our torsos and soap our backs wondering aloud how we got so filthy. 'And this cut?' she would ask in an exaggerated voice. 'Where did this one come from?' She would wag a finger playfully and smile. Her staged anger made us laugh and her delighted voice was like honey in warm water. We knew that other mothers hated it when their kids came home with torn dungarees and bloody knees, so Mummy's revelling in our constant state of raggedness was a novelty of which we never tired.

Mummy loved the small casualties of childhood that marked our bodies. She was riveted by our stories – playground triumphs and the physical indignities of falling and getting scratched – because she knew that the little dings and nicks on our bodies would forge our personalities. We were wriggly and outsized because she encouraged us to exaggerate and amplify. In our retelling, every cut was actually a gash, every scrape a laceration. At home, we were brave, even if outside we navigated with a little more caution.

We were little black girls born into an era in which talk of women's rights swirled around in the air, but in which those rights were still far from tangible. The first ten years of my life coincided with the UN Decade for Women, so there were always speeches and conferences bringing people together to talk about the urgency of equality. Africans took the UN seriously back then; so, perhaps sensing the imminence of women's liberation, Mummy set about raising us to be ready for the tipping point – the moment when assertions of female independence would be met with praise rather than admonition. She did this deftly. Somehow she knew that the key would lie in the cuts and the bruises and the shared laughter of our baths.

◆ ◆ ◆

Although most of the Burley Court mothers didn't work, in our house Mummy earned the money and Baba – being a botany and entomology student at the University of Zambia (UNZA) – went to school to learn about plants and insects. Baba's other job was being a freedom fighter, but the income from that line of work was negligible. Before he met her, he had been wedded to the Movement for the Emancipation of his People. But then he had seen her one day and liked her smile and liked her legs. They had talked and he had discovered that she played tennis and there was something about that he liked, too. Soon he began to think about her all the time: the Swazi girl with a killer backhand who pretended not to notice him when he and the other guerrillas stood at the courts, watching.

For her part, Mummy liked the tall handsome man whose corduroy pants fitted him just so. She liked his sense of moderation. He drank, but seldom to the point of forgetting. He spent time with the others, but was often on his own. He smiled often, but wasn't the type of man who laughed gratuitously. In her experience, those types of men always had something to hide.

She qualified as an accountant the year after they met and soon after that he borrowed a tie and she wore a pair of white knee-high boots and a cream-coloured mini-dress that barely covered her swelling belly and they got married at Lusaka City Hall.

The women of Burley Court gossiped about all manner of apartment business but nothing occupied their time and energies quite like a good discussion about the Guerrilla who refused to work and the Swazi who was so in love with him that she allowed it. Whenever the subject of my parents and their relationship came up – which was often – the women would speculate about the peculiar madness that besets some women when it comes to matters of the heart.

Because their area of specialisation was rumour-mongering, Mummy and her friends referred to them as the Hungarers Mama Inwono was the lead Rumgurer. She couldn't accept the unchristian relationship that was unfolding before her eyes: Zambia was then, as it is now, a deeply conservative society. Women and men had separate domains and never the twain should meet except where it was sanctioned by God.

Mummy was casually pretty and had nice fit legs, which she was always showing off in miniskirts and dresses that stopped far too high above her knees. She knew how to drive a car and generally lived her life as she wanted. Yet in the eyes of the Rungarers Mummy possessed a number of traits that would doom her to a failed marriage. For one thing, she worked too much, sometimes only arriving home after six, while her Guerrilla came and went whenever he pleased, collecting insects that were ostensibly related to his 'studying' and dragging the children along with him in dungarees and denim. They always came back muddy and sticky. It was obvious that he wanted to turn those three poor little things into boys – their hair was cut short and they did not have pierced ears, among other notable offences. Worse, they never went to church. There just didn't seem to be any order in the lives of the Swazi and the Guerrilla and their children. It was not clear what the organising principle was that kept their household together: it was not God, nor was it family or tradition.

The Rungarers often huddled together in the hallway next to Mama Tawona's house, bent towards one another in conversation. When they were not laughing loudly, they spoke in hushed tones. They cackled with their mouths behind their hands and then smiled and said hello and imitated politeness when someone walked by. Mummy couldn't stand them. She smiled broadly whenever she passed them in her smart work suits, but never slowed down to have a conversation. She did nothing to cause them to twist their faces and turn their lips upside down at her but they did it anyway, rolling their eyes as she passed, staring at her new shoes or eyeing her old handbag. She couldn't win and knew it. She was either a show-off for having too many nice things, or a pitiable mess for having too many items requiring mending.

She gave them as little attention as possible. Her apparent lack of interest in them only fed their envy, though. It stoked the fires of their outrage. On Saturday mornings Mummy would leave early for her French class and as she passed they would harden their eyes. Heh! Maybe this is how people behaved in her country, but in Zambia, she would lose her man if she kept leaving the house for unnecessary things like French classes and tennis matches.

For the most part, the contagion of the Rungarers did not spread beyond their small group. Adult business was largely adult business and kid business stayed among us kids. But there were moments of crossover, when the mutters moved out of the shadows and the hurts that grown-ups inflicted on one another writhed before us like the grass snakes we would occasionally catch and kill when they strayed onto the playground.

◆ ◆ ◆

One day, we were playing a game of hide-and-seek and Terrence was 'it'. I hid in a stairwell. I knew he wouldn't think to look for me in that particular area because it was in Building One and Mama Tawona lived in Building One, which meant we rarely played in Building One. I took the chance, though, because I had seen her and two of the Rungarers standing at the bus stop waiting to go to town earlier. I thought I was safe.

I was wrong. Just as I settled into my spot, Mama

Tawona and the Rungarers trundled down the hall, loud and out of breath. Perhaps the bus had not come and they were complaining about how unreliable public transport was becoming; perhaps they had been to the market and were back for lunch. I don't remember precisely but I remember feeling the way they always made me feel – on edge. It was a hot day and they talked freely and easily – the way women do when they are not in the presence of their husbands or their children.

They stopped in front of Tawona's house and their minds turned to gossip. Soon, they were talking about Mummy. Mama Tawona wondered aloud how stupid that woman could be taking care of that man. She suggested that Baba was not a real man in any case – just a boy chasing childish dreams, playing with guns and travelling all over the place using the Zambian government's money. And all those parties and all that coming and going by the other guerrillas at all hours of the night! Always someone new sleeping in the house – men and women, men and women, sometimes children also there, inside. What about their own children? Some of those people were criminals. The Rungarers were convinced that a lot of the exiles coming from South Africa were actually just common folk, ordinary people who had concocted elaborate stories to escape punishment for being thieves and muggers. It was so easy to pretend to be a hero – meanwhile, they were just common criminals! Eh. Most of those ANC people were just crooks.

It had never occurred to me to think about my parents as dreamers nor had I thought about our family as being all that different from others in Burley Court. The aunties and uncles and the students who slept in our beds for weeks on end and then disappeared were just a fact of life. This was precisely why I would never make the jokes

Terrence made – my difference made me vulnerable to derision.

Until I ran into Mama Tawona's outrage and consternation, I hadn't thought about the fact that there were other ways to live. Mama Tawona and the Rungarers represented the moral police. They were arbiters of who would get into the Kingdom of Righteousness and who would not. It was they – and not the landlord – who decided whether you belonged in Burley Court or not.

Mama Tawona was nothing like the other women who populated my life when I was a girl. The rest of them were like my mother. They were members of the ANC or they were students with strong ties to the liberation movement. Many of them were members of MK, a paramilitary wing of the ANC, which meant they were training to become soldiers.

These women were the ones I loved the most. They were sharp of tongue and hungry of gaze and they belonged together in the way of a pack. They were glorious in the multi-toned way of African women – long and lean with upturned buttocks, or sturdy and wide-hipped with slender ankles and wrists tapering neatly into broad feet and slim fingers. They were richly dark with closely shorn hair, or they had pitch-black just-so afros haloing their walnut skin.

They smoked and drank and laughed out loud; free in one sense, you see, but not free at all in the ways that mattered the most. They wore minidresses and long boots and jeans that allowed them to move quickly and jump effortlessly, to run the way women weren't supposed to. They had arms strong enough to carry AK 47s and their braided hair was pulled magnificently tight; brows always plucked to perfection. They radiated a strange sort of lawlessness. It was as though their half-smiling, half-sneering lips had been moulded to defy the rules. Their ease with words, their comfort with the art of flinging barbs at one another, at women who happened to be passing by – at rival and friend alike – made my heart jump, pump, *barapapumpum, barapapapum*. I was in love with them.

Plump bums, bony haunches, spread thighs; they sat on our kitchen counters, calves swinging, shoulder to shoulder in sisterly solidarity. When someone put on a Boney M record, they would crowd into the centre of the living room, laughing into each other's eyes. '*Haiwena, sukuma!*' they would shout, urging anyone who still thought they might sit down while the music was playing to stand up. '*Sana, ngiyayithana le ngoma.*' And there they would be, doing the Pata Pata to 'Brown Girl in the Ring'.

I realise, now, these were new girls, stepping out of old skins. They roared, these young lionesses. They snapped gum and talked about how long they would wait before they were called to the camps. They laughed at their elegantly shabby men. They smiled sideways and sucked their teeth when a beautiful man they could see themselves loving happened to pass by. They breathed fire and revolution and I longed to be them.

The men were just as glamorous. The men who came to drink and laugh late into the night with my parents, the ones we called Uncle, and whose laps we climbed into and who tickled us and gave us sweets, these men were all 'firsts'. The first African accepted at such and such university, the first black man to live in such and such a place, the first black to lecture at so and so university. Because of this, they had an air of invincibility and supreme confidence about them – even when they were falling-down drunk.

We were mesmerised by the poetry of their intellect. Every weekend there was a debate about when Africa was going to put a man on the moon. And because they didn't snicker or seem to think this was absurd, neither did we. In the Lusaka of my childhood it was perfectly plausible that we could go to outer space under our own steam. I had no idea that a man had already been sent to the moon and that his name was Neil Armstrong. When I was little we only compared ourselves with the West in ways that favoured us.

In escaping apartheid, the men who crowded into our flat were part of a new breed of Africans who had left South Africa and Zimbabwe and Mozambique determined that they would shine and shine and shine. They were possessed of the secret of freedom, a sort of inner spirit that propelled them forward and made them look – to my wide eyes at least – as though they were soaring.

They were heartbreakingly handsome, these men. They lounged loose and long-limbed across our couches. They had guerrilla beards and unkempt hair, and sinewy thighs and bell-bottom jeans. They drove beat-up falling-apart cars, laughed as though their hearts were not burning and drank as though their nightmares would never stop.

They were idealists and gangsters and hustlers and bright-eyed students who had left girlfriends and mothers and wives and babies who would never know the circumference of their fathers' arms – little ones who would grow into girls who would grow into women who would hate the men who loved them for not being their fathers. But in our house, they were heroes. My sisters and I knew nothing of the lives they had left behind and so to us they were new men, unmarred by responsibilities and ties to painful pasts and mundane yesterdays.

In exile, they created themselves as though from mud and ochre.

Upon leaving South Africa, they had shed their old skins and become the men they had been born to be. Their backs straightened as they descended into Moscow's frigid embrace; their muscles lengthened as they marched across bush and mosquitoinfested swamps in Angola; their spines elongated as they squelched through bog and marsh. Nonsense may have spewed from their malarial lips in Kongwa but they were free. They marched across Africa singing freedom songs until they lost their voices. They sang until they were dry-mouthed and croaking so that, by the time they arrived at the end of all their convoluted journeys in Lusaka, this place of cigarettes and laughter and hard-soft women, they were exhausted and ready to smile.

Having made it to the headquarters of their movement, which was supposed to emancipate the people, many of them simply collapsed. I see, now, that this is how we found them. We found them fathering fat brown children and loving free women. We found them sitting on red polished verandas feeling the warmth of the Lusaka rain on their brown shoulders. We found them smoking *zol* and singing Bob Marley's 'Buffalo Soldier'.

They came to Lusaka broken by many more things than the struggle for justice. But their demons did not matter here. What mattered was that they had decided to make our little city with its outsized ambitions and its orderly roundabouts their place of safety. For them, Lusaka became the place where black was equal to free, where nobody, not Queen Elizabeth or John Vorster or Richard Nixon, could tell them anything. Lusaka – in all its peaceful futuristic pan-African glory – was theirs and they meant to burrow in its peace for a while.

Some of the residents of Burley Court did not find the women and the men who visited us especially interesting. They found them loud and they resented the fact that their president – His Excellency Dr Kenneth Kaunda – had given all these revolutionaries special status in the country. Dr Kaunda was a dreamer who believed that Africa belonged to Africans. He had said that independent Africa had a responsibility towards the parts of Africa that were still in chains. And so, because Africans in South Africa and Zimbabwe and Mozambique were not free, Dr Kaunda had given us refuge in Zambia.

For ordinary Zambians, our presence was a daily reality, not just an empty political slogan. Most were gracious and embraced our cause. But for others, like Mama Tawona, we were rule-breakers and layabouts. For them, the word 'refugee' was a slur. The refugee women took Zambian men while the freedom-fighter men caroused and broke Zambian women's hearts.

I crouched on the ground, waiting to be found. But the problem with Mummy and Baba was bigger than their being refugees; problem was, they were in love and that idea struck her as laughable.

Their gossip was about this strange and laughable fact. Mama Tawona threw her head back and cackled, talking about my mother as though she were a silly child. 'Ha, *mwana*! That love she is feeling for that man makes her think he is wonderful. Meanwhile we all know that is just foolish. Isn't it that when you are in love even a desert can have the appearance of a beautiful forest?' She roared with laughter, and Mrs Mwansa (who had no children but at least had a husband, so she was spared from total irrelevance) and Mama Terrence nodded their heads in agreement.

'She will learn,' said Mama Terrence.

'Ehe, she will learn. It will be pain that teaches her,' said Mrs Mwansa sagely.

Mama Tawona continued. 'Mmn, but you know men. One day he will wake up and decide that the only thing he wants in this life is the one thing that she has not provided him. Then we will see if she still smiles and says "Good morning" like that in her high heels. Eh! I don't think so. No. Instead she will be crying, crying, crying tears of sorrow. Eh-eh! Because men are like that. If they don't get their heir, they will leave you. Until she has a son, she will never be guaranteed that man's love.'

And so the world's obsession with boys revealed itself to me. We needed to have a baby brother and it needed to happen soon because my sisters and I would never be enough. The absence of brothers would bring untold misery to our parents. I hadn't known boys mattered more than girls, that one fictional first-born boy was more important than a fistful of girls. This revelation – that a family without boys is really no family at all – was so significant I didn't hear Terrence thundering around the corner. I was sitting there turning over our family's boylessness in my mind, thinking about how I would formulate the question to Mummy when she got back from work, when I felt Terrence's skinny knee connect with my face. I screamed, and the Rungarers jumped. My cheek puffed out instantly and I saw no sympathy in Mama Tawona's eyes. She looked at me as though I was a thief.

It hurt.

I only learnt the word 'primogeniture' much later in life, but this was my first lesson in the concept. What an absurd idea: that my father may have grounds to find another woman so they might make another child, a boy who would ostensibly be made more in my father's image than any of us. With my cheek swollen and this new idea thudding in my head I wasn't sure if I should laugh or vomit.

How could anyone be more like Baba than me? Wasn't his face in mine? Wasn't he our dad who loved us more than anything in the world because he took us places – to the market and the mechanic and to visit with his friends to show us off?

Yet once it had been spoken I understood it. It explained all the other times Mummy had been asked – by women she had just met – whether she was going to try one more time. It provided a basis for all the times someone had said, 'You can't stop until you get a boy,' all the times Mummy had turned her face away in anger and pulled us along quickly.

◆ ◆ ◆

A few days after the hallway collision, my cheek was still tender and slightly bruised. Tawona and I were playing hopscotch and – unusually – she was losing. I threw the stone and it landed firmly in its box. I began to hop. 'You touched the line,' she shouted.

I hadn't touched the line. 'I didn't,' I said.

'You did. You're a cheater.'

'You're the one who's cheating. Because I'm winning you want to make up stories? You get out of here and go and cheat somewhere else!' I shouted. I was still angry with her mother, still mulling over the conversation I had overheard, still mad that my face was sore.

Tawona was never one to take an insult lying down. She shouted, 'Maybe it's you who needs to go to the witch doctor, and not your mother!'

I had no idea what she was talking about but I felt my face flush. 'Oh! Now you have no words, eh?' she continued. 'Let me tell you something, you stupid girl. If your mother was from our tribe they would have taken her to the witch doctor by now. Anyway, maybe it's because you people are foreigners. In Zambia we don't have such things. How can a woman have three girls in a row?

Non-stop. Three? Two is okay. But three!? Eh! Three is a curse.' She ploughed on, determined to do maximum damage.

'If she doesn't fix this problem your father will leave her for a woman who can give him what he wants. No man on this earth doesn't want sons. I mean! Eh! She should be careful. Do you think that man will stay in the house where there is no one to inherit?'

She continued.

'A man can never ever love his daughters the way he will love his sons. Boys belong to their fathers. So now, what does your father have? Just girls? So then? Eh! So then he has nothing.'

I don't remember going for her. I only know there was blood everywhere and I was not sorry that I punched her. I was not sorry at all and she was shocked and no longer smirking and that made me feel better although not much because she had just broken my heart.

Then there was a ring of screaming excited kids around us and she was up and livid, and storming towards the stairwell with the crowd billowing out behind us as she cradled her split lip and smoothed her bloody dress over her paunchy tummy. I hung back, afraid. Terrence turned, then ran back to me. His lips were dry as usual but he was serious. The gravity of the situation was clear to him. 'You better come, you'll just make it worse if you don't.'

Terrence took my hand and led me to the front. We stood, facing Tawona, who was a bloody mess by now. Someone handed her the tooth I had punched out of her mouth. It was dirty and very small and looking at it set her to wailing once more and it made my lip quiver too. I hadn't meant to knock her tooth out. I was scared; terrified, really. Mama Tawona would have my head.

By the time we reached the top step, Mama Tawona was waiting. Tawona's little brother had run up to tell his mother that his big sister had been beaten and that I was the culprit. She stood there with murder in her eyes. I didn't wait for her to start shouting. I couldn't. I committed an even worse sin: I bolted. I broke the cardinal rule of all African households and ran from an adult who was trying to discipline me. I pushed past her and ran down the hallway and into our house. I was desperate for Baba to be home.

He was. He was sitting at the dining room table with his books on the table and a few beetles spread out in front of him. Mummy hated it when he labelled his specimens on the table and under normal circumstances I would have told him this but this was an emergency and so I rushed forward and crawled into his lap, which I was getting too big to do, and I started to cry. In the chaos of those few moments he thought I was hurt and so he looked for the cut, searching my body for the place where the skin was broken.

'Are you hurt?' he asked, confused.

'No,' I cried. 'No. But, but Tawona said you won't love me because I'm a girl.' The words were a jumbled tumble of snotty rush. 'She said that, that you only want boys and that we don't belong here in Zambia, we are foreigners and we should go back where we came from, and then she said we don't even belong to you, that only boys belong to fathers, girls are a curse.'

I wailed. Ruptured.

He said nothing and this calmed me because, as every child knows, silence is always the beginning of listening.

Baba bent into my hurt and pulled me close. His insides thumped a sonata, his heart thudding dully against my chest: 'You are mine, you are mine, you are mine.' Tawona's words lost a bit of their edge. My own little heart thumped back: 'I am yours, I am yours, I am yours.'

That night, after she came home from work and heard the story, Mummy made me apologise to Tawona. We went to her house together and knocked on the door. Mama Tawona peered out imperiously.

'So you have come to say what?' she said abruptly. Mummy didn't let her continue. She was curt.

'We have come to apologise,' she said. 'Sonke should not have hit Tawona.'

Mama Tawona began to interrupt her. 'You think that just saying sorry will be enough—'

But Mummy cut her off. She was not finished.

'But understand this: your bitterness needs to find another home. It is not welcome in mine. And if it doesn't, if you insist on this nonsense, then you will see. You will see me and you will know me. That same curse you think has been put on me will be on you. You will be cursed in ways your people do not even understand. Do you know the Swazis? The Zulu people? If you want to see powers, you will see them.'

Mama Tawona's hands had stayed on her hips in defiance as Mummy spoke, but her face was frozen. Mummy gave her a hard and thorough look and then asked, 'Do you understand me?'

Mama Tawona remained silent. Ashamed.

'Heh?' Mummy repeated, sounding rougher than I had known she could be. 'Do you understand me?'

Mama Tawona nodded. Then she looked down. She was not the type of woman who admitted she was wrong. That would have required the kind of introspection that women like Mama Tawona studiously avoided. Observing the rules of respectability, and policing the gates, requires a kind of hard-nosed vigilance that precludes sensitivity and thoughtfulness. My mother knew this so it is unlikely that she expected an apology.

But I was still young and so I did expect it. I thought we would wait for her to say, 'I'm sorry too.' It was obvious that both Tawona and her mother owed *me* an apology. That would not come. Mama Tawona shrank in the face of Mummy's anger, but she was not convinced she was wrong; she had just been caught.

Mummy took my hand and we walked away. We entered our flat and I imagined Mama Tawona still standing at the door – rooted and, for once, speechless.

Baba put us to bed as usual. He told us a story about a girl who found a rock that turned into a star that shot across the sky and I was very tired but I knew that he intended me to know that I was that girl and also that rock that turned into a star and maybe also that sky. He wanted me to know that I belonged in his heart and in his imagination and that I was the centre of the universe.

S.E.X.

MY EARLIEST MEMORY of sex is bound up in pleasure and voyeurism. I was only six when I stumbled upon a man and a woman in flagrante, but I was old enough to know that she was having far too much fun. I knew this because I could hear it in the way she chuckled, which I knew she was not supposed to do because what she was doing was something only men were allowed to like. I knew it even though I wouldn't have been able to tell you why. There was something off limits about the way men turned their heads whenever a plump-bummed woman passed them by. Women were supposed to pretend they hadn't noticed, and other men were supposed to look as well.

I was very young when I realised men were supposed to like things to do with women's bodies and women had to guard themselves against the things men liked. They had to not smile and pretend they didn't notice. Men were fools over sex and women were silly about love.

The women around me must have talked about men and sex and pleasure but those discussions were never fit for children's ears so I didn't get to hear them in any detail. I heard only the talk about love and romance. I saw the looks exchanged, and sensed what it was they weren't saying, but I never heard them talk about sex.

The men were different. They talked about everything in front of us: white settlers and ditched lovers and fallen women they had picked up. Often, they had drunk too much. They leered and laughed and didn't mind their manners unless they were told by the women that there were children around and they should shush.

◆ ◆ ◆

My sisters and I spent a lot of time at Aunt Tutu's house. Aunt Tutu was one of Mummy's best friends. She had married a Zambian man, Uncle Ted, and they had three kids, the same ages as my sisters and me. We were a crew, a less raucous group than the Burley Court group, but only because we were fewer in number.

At seven, Masuzyo (Suzie) was a rotund dispenser of wisdom, a slit-eyed know-it-all whose spectacles made her seem far older than her meagre years. Wongani was five, only a year younger than me but she, too, seemed far older: she was her mother's child. Tapelwa was only four, an age so inconsequential that he was relegated to shuffling around on his own, not small enough to be with the babies and not old enough to be with us big girls.

Mandla and Zeng were always toddling around in the background, oblivious to the ways in which they were being excluded, while Wongani, Suzie and I spent most of our time discussing the latest news, gossiping and arguing about episodes of *Wonder Woman*. Aunt Tutu was rarely home. She spent her days driving around town, visiting people so that she could remark upon the state of their houses, the quality of their biscuits and the cleanliness of their servants.

Despite its downsides, one of the best things about Suzie and Wongani's house was the guest bedroom, which was just big enough to accommodate a beige couch and king-sized four-poster bedroom suite. As we played, we would listen out for the crunch of Aunt Tutu's car coming down the driveway. We knew that if she caught us in there with our dusty feet, and our grimy nails, the consequences would be dire. Invariably, we would get carried away and the person assigned to keep their ears pricked would forget and it would be too late – she would be standing right there behind you. One minute you would be mid-jump, giggling and about to land on the plump mattress, and the next your arm would be pinned behind your back and Aunt Tutu's voice would be an edgy vibrato, oddly sing-songy and menacing and urgent and hot in your ear:

'Didn't I tell you not to play in this room?'

During the school holidays before I turned seven, our enjoyment of the guest room was interrupted for two weeks. Aunt Tutu's brother and his German girlfriend visited from Berlin. When they were in town, our de facto playroom was off limits. This meant our relationship with them was initially antagonistic. Long before they arrived at the gate, crammed into a rickety metered taxi in a dishevelled, cigarette-stained heap, we decided we didn't like them. They weren't our visitors. They weren't in town to keep us company and make us laugh. No. They were just a two-week-long inconvenience. The Uncle and the Girlfriend turned out to be more than that, of course, mainly because they were nothing like the adults we were used to. They lit incense, which reminded me vaguely of the Indian restaurant in the centre of town we sometimes went to when there was something to celebrate.

Also, they dressed very strangely – the Girlfriend especially. Whereas Mummy and Aunt Tutu poured their still-trim figures into tight polyester trousers and white knee-high boots, the Girlfriend wore long, flowing skirts and gypsy-like tops. A sliver of her hollowed-out belly was almost always showing, which we found somewhat disgusting and alluring all at the same time. The women we knew would never have bared the flesh on their stomachs. Legs and arms were one thing, but among African women, even those who defied stereotypes, tummy skin was an altogether different story.

As for him, unlike our fathers, the Uncle looked dirty. Baba's scraggly beard and afro had a certain air about them: a cultivated unkemptness that nodded to forethought and therefore to some form of guerrilla stylishness. Not the Uncle. The Uncle looked positively downtrodden. His hair was beginning to mat in some places like the madman who used to dance lewdly in town right next to the Playhouse, the one who cackled at any woman with a big bum who happened to walk past and who picked up newspapers as though he would be able to divine the future if he just collected enough of them.

In addition to their shaggy appearance, the Uncle and the Girlfriend spent much of their time engaged in what they called 'jousting'. When an exhausted adult wished to end a heated debate with the Girlfriend, she would retort, in her guttural German accent, 'You caaan't be afraid of jousting. That fear of questions and questioning, it represents the death of curiosity, which is the beginning of the end of any society yearning to be free.' The Uncle also liked the word. He would say things like, 'What will Africa become if those entrusted with its empowerment aren't capable of intellectual jousting?' He shook his head and sighed a lot.

Suzie and Wongani's father was Uncle Ted and he was very important because he worked for Zambia Airways. Instead of letting him rest when he got back from work, the Uncle and the Girlfriend insisted on talking to him about the Anti-Colonial Project. We all knew that once Uncle came home we were supposed to go outside and let him rest. The visitors did not know this. So, they badgered him with questions and ignored our wide-eyed looks. Uncle Ted would take on the baffled and exhausted countenance of a man who had been working too hard to have to worry about thinking after he had knocked off and he would try to steer the conversation towards safer, more intelligible territory. Uncle Ted was not particularly interested in social interaction. So, even at the best of times, he let Aunt Tutu do the talking, preferring to smile aimlessly into his beer.

The Uncle and the Girlfriend weren't concerned about his baffled expression or his body language. So intent were they on making their own points that they simply couldn't see his signals of distress. Every night they hounded him, peppering him with questions to which they already had answers, walking him through analyses to which they had subjected him already. Their favourite topic was Zambia Airways. It was a Vanity Project, a useless money-guzzling enterprise designed to appease the mighty Nationalist Ego. 'How ironic,' the Uncle would spit out, 'that the great nationalist agenda has now been trampled by the forces of neocolonialism.' They argued in forceful, spittle-inducing paragraphs, saying things like: 'All these African presidents flying in and out of Jakarta to foster consensus amongst the non-aligned movement will do nothing to build basic infrastructure! They are just robbing the poor of the revenues that are rightfully theirs.'

Now Zambia Airways was the pride of the nation and it was well known that it only hired those who were enthusiastic about the project of African unity to work in its sales and marketing department. This meant that Uncle Ted had no idea what the Uncle and the Girlfriend were talking about with their critiques of nationalism and neocolonialism, which was lucky for everyone because it prevented hurt feelings all around. In fact, one of the best things about working for Zambia Airways was that its employees were not required to be anything other than patriotic and enthusiastic.

To most Africans in newly liberated countries, the national airline symbolised, in all the easy and trite ways, everything that was possible for a new nation. Airlines were the gleaming future. African pilots, resplendent in their uniforms, demonstrated the intellect and sobriety that colonialists had long accused Africans of lacking. However, their ground staff were something else entirely. They were sycophants, whose role was to burnish the reputations of their countries and herald the greatness that was yet to come.

Men like Uncle Ted, obsequious enough to have secured jobs with the national carrier, were elevated in society by mere association with the airline. His employment at Zambia Airways, and the fact that his office was *physically* at the airport, made Uncle Ted a big man in a small society. His position as a senior figure within Zambia Airways also made him singularly unqualified to critique the institution, certainly not in the way the Uncle and the Girlfriend were attempting.

In fact, it was quite the opposite. Uncle Ted's role was dependent on his being a yes-man. Whenever President Kaunda returned from one of his whirlwind world trips, his arrival at the airport on a Zambia Airways plane would be marked with ululation and thanksgiving, but also with the awe befitting one who has just alighted from an aircraft. Uncle Ted was always there, on hand to greet him and to ensure everything functioned smoothly as the president made his way through the airport.

Since he was the president and there was no paperwork to be done, and since the chief of protocol, the minister of foreign affairs and most of Cabinet were also always present to welcome the president home, there was technically very little for a Zambia Airways manager to do on these frenetic days, but this never occurred to Uncle Ted.

As the spouse of a senior Zambia Airways manager, there was even less for Aunt Tutu to do at the airport when the president arrived, but this never occurred to her either. Indeed, sometimes, if the trip had been an especially important one – say to Moscow or Beijing – Uncle and Aunty dressed up Suzie and Wongani in their frilliest, whitest dresses, as though they were going to be christened, and they would shroud Tapelwa in a charcoal-coloured suit that was three sizes too large. Thus appointed, they would drive to the airport to stand in the VIP section on the runway in the hope that senior members of Cabinet would note their loyalty to ruler and country as they sweated in the glare of the concrete.

On those days, my sisters and I would watch on TV, hoping for a glimpse of Uncle Ted and Aunt Tutu and the kids. When he landed, the president always stood at the top of the stairs of the plane with his white hanky in his hand, waving to the crowds and officials gathered to greet him before he descended. There were always busloads of supporters dressed in UNIP colours – women wearing green for the land and orange for the copper that lies beneath the land and schoolchildren in checked uniforms sweating in the sun.

After waving and smiling, the president would make his way, in a slow-moving convoy, all the way to the stadium. There, he would shout in a voice quivering with patriotism, 'One Zambia?' It always sounded like a declarative statement blended into a question, the first part of a trademark call and response that all Zambians knew. In our tiny living room, my sisters and I would scream back along with the crowd, 'One Nation!'

Having been raised in a one-party state, we understood that our role was to respond in the affirmative when the great leader called upon us to do so. Although we never saw Aunty or the children, more than once the back of Uncle Ted's bald head was beamed into our living room in Burley Court. The fact of his having been on TV made him seem larger than life. To us, Uncle Ted seemed a little bit like Clark Kent. He appeared to be a mere mortal, an ordinary man who went to work every morning, but, in an instant, there he was, standing within spitting distance of the President of the Republic of Zambia.

Uncle Ted wasn't someone you questioned about whether the airline could be viewed as an expensive monument to the ego of the president. Had he understood the nuance and complexity of the argument,

Uncle Ted might have booted out his guests. But he didn't get it. Uncle Ted could not have fathomed that anyone might suggest Zambia Airways was a waste of taxpayers' money and so he simply looked at them quizzically across the dining room table and made no comment. It was as though they were speaking a different language, as though they had come from a distant planet where words were a form of nourishment rather than a set of sounds used for the purposes of communication. He simply ate his *nsima* and smiled in exasperation, content in the knowledge that they would soon be gone, and that in the meantime they would make their funny eating words and he would ignore them and pretend that they were making sense.

While the ANC comrades who gathered at our house every weekend may have appreciated the robustness of the arguments made by the Girlfriend and the Uncle, they were also beneficiaries of President Kaunda's largesse and were unlikely to be so direct as to suggest that their free flights should be stopped in the interests of the common man and woman on the street. They were so deeply invested in the Zambian nationalist project that pooh-poohing the idea of a national carrier would have felt counter-revolutionary even if its logic was sound.

The hippie lovers, on the other hand, didn't care. They weren't tied up in Africa as an idea – they were only interested in The People as an idea and, although that had its own problems, it allowed them to be more critical than many others. When they weren't debating the post-colonial condition, the Girlfriend and the Uncle spent a lot of time looking deeply into each other's eyes, smoking cigarettes and holding each other's faces: often simultaneously. They also complained that they were tired a lot and often they had to retire to their room to sleep off their fatigue.

They developed a pattern. They would get up late and join us kids for the midday meal. For lunch each day the maid fed us a steaming plate of *nsima* with greens and tomato relish. We gobbled it up and giggled as the two of them stared at each other dreamily over our heads. The Girlfriend struggled to eat the food but liked the fact that she was eating in the same manner as The People and so she persevered. We were amused by the awkward way she used her hands to scoop up the relish and in a way this endeared her to us. She may have had strange clothes and odd manners but she was sort of childlike in her attempts to act like she was one of us.

As we ate, the Girlfriend peppered us with questions. In these moments, we saw that she wasn't like us at all, nor would she ever be like our parents. 'How do you feel about the *way* the teacher teaches you at school? Aren't you tired of being told what to learn?' The Uncle chimed in, 'Wouldn't it be more fun if you could learn what you want to learn rather than what The System,' (here he would grow more vehement) 'what some strange people in a distant land, decide you should learn?' We could understand the words, but it all sounded like gibberish.

❖ ❖ ❖

On the fourth day of their visit, the Girlfriend and the Uncle disappeared as usual into the guest bedroom to 'take a nap'. Suzie, the oldest and bossiest, explained that they still had Jet Lag. 'That happened to me when we went to London,' she said authoritatively, dragging out the word *London* the way I imagined Londoners would. 'I couldn't sleep for weeks because my body clock was ticking all night and the tocks kept me awake.' I wasn't sure whether ticks and tocks worked in this way. Still, I rarely questioned Suzie on matters of international import. Instead, I whispered to myself in a Benny Hill voice, 'Let me hold my bloody tongue since I've never been to mother England.'

Her sister did not show Suzie the same courtesy. Suspicious by nature, Wongani was not convinced by the jet-lag theory. 'They are doing something naughty in there,' she declared. Half a decade into her life, she already had an air of resignation about the state of the world. She was prone to sighing and referred to everyone as 'that one'. For example, apropos Daphne, the maid, one morning Wongani suggested, 'Hmmn, that one thinks we haven't noticed she's visiting her boyfriend at the kiosk? How can we need to buy milk so many times a day?'

Having surmised that Uncle and his guest were up to no good, Wongani decided to undertake an investigation. Once she had asked the crucial question, 'What exactly are they doing with the door shut in the middle of the day when normal people are busy?' – it was impossible for any of us to ignore the possibility that they could be up to no good.

It was on the basis of this question, and this question alone, that we found ourselves standing in front of their bedroom door, peeping through a slight crack. Inside the room, the mad visitors were wriggling under the sheets. Their legs were intertwined; their fingers and lips and hands and hips grinding ever so slowly. We got an eyeful and, for our sins, we were struck dumb and momentarily paralysed. We watched the contortions with our heads cocked to the side. We were caught flat-footed, our mouths agape. After a few minutes, we began to move, our grubby fingers clutching one another for balance as we strained on our tippy toes and struggled to take in everything that was happening under the covers.

Then reality hit.

'They're gonna see us,' I whispered. 'Let's go!'

'No,' Wongani and Suzie hissed. They were mesmerised.

We watched for a few more minutes until we heard someone coming down the hall. Petrified that it might be Aunt Tutu, we scampered away. We ran outside and stood in the dusty yard. We looked at one another and then looked away, flushed and embarrassed and aware that we had just witnessed something that was Absolutely None of Our Business.

For weeks after this we could talk of nothing else. We discussed the Girlfriend and the Uncle long after they had gone. They had disappeared as abruptly as they had come, leaving Aunt Tutu a vegetarian cookbook and pressing a ceramic hand-painted bird whistle from Hungary into the palms of a startled-looking Uncle Ted.

We agreed that we had actually seen them having S.E.X. We always spelled it out when we said it, in case the babies heard us, and we always, *always*, whispered it.

Until this incident, I had only had a vague sense of what sex was. I knew that it was something private and forbidden but now – thanks to my astute companions – I was also aware that it was simultaneously bad and pleasurable. Wongani was clear that people who liked doing it were dirty. Given that the two people we had witnessed in flagrante delicto were not exactly models of hygiene, it was hard to disagree with her on this score.

We weren't just fascinated with what we had seen, though. We were especially fascinated with *her*. We spent inordinate amounts of time talking about *her*. In part it was because, as we peeped into the room that afternoon, she was the one who was sighing and moaning and generally carrying on, while he whispered and grunted a bit but generally kept his cool.

Perhaps we talked about her because we were girls and she was the girl, and we knew from previous sources of knowledge that she shouldn't have let him do those things to her in the first place. We had known this from before we suckled our mothers' breasts. Every girl knows this. The rules are different for us than they are for boys and any girl who pretends that she doesn't know this, or who momentarily forgets, will find out sooner or later. As different as we were from one another in temperament, the three of us could agree on this. There are some things you just know.

A few days after the peep show, I was sitting outside in the barren yard next to Suzie and Wongani. Their heads had just been shaved and Aunt Tutu had slathered a liberal dose of Vaseline onto their scalps to ward off lice. She had ordered Daphne to ensure that they sat in the sun the whole morning to burn off any vestiges of the bugs. Given her relationship with Wongani, Daphne relished the opportunity to enforce Aunty's instructions. I sat next to them and drew a line in the ground as Vaseline dripped down their necks and onto their shoulders. Every time one of them tried to move, Daphne ran out of the house and said, 'Your mother said three hours. You stay there. It's not yet time, not yet.'

Aunt Tutu may have known the burning sun would do nothing but bake her children's heads, but the shame of having lice in her house had most likely driven her to administer this particular cruelty. Aunt Tutu did not want it said that she had known about the lice and done nothing to prevent their return.

So we sat and sweated together in the grassless yard –

a sacrifice to appease other mothers who would ask where the girls' hair had gone. Aunt Tutu would say, 'They had lice so I shaved it and made them sit in the sun to burn the germs,' and the other mothers would respect her in that fearful way and inflict the same on their own children next time, repeating both the unnecessary punishment and the boastful pretence of motherly sternness. Suzie wiped a trickle of runny Vaseline, preventing it from seeping into her eye, then picked up the conversation where we had left it when Mummy had come to take us home the day before.

'As I was saying,' she began.

Wongani and I swivelled our heads to face her and she continued, 'They aren't even married.'

'Yes,' her sister agreed, 'which is a pity because they are going to burn in eternal shame.'

'Straight to hell,' I sighed, 'especially her since she's the lady.' I was surprised by how nonchalant and worldly I sounded.

We nodded and then shook our heads in resigned consternation.

In the coming weeks, we went into overdrive, spreading the story far and wide. My friends at Burley Court could have told you what happened as if they had seen it with their own eyes, as could my other set of friends at Uncle Stan and Aunt Angela's house, which was where I spent most of my weekday afternoons when school was in session.

Once the juicy details were shared, and on every street where they had been disseminated, there was almost unanimous agreement that the Girlfriend must have been A Lady Of The Night, brought to Lusaka specifically for the purposes of Doing Sex.

Again and again we returned to the scene in feigned

horror. Suzie was especially good at recounting the most salacious details. She always seemed to circle back to the one point: 'Did you hear her saying "Yes, yes, yes!"?' She would pant in a lurid pseudoGermanic imitation of the Girlfriend's voice. We would giggle, and shift uncomfortably. Invariably one of us would wind up the conversation by saying, 'Everyone knows, it's only Street Walkers who like S.E.X.'

I felt increasingly uncomfortable when the subject came up. The Girlfriend had actually been nice to us. It had only been for two weeks, but she had lived with us. She had shared our *nsima* and made us laugh. She had even made us think about school and about President Kaunda. With her questions and her wispy shirts and lowhanging skirts, she hadn't been a monster – she had just been a girl. She had given me a fragrance stick that smelled like vanilla, and she had given Suzie an empty matchbox with a picture of a dragon on it, and had left a tiny little square of magenta-coloured felt for Wongani. The Uncle had not even bothered, yet here we were saying nothing about him and telling every kid within a fivekilometre radius about her moans and groans.

The Girlfriend's mistake was not that we had caught her; it was that she liked it. We may have been little, but we knew enough to forgive him and call her the sinner. We were big enough to see that she was not ashamed and this seemed deliciously wrong and also it seemed to explain everything that was off kilter about her. The Girlfriend said what she liked and did what she pleased and, because of this, and because I was a girl just like her, I wondered what it might be like one day to lie as she had, legs spread and arms held high; heavy-lidded, slack-jawed, writhing and unashamed.

Gogo Lindi

LINDIWE MABUZA ARRIVED in Lusaka the year I turned five. She was the kind of woman who made people nervous. She had been living in America where she had mastered the art of not caring what anyone thought – of being a thoroughly independent woman. She had always possessed this trait; no doubt it had carried her to Lesotho and then to the US and back again. But living in America in the 1960s must have honed it.

She was surly sometimes and unconcerned about what it meant to be a bad tempered woman. She did what she wanted and argued as vehemently as she saw fit. She disagreed with people and didn't care if they got offended. Men especially. She didn't talk about feminism. She just stuck her nose in the air and looked down on men who were not as clever as her. She didn't care what her intellect did to their egos.

When I met her, she was almost forty, divorced and highly educated. Because Baba was technically her nephew, she insisted that I call her Gogo, despite the fact that she was far too young to actually be my granny. She was odd sometimes. Obstinate, even on minor points like this, but people learnt to back down and let her have her way. They said she was 'difficult' and she was.

There were all sorts of problems with being almost forty, highly educated and divorced in those times, but I didn't know about any of those problems. I just knew that she came along at exactly the point when I needed someone who would be all mine, someone I would not have to share with the big-headed toddler and the milk-smelling baby who seemed intent on ruining my life. When it all seemed too much, Gogo Lindi arrived with the express purpose of adoring me.

Before moving to Lusaka in 1979, Gogo had earned a master's degree in America; then, she had gone to Minnesota to teach. In Minnesota she had fallen in love with a man but when that ended she picked up the pieces and stayed revolutionary. So, when she met me, I suspect she was still a little bit heartbroken and trying to find pieces of herself that she had left on the other side of the ocean, miles away. She was also searching for somewhere new to belong and for someone to belong to.

She had a daughter, Thembi. Their relationship was complicated and by then Thembi was already a teenager – a big sister to me. What Gogo needed was a little one, someone who would simply adore her and not ask complicated questions about where she had been and why she had left her. And so, on the cool evening when Lindiwe Mabuza arrived in Lusaka, she found me, the little girl who had been waiting for someone just like her.

Gogo looked straight through my little ribcage into my full-full heart and realised that I was a precocious and lavishly jealous little girl who could not get over the arrival of not one, but two, baby sisters. She recognised in me a fellow traveller, a little soul who could be tough if she wanted but also needed more than she was getting from the adults around her. She could see I was unsettled by all the faces and the voices and the comings and goings in my revolutionary house sometimes – as any child would be. She could see, too, that I dared not give voice to my worries: I had already worked out that there would be entirely no point in complaining. This was life.

Gogo Lindi saw all this and set about doing what aunts have been doing for girls for centuries: standing in. She stood in for the attention Mummy could no longer afford to give, and for the ideas I could not yet shape about what it meant to be a girl. And, later, when I was old enough to decide for myself what sort of woman I would be, Gogo Lindi gave shape and colour and contours to my ideas about how to be strong. She was one of the first women I ever loved who didn't give a damn about the rules. She taught me above all else how to belong to myself first before I let myself belong to someone else. This is a lesson that is never fully learnt; wherever I have failed to use it as a guide, I blame only myself.

No one quite seemed to know what to do with Gogo. She didn't fit into any of the pre-assigned boxes. This didn't matter to me, of course. I had no idea at the time how important the boxes were. I only knew what I thought, which was that she was the most beautiful and prettiest-smelling person I had ever met. With the innocence of the child who believes in the kindness of grown-ups and the fairness of the world, I thought she had arrived solely to give me love and affection.

Our favourite game was called Olympics. In this game Gogo Lindi was the coach and I was the athlete. Each time we played the game we were catapulted into the future. In the imaginary world we constructed, it was 1992 and I was eighteen years old. I was the World Champion of gymnastics, representing a free South Africa. The games were hosted in Addis Ababa, the headquarters of the Organization of African Unity, because – well, because nothing else would have made sense. Even our games were pan-African.

Gogo would stand at one end of the Sangwenis' yard and I would stand at the other. The Sangwenis were extended family. Aunty Angela and Uncle Stan were like parents to us and Lindiwe and Dumi were the big sister and big brother we didn't need to imagine because we had them in the flesh. I spent most days at their house when I was a toddler and, of course, a weekend would never go by without us going to their house. Gogo Lindi was Uncle Stan's younger sister. So, when she arrived in Lusaka, naturally she stayed at Aunty and Uncle's house and naturally she insisted that Baba call her Aunty in spite of the small gap in their ages. So it was here – at the house on Kalungu Road – that we began our lifelong adoration of one another.

'On your marks!' she would shout. 'Get set. Go!' And I'd be off, running as fast as I could. It was me against the clock. 'Good time,' Gogo would say. 'You beat your previous record by about five seconds.' Then I would begin my tumbling routine. I would cartwheel and handstand and roll for a few minutes in some order I had decided made sense. 'Beautiful,' she would say. 'Absolutely stunning. Even better than Nadia Comăneci.'

We were a conspiracy – a secret shared in hot breath and stifled giggles. She knew I was smarting from the pain of having new siblings, so she gave me whatever I wanted. Others could get sidetracked by the antics of Baby Zeng or the cleverness of genius Mandla, but she remained unmoved. Gogo kept her eyes fixed firmly on me, never once even vaguely interested in the other two. They didn't notice, so they never harboured a grudge. But I knew and it meant the world.

Most nights Gogo was in the studio broadcasting stories into South Africa. She was in charge of Radio Freedom and was the head of culture and arts for the ANC in exile.

Lindiwe Mabuza had earned her master's degree in American Studies in Ohio. I only realised later what a feat this was. For a black South African woman, born in 1935, to have made her way out of Natal, to the Transvaal, to Lesotho and then on to America, was pretty remarkable. In the 1960s she had become a professor and married a man there, a black American.

She talked a lot about these people who were risen from slaves, about the parallels between us and them, about how our struggle was intertwined with those 'brothers and sisters from across the pond'.

Whenever she said this I imagined a lost tribe of jive-talking afro-wearing urban negroes (as we called them) wandering the plains of America bumping into Indians. What I knew of America was incongruously derived from a combination of old Western films full of Apaches and Navajos on empty expanses of land... and sitcoms like *The Jeffersons, Sanford and Son* and *Good Times*.

For many years, the brothers and sisters from across the pond would occupy this curious place in my mind.

I would dream about them speaking a version of English that I struggled to understand and humming 'Kumbaya'. Perhaps this was the reason why, when I finally made it to America, I embraced them like long-lost cousins. Gogo Lindi's ex-husband had carried a white man's name – Brown or White or Brody or something like that – but he was black as midnight. Years later, when I became a teenager, I would stumble across his pictures in a trunk of things she had left with Aunty Angela for safekeeping. I felt that I had looked at something I wasn't meant to see, so I carefully put them back, even though she was miles away by that time. Still, I got enough of a glimpse to see he was as handsome as Sidney Poitier and looked as though he loved her very much. The marriage hadn't worked out and I loved her because she had been strong enough to mind terribly but not to have been broken by it. After all, hadn't she stood on the streets of Jobstown, with her skirt hitched up, when she was only nine years old, watching the man who denied that he was her father through slit eyes? Hadn't she yelled at him on the streets of that barren Natal town where she was born?

'Hey you, I know who you are.'

Hadn't she shouted it so loud that he had turned on his horse and tried to bore a hole into her unwanted head with his eyes? And hadn't she refused to back down?

She had said, 'You are my father, you must buy me shoes.'

And hadn't he finally turned disdainfully and just kept on riding?

This had been about 1943 when she was a poor child to a single mother. She had been born into hatreds both resilient and limber, hatreds that told her that she was nothing.

Gogo Lindi could cook but chose not to when she didn't want to. She was in a bad mood sometimes and that was just life. On those days, she would sit in the Sangwenis' house like a visitor, expecting to be served. Her immaculately plaited head would be in the clouds as she stewed in a spectacularly bad mood that was often of her own making. Everyone would tiptoe around her.

Except me. She was my special friend.

I loved her because she was not my mother and didn't want to be. She loved me because she liked the light in my eyes, not because she was my flesh but because in my veins there was something of her – something restless and yearning that wanted to belong and also to be free.

The odour of teeth

IN THE MIDDLE of 1981, just before my family left Lusaka to go to Nairobi, I experienced an unexpected violence on the quiet edge of a big yard.

The scene of the crime is 10 Kalungu Road and on the morning of the violence I am dropped off at the Sangweni house, as I am on most days. Mummy greets Aunty Angela with a wide smile and they discuss the pick-up plan. Aunty nods at Lindi and Dumi who are wolfing down their breakfasts and says, 'These guys have sports after school today so I'll go out and fetch them at about four-thirty but Praisegod will be here to look after Sonke.'

Mummy says it's fine and tells Aunty that she will

come by at five, five-thirty. She waves goodbye and I dig in for a second breakfast. Ten minutes later, as Lindi and Dumi pile into the back of Aunt Angela's car, I hop onto Praisegod's bike and he rides me to school. Praisegod is a dutiful servant. Compared to others, his life at Kalungu Road is easy. There is little need for protocol with the Sangwenis. Uncle Stan works for the United Nations as a fairly senior official, which means a lot in terms of stability and comfort. Mummy often says that, despite the perks and benefits that come with a UN job, Uncle Stan is completely without Airs and Graces. To which Baba always says, 'That's good because Aunt Angela would not know what to do with him if he suddenly developed them, given what a humble soul she is.'

◆ ◆ ◆

On the day in question, Praisegod whistles a joyful tune. As he works, clipping the hedges and sweeping the ground underneath the mulberry tree, he hums and chirps as though there is an assortment of birds in his voice box. He sounds like he is hiding an exotic and dying species in his throat. Maybe he is mimicking birds he kept in his youth.

This is not unusual. He is the best whistler I have ever heard – even to this day I have never met another person who had the gift Praisegod had. When he whistles is he imagining that he is flying? Is he imitating a bird that he heard in his youth? Is he even conscious of it or does the sound merely come out?

I never ask him these questions, which is a pity but not strange. It isn't that I am not inquisitive. I have plenty of questions about worms and moths and neighbours and cars and the shape of the clouds. It simply doesn't occur to me that he might have another life. In my mind, Praisegod exists for the sole purpose of tending to the garden. He would not breathe if there weren't packages to be carried to and from the car. If it weren't for me to take to school and keep company maybe Praisegod would turn into an overgrown statue standing in the middle of the garden.

Like all middle-class African children, I am accustomed to living with domestic workers. I know that they are always to be spoken to politely and respectfully. In our house we call women servants Aunty and, later, when we move to Kenya and there is an *askari* planted in front of our gate, we call him Brother Patrick because he is only a few years older than me.

Although Mummy and Baba tell us all the time that we should be respectful to servants – both in our home and in the homes of our friends – we understand that there are alternative ways of treating The Help and that, in other households, The Help are treated very badly indeed.

Sometimes when the grown-ups are talking in the sitting room we overhear things that are not meant for little ears. This usually happens when we are deliberately still, crouched in the flowerbeds underneath the big living room window. We hear things we should know nothing about: madams beating The Help until the vessels in their eyes burst; The Help that has to be carried out of the house by The Boy who has stood as a silent witness to the crimes of the madam. Our eyes widen as we hear about village girls sent home abruptly when the swelling of their tummies can no longer be ignored.

The Help are whispered about when children are around.

'That child was only fifteen when she started working

there, but you know how Malawian men are. They will marry a twelve-yearold if their mother tells them to.'

We giggle and make sick eyes when Aunty Pulane – one of Mummy's closest friends, who has a sharp tongue and even sharper eyes – says, 'No wonder that man has never spent a single night in his own bed. She caught him fondling the helper's son.' They invoke God's name and somehow it is insufficient to say it in English.

'*Thixo!*' says Aunty Angela, invoking the deity herself. The rest shake their heads in knowing disbelief.

When certain visitors come over, it is hard to forget the things that have been said about them from the safety of the Kalungu Road settee.

The women's responses – their rejection of the acts, but their tacit acceptance of the inevitability of this behaviour – make the abuses seem like a natural extension of men's bodies. They never ask why men do the things they do. What some men will do is taken as a given. Instead, they are interested in why the child was not better protected. They want to know how the mother could not have foreseen that this would happen. They have unflinching common sense, so they are not concerned with the politics of blaming women. Instead, they want to know how to keep their girls safe. They are the kinds of mothers who don't let their guards down for long enough to let their daughters get close to fire.

Though there is never any significant drama with our servants, the general rules of engagement for maids and madams are very clear. Middle-class men are allowed to do what they like to maids. They can lurch for breasts. They can get home early and lock all the doors so that no one knows what they are up to. Boys can bed the neighbours' housegirls and learn how sex works, and they can deny the children that swell bellies after those liaisons.

Servant women are given no such leeway. The most minor infraction – a slowness in standing up when the wife of the house comes in, or a long face when a request to borrow money is declined – can signal the beginning of suspicion, or worse, the end of patience.

This possibility of brutality, no matter how remote (and often it isn't remote at all), keeps the domestic labour system in Africa running smoothly. Because of this, African servants are trustworthy and hard-working and generally mute on matters that do not concern them. There are those who pilfer and, yes, there are some who beat the children in their care. But these are relatively rare exceptions.

By and large, servants are loving and kind and reliable. This is not because the poor – who have no choice but to clean our homes and care for our babies – are better or humbler than the middle classes. It is because they have no choice. This is as true now as it was when I was a child. The exploited have much to lose, so they stay in line.

Praisegod, it turns out, is a rare and malevolent exception.

◆ ◆ ◆

Look at him. Watch him now as he fades into the trees, into the soil and the grass. He knows how not to be noticed. His skin is the colour of amnesia; his eyes have the dark-brown tint of forgetting. His features are nondescript. He is a man who looks down all day, sweeping and raking and planting. You can assign him whichever lips and nose you wish because you will soon forget them anyway. There is nothing about him that will make you think twice about his character or his intentions.

You will assume that he is here only to collect his wages and to excel, in his own private ways, in the menial tasks at hand. You tell yourself, as you look at his blunt face, that he finds some satisfaction in sweeping the driveway and stacking logs. Look carefully, for this is a young man. He is gentle with children and deferential with the father of the house. Barely out of his teens, he listens carefully to the instructions of the madam and inspires confidence because he so rarely meets her eye.

This everyman, this most lowly of African men, a mere uneducated servant, is broken. His soul had probably already been smashed by the time I was born. It must have happened when he was only just a boy. Maybe his father wounded him. Maybe his mother pummelled him. Maybe, because he was left-handed, they tried to drown him in a stream to see if the demon inside would come out. Maybe, on his first day of school, the letters began to swim before his eyes and, in fear and misery, he wet himself. And maybe, after the welts had risen on his buttocks from the caning, as he was running home to cry in his mother's arms, maybe he was hit on the back of the head by a stone, and maybe he fell, then, and awoke alone and concussed.

And maybe after that, after the headaches and the vomiting had subsided and he was left only with the memory of not being safe, maybe from then – which may have been from as early as he could remember – maybe after all that, everything was too hard and too complicated and little girls like me, with our endless questions and beaming smiles, with our almond eyes and neat braids, with our impossible expectations, and our offerings of brimming cups, maybe we now make him remember the times before he was broken. For those who have never been consoled, remembering is an awful burden to bear. What better way to ease a load than to forget it was ever there? What better way to forget than to be a child again, to play the games that children play, to exist as an innocent, in the time before wounds and pain and memory?

I am speculating, of course. But I have the luxury to do so: I have been a resilient victim, far more capable of survival in the end than a poor, broken man who himself was a casualty – the victim of a stunted revolution. I am not being brave – only honest. What happened to me was a bad thing, for sure, but worse happens every day to people who are in no position to recover. I tell it to show that it is awful and also that it isn't the end of the world.

◆ ◆ ◆

So let us go there. Let us begin with the minute when he says to me, 'See?' with all the gentleness of a mild summer day. 'Come. Come see this.' He is smiling as though he has a secret to tell, so I crouch down beside him and look at the grasshopper he has captured in his hands. I marvel. 'Can I hold?' I ask, fearless as ever. He has something else to show me, he says and so I follow, traipsing behind as he leads me towards his quarters.

This is ancient history now, but I can never tell it without wanting to stop the reel at this moment; without wanting to make myself turn around and walk away before I enter the cool, well-shaded room at the edge of the property. I want Aunty Angela to come out, wiping her hands on her apron, to say, 'Sonke, let's go and buy some bread at the French bakery,' but it's too late for that now.

I hesitate at the door: I have been warned many times

before not to go inside his room, because nobody wants me badgering him and disturbing his privacy. The room is cool and dark and sparse.

His bed is narrow and neatly made up and the room smells like he does: old sweat and tobacco and something acrid and musty and strong.

I enter.

He sits on the bed and pats the space next to him so that we are seated side by side. My legs dangle loosely and I am not afraid. He moves quickly and is suddenly on top of me and then I am afraid. I am very afraid and there is fear in my bowels and drums in my blood and everything in me wants to live and die at once. But it is too late to decide which way it will go – life or death. It is too late and my powder-blue shorts are off and I am fighting to keep my panties on and he is trying to snatch them down and I am clenching so hard that he cannot roll them down any further and then he is ramming against me with his body and trying to prise my legs apart and then his breath is in my face and he is heavy and he smells so awful I want to cry and vomit at the same time and then he asks, 'Is it nice?'

I say yes.

The 'yes' unlocks a door and he tenses up. He stops holding my arms so tightly and he just lies there. He is sticky and so am I. I am sore from where his fingers have gouged, and from where his penis has tried to enter me. He has not succeeded but he has hurt me.

I am hurt.

I lie underneath him and he is hot and he smells awful and tears leak from the corners of my eyes. Then he sits up and buttons his trousers. He does not look at me. I get down from the bed and put my shorts back on and I do not look at him either. I move away from the bed and stand a few feet away, next to the door, waiting as he finds his own feet. Then he takes my hand and we walk, as we have walked many times before, hand in hand. We walk into the bright blinking day and I am not crying. I let go of his hand somewhere in the garden and I pick my way across fallen mulberries and papayas. I slip quietly into the house and then, once I am there, in the cool of the kitchen, away from the garden and the over-lush smell of ripening fruit, once I am leaning forward at the sink and drinking a glass of water, I make up my mind about what has just happened. I solemnly swear that he will never touch me again. I do not even cry, because I just know, in myself, exactly what I need to do to be safe.

◆ ◆ ◆

Afterwards 10 Kalungu Road no longer feels like home. Mummy still drops me there before school and I continue to stay after, but now I cross the veranda quickly and never stay in the back yard. In the afternoons I am Dumi's shadow. I stick to him and Cousin George, even when they are being mean and telling me they have boys' things to do. When Lindi is home, I glue myself to her side and I don't even care when her friends call me the tape recorder and shush each other when I appear at her bedroom door. 'You know she's just gonna run and tell the grown-ups what we're saying,' they snicker. It doesn't bother me one little bit. I am a hard little ball inside and my mission is simple, clean, crisp. I will be fine, as long as I avoid the garden.

A couple of days after the incident, Aunty asks Praisegod to ride me to school on his bike – as he has many times before. 'No,' I say, interrupting her instructions to him.

'Why not, Sonke? I have to go into town today. It will make everything much easier, big girl.' No. I begin to cry. It is the first of many times that I will break my crying rule in the long months that follow.

A few times, when Aunty Angela needs to go to the shops, she suggests that I stay behind because 'Praisegod is here.' I refuse. I join her, each and every time, and soon she doesn't bother asking. She simply says, 'Come dear, I need to quickly run to the bakery.'

While my confidence grows with each new act of rebellion, it doesn't occur to me to tell anyone about what Praisegod has done to me. Not for one minute do I even consider this. Not as I straighten myself up and walk into the house. Not as Aunty Angela says, 'Where were you?' Not when Mummy comes to fetch me. Not when I am in the back seat looking out of the window as we drive home with my babbling sisters putting their jammy fingers all over me. Not even on that day when they try desperately to put me on the handlebars of the bike so that he can ride me to school. Not as I squirm and kick and finally manage to break loose and run up the tree that stands over the gate.

Telling would put everyone in the unbearable position of having to do something about it.

'Why did you go there when we have told you not to so many times?'

'What happened?'

They will ask this with panic squawking through their voices.

And in the telling of the tale, when I respond, I will not know how to explain the quietness of the room and the awful betrayal of my lungs which never once gave me breath enough to howl.

Telling someone, telling anyone, will be the same as

telling them all and it will box me for them. It will make me an outsider, a child who trails whispers and who will grow up and be followed by the lingering scent of 'Why?' If I tell them they will soothe me and hold my hand and tell me it will all be fine, but I will be marked. From then on, they will wonder, quietly and perhaps in my presence. They will ask why I never screamed. I will still be their child but I will be altered – damaged and no longer innocent. They will no longer be able to say of me, 'Oh, that one never bothers anybody.' I will be troubled.

◆ ◆ ◆

A few months after the incident, Mummy and Baba tell us that we are moving. We are going to Kenya because Baba has a new job working for one of the agencies of the United Nations, just like Uncle Stan. This news is no surprise. For weeks Mummy and Baba have been sitting together at the kitchen table, talking late into the night, discussing Something Important.

I am floored when Mummy says that they aren't taking me with them. I will have to stay in Lusaka for three weeks after they have left so that I can complete the school term here, while they set everything up in Nairobi. Baba's contract begins a month before the school term ends, so Mummy explains that it makes the most sense for them to leave me here.

She announces it very matter-of-factly. 'We will drive to Nairobi, and you will stay here. Baba will use the ticket the UN has given him to fly back to Lusaka to get you at the end of term. Then the two of you will fly back together.' I start to cry, and Mummy doesn't fully understand why. 'You love that house, Sonke. You'll be with Lindi and Aunty and Uncle and Gogo Lindi will come and see you every day if you want. I'll ask her myself.'

I am mortified and petrified and resolute in my opposition to the plan. I am not opposed to moving to Kenya but I am dead set against sleeping in that house.

◆ ◆ ◆

On the day of the big departure, we drive over to the Sangwenis' house in the fully loaded car. The adults talk for a while and drink tea to delay the inevitable. After some time, Baba and Mummy exchange looks. He stretches on the couch, a long languorous unfolding of his limbs, which signals to Uncle Stan that the time has come.

Uncle clears his throat and marks the occasion – as is his wont – by giving a speech. With his combed-back thicket of hair that is delicately greying, and his professorial maroon-and-green argyle cardigan, Uncle Stan is nothing if not sublime. Even when he is angry – which is rare – he speaks slowly and carefully. He is not a man prone to outbursts. And so it is that when he draws himself up to his full height to deliver a farewell sermon, he imbues today's departure with an air of serious quietude.

He talks firstly about where we come from. He speaks of Humble Beginnings and Man's Capacity to Triumph Over Adversity. These are phrases he uses often, especially when he refers to Masondale – the village in the Natal Midlands where he and Baba were raised.

He takes the opportunity to remind us that the architects of apartheid did not intend for Masondale to 'produce men of courage and conviction and dignity. And yet all our stock is like this. We are sprung from the loins of people who have never allowed themselves to be conquered.'

As he speaks, he uses Baba's home name, the name that he grew up with. In exile, Baba has assumed a new name: Walter, which was his father's Christian name. He shed Matthew, the one given to him at birth, when he crossed into Francistown in 1962.

Uncle Stan continues, speaking slowly and with great deliberation. 'We are descended from people who are noble both in word and in deed. Matthew, Ntombi, girls – travel well on this new journey. Make us proud.'

Then it is hugs and kisses and waves and smiles, and everyone is saying how brave I am to not even be crying and the car is pulling out of the driveway and onto Kalungu Road. Aunty Angela takes my hand and we turn to walk back to the house.

I cross the veranda and go to the sink in the kitchen to get a glass of water. I look out and see Praisegod sweeping under the mango trees in the back garden and suddenly I feel, in the most intense way possible, that I am only seven years old and it feels like too small a number in the face of so big a task and so I drop the glass and find myself running.

There isn't really anywhere to go, so I dive under the dining room table and I start to wail. I lock myself behind the sturdy legs of the chairs and grip the chunky wooden knees of the table as though my life depends on it. Aunty Angela – bless her – thinks that I am embarrassed that I broke the glass. Correcting her would be too difficult. It would raise too many other questions and so I don't.

Instead, I sniffle and look out at her through the wooden bars, my limbs indistinguishable from those of my mahogany refuge. 'It's okay, Sonke,' she says, coaxing me to come out. I can only heave; words may hurt, but the sobs offer release.

After some time Aunty pads away and goes to the bedroom. I sit under the table no longer weeping. I can still hear him sweeping outside. Then that, too, stops and all I can hear is the distant sound of a manservant whistling.

◆ ◆ ◆

In the three weeks that pass between their departure and Baba's return, I do not utter a single word to Praisegod, and nobody notices. The initial battles I fought to prevent him from taking me to school have been won so there is no need for me to restate my position. Aunty takes me to school, and Praisegod stays well away.

I survive the weeks by playing on the streets and staying out of the yard in this place that is no longer really my home. At night I think about his breath. I hear myself say yes and blood warms my face. The softly grunting tangled and dirty man who, on that day, was not the Praisegod I had come to know is never far from my thoughts.

Then it is over. Baba comes back and we drive to the airport and I am sitting on a plane next to him and Kalungu Road is on the ground and we are up in the sky and the clouds are beneath us and Praisegod is getting further and further away. I am moving at what feels like faster than the speed of light and underneath us Zambia has disappeared and instead it is the Serengeti and within it are thousands of acacia trees and scores of brown rivers, and wildebeest and elephants and ostriches, none of which I can see but all of which are in a picture book on my lap. My eyes and my mouth are a triad of awestruck Os and I have finally allowed myself not to think about the fear in my belly. I am all imagination now and Praisegod is far, far away.

When she sees me at the airport Mummy hugs me longer and harder than she ever has before. She tilts my face towards her and says, 'Ha! No scrapes on your knees?' I shake my head, grinning and trying not to cry. 'Nothing?' She inspects my arms and my legs and for a minute I wonder if she knows and I secretly hope that she does so she can march back to Lusaka and Crush His Skull, the way Baba always threatens to do to other drivers when they block him in traffic. But the moment passes and instead she says with a wistful smile, 'Well, then you must be growing up, my girl!'

In Nairobi there is no Praisegod and no back garden, only a maisonette on Ngong Road. This is just at the turn-off to State House, which means that every day motorbikes and police cars wail past us, with the president somewhere in the middle and a body double pretending to be him in another car right in front of him or right behind him or, who knows, perhaps sitting right next to him prepared to be sacrificed in the event of an assassination attempt. I am trying to say that I am in this new place where I can breathe again. I am in this new place where, this time, I will know better than to trust a man who whistles like a bird and whispers like a friend.

I fold away the stink of his fingers and the odour of his tobaccostained teeth. In time I will force myself to forget his face; its contours will shadow. His body will not be so easy to displace but I will teach myself that I was strong and I will remind myself of all the ways I fought him and made myself live. And my memories will be rich and they will be bigger than him. They will click in my head like a showreel and make me everything that I am. They will tell me the legacy of my childhood is so much bigger than anything one man could undo.

Mummy puts purple iodine on my knees and kisses me before bed.
The German Girlfriend tells me not to trust The System.
Dr Kenneth Kaunda believes in us all.
Copper is the colour of the mud after it rains.
I pin a tag on which Baba has written 'Danaus chrysippus'
onto his pinboard and the powder from the butterfly's wing
smudges on my thumb.

Even in my frightened silence I believe in the strength of my own bones. I believe in the tough sinew that keeps my legs moving. I have faith in the muscles of my arms that pull me up and swing me over. I trust in my pumping heart and in the sturdiness of my ribcage. Through those weeks that turn into months that become years of what you might want to call silence, I speak to myself. I tell myself the truth, which is that he is wrong and everything about me is right. I believe in my bones because I have others who believe in them too.

Today, across the yellowing decades, I remember the tobacco on his tongue and the marijuana seeds under his nails; and beneath them I can still taste his sweat. I still feel the weight of his dead dreams some days when I wake up, and this is fine. What matters most is that – like Scheherazade – I said yes so that I could live.

Kenya

KENYA NEVER OWNED us the way Zambia did. The ANC community in Nairobi was less structured; while Lusaka had been our home because it was the headquarters of the ANC, Nairobi was our home because Baba had a job there and his job had nothing to do with the revolution.

This one fact – that Baba now had a place of employment and was not a full-time member of the ANC – began to open up possibilities for us. We went from being refugees in Zambia – a country whose entire foreign policy was built around our protection and emancipation – to being expatriates in a city concerned with feeding its rich and distancing itself from its poor.

On weekends we would drive across town to visit other South African families. A year after we arrived in Nairobi, Uncle Stan and Aunty Angela joined us. By now Lindi was in boarding school in Swaziland and Dumi enrolled in Nairobi Academy, where we also went. Having our old friends in Nairobi made it feel more like home, but the city itself remained a mystery.

To get to the house where the Sangwenis lived we often took Arboretum Drive, which was flanked on one side by a micro-forest with ancient trees hung with vines. It was a lush, impossibly green daub of paint that seemed to emerge from nowhere, just past the busy shopping area of Westlands. Once we were past Arboretum Drive, we were in a proper suburb – on our way into Kileleshwa. I would look out of the window, catching glimpses of colonial villas behind high walls covered in Bougainvillea vines. The flowers – purple and peach and red – bounced across the tops of wrought iron gates and tumbled onto the dark green of hedges that made me want to jump out of the car and smell them. That would have been impossible, of course; a wall bordered every house and every gate was guarded by an askari – a man whose only job was to keep strangers out.

Like Lusaka, Nairobi had many roundabouts. These intersections were still elegant, in spite of the increasing traffic. They were beautiful places of near-lawlessness. On weekends, Baba sped through the city's roundabouts without slowing down. In the back, my sisters and I would slip and slide, giggling at the motion, certain that the car looked like a cartoon – on the verge of tipping over.

During the week, the city was completely different. From Monday to Friday traffic was controlled not by lights and careful observance of the rules, no; our car moved on the basis of the instructions of white-gloved traffic police. Both hands up meant stop. A slow deliberate arm with a hand pointing told us to proceed left. The right hand would continue to signal stop to oncoming traffic. The drivers would do as they were told until the cops turned away. Then they would sneak forward, hoot and carry on without regard for decorum.

The officers wore braided hats and crisp light-blue shirts and navy-blue shorts. Their sinewy African legs were familiar. I had seen them in Lusaka, motioning in the same way, standing in the sun yet somehow not sweating. I was in another country, but somehow things were the same.

Except, they weren't. Nairobi had harder edges. It was faster-paced, noisier, and much bigger than sleepy Lusaka. Nairobi screeched and clanged and was in a hurry to go somewhere important. Kenyans were sure-footed and confident. They were brash and impatient where Zambians took life easier, moved more slowly. Perhaps it was because the recent past was so bloody in Kenya. The country preferred to look ahead, because looking back was too painful.

I was only eight when we moved to Kenya. I did not know that, in the decade leading up to Kenyan independence in 1963, the British had behaved like violent thugs. Kenya's colonial history is as bloody as any other in Africa, although until recently Kenyans had managed to pretend that theirs was a history that never happened.

So, had I asked, no one in the city would have willingly told me about the Mau Mau. They would have avoided telling me stories of the hundreds of Kikuyu women who took oaths and picked up machetes to defend their land against the British. They would not have said a word about the Mau Mau men who were killed in their thousands in the 1950s in a brave uprising that dared to kill whites. Kenya was a place of secrets and Nairobi was a city whose residents knew far more than they were prepared to say.

Daniel arap Moi was Kenya's president. He was different from President Kaunda, who cared about Zambia to the point of tears. President Moi seemed unmoved by the slums and the potholes and the malnutrition. He wore dark suits and had red eyes. He rarely smiled on the television.

In Lusaka Mummy and Baba used to say, 'Say what you will about President Kaunda, he certainly loves his people.' In Kenya, I never heard them say this about President Moi. Instead, when the evening news came on they would shush us and we would watch as the unsmiling president opened schools and addressed conferences. He did not cry when he saw the goitres and the thin legs of the children who gathered in their school uniforms to greet him.

While the sight of President Kaunda had inspired excitement in us, here we watched the president with a sort of fearful awe.

Everywhere you looked in Nairobi there were unfathomably poor people. Many of them were children. They chased us in hordes on nights when we went out to restaurants in the city. Their eyes would bore into our backs as we rushed quickly back to the car. Then they would look on in silence, staring at us through the windows as we pulled up to traffic lights.

On the weekends they spilled onto the roads, too poor to buy anything to sell — not even food. Their hands were always cupped and their faces looked as though they had never been clean.

I wondered how they didn't get run over by the reckless *matatus* whose drivers sped past them with deadened eyes. They lived on the centre line of Nairobi's busy roads, between whizzing cars, and learnt to give way to big men whose tyres drove relentlessly across lanes so dilapidated it was hard to imagine that they could take the country into a new kind of future.

The Nairobi of my childhood refused to look up. It was interested only in the midline, in the space between the stomach and the wallet. It was intent on avoiding eye contact at all costs. That was how you managed the city – by shrinking into yourself and closing your eyes and covering your ears to block out the noise of it all.

There were places in that city too violent or too dirty or too terrible for us to enter, places where armies of children lived and slept and which they never left. There were children in Nairobi whose particular corners of misery might as well have been another country. I was shielded from the pain of this sort of belonging. The children of Nairobi's underclass knew their place, and the children of the upper classes expected them to stay there. Kenya's leaders were not planning for growth. Their strategy was premised not on building the middle classes, but on empowering the elite.

Uncle and Aunty and Mummy and Baba decided to buy a whole sheep and have it slaughtered and butchered. The idea was to share the costs of the sheep and then to divide it and put its pieces into the deep freezer. That would be cheaper than buying fresh meat every week. Baba asked the askari posted at the front gate of the small complex where we lived where he might find the place where this sort of service was offered. The guard told him he could buy a sheep at Dagoretti Corner or in Kibera – the massive slum across the road and past the golf course. He urged Baba not to go there himself. 'I will do it for you, sir,' he suggested. He wanted to earn some extra money, but there was something else there, something more urgent. He wanted to protect us – with our polished shoes and our pan-African aspirations. He wanted to prevent us from seeing Nairobi's gaunt and pock-marked buttocks.

◆ ◆ ◆

At Nairobi Academy, the roster of students was an amalgam of Patels and Richardsons and Kariukis. All our parents were intent on providing us with a sound British education. Every morning we would start the day by singing the Kenyan national anthem. Then we would recite our times tables by rote. 'Three times one is three. Three times two is six. Three times three is nine.' We spoke as one. Those who stumbled were rapped on the knuckles. We only stopped when we had done the twelve times table. The ones who sat at the front, with their uniforms orderly and neat, were always correct. Mrs Richards kept her eyes on the ones who sat at the back. They mumbled and messed up though they were less afraid of the ruler than I ever was.

Although we read *Nancy Drew* and the *Hardy Boys*, and idolised them all, it never occurred to me to want to be blonde and American. No one at school was as confident or as beautiful as Ethel Wanjiku. While my socks inevitably drifted down to my skinny ankles, Ethel's stayed up all day, every single day. Her legs were straight and brown and slightly plump in that perfect way. She had calves that were not too skinny and her pinafore never seemed to crease. She had plaited hair that touched her shoulders and was held in place by two immaculate dark-green barrettes that perfectly matched our dark-green cardigans.

When I tried to get Mummy to do my hair like that she said it wasn't long enough. I had to be content with six scrappy cornrows going backwards. No ribbons, no barrettes. Not even a hairpin. When I begged Mummy at least to let me have green rubber bands to go with my uniform she said, 'School is not a modelling competition. Concentrate on your books, not your looks, my girl.' Often by the middle of the week there were little kinky balls at the nape of my neck and the lines of scalp between each braid were no longer so clear. It was hard not to be jealous of Ethel.

Still, I had a few things going for me. One of them was my love of reading. I don't remember a time I didn't know how to read. When I was still very small – maybe four or five – I would crawl into Baba's lap and read along silently, not understanding the meaning of the words but knowing how to put them together.

Shortly after we started at Nairobi Academy, Mummy came up with a new rule. If there were no visitors, then we would do our chores and play, and then, by 3 p.m., we would be in our bedroom, reading. Mandla and Zeng would sometimes giggle and try to talk. Often, they would fall asleep.

I never did. I curled up and read, even if my eyes were droopy. The stories were a respite – I could be a dragon or a princess, a beggar or a thief. And after a while I realised I could write, too. In real life, I may have envied Ethel, but on the page I could be her or Gogo Lindi. In the stories I scribbled on those quiet Sunday afternoons I could be anyone, anywhere.

We could afford to go to Nairobi Academy because Baba was now an employee of the United Nations. In

Lusaka he had volunteered for the United Nations Environment Programme. After he finished his degree, he had been offered a chance to go to Kenya as a proper employee. The transition served us well but it wasn't enough to allay the bigger fears he and Mummy had.

The ANC had a tenuous presence in Kenya. The community that had nurtured us in Zambia simply didn't exist here. For one thing, Zambia was geographically much closer to South Africa. It was a leading member of the Frontline States, so the threat and fear of apartheid among ordinary Zambians and within the ANC community had been more significant. But more importantly, unlike President Kaunda, President Moi was not invested in the future of black South Africa, so our fate was not inextricably linked to the fate of his own country. Moi was hardly enthused by the idea of educating and ministering to the health needs of his own people. Like many of Africa's rulers in the 1980s, he had no great moral agenda and was interested in little beyond maintaining power.

Kenya pulsed with money. It was East Africa's regional financial nerve centre, yet it had no real political heart. Mummy and Baba knew that, unlike Zambia or Tanzania or Mozambique – countries where the Big Men understood the power of ideas – Kenya would not defend or protect them if times got rough. It would offer nothing on the basis of solidarity.

Our situation was compounded by our legal status, which was ad hoc and tenuous. It was clear that my sisters and I would need citizenship. The older we got, the more urgent this issue became.

At the same time, inside South Africa the fight against apartheid was heating up. The regime was getting more brutal and, in response, activists were becoming increasingly militant, as were millions of ordinary black South Africans inside the country. Week after week there were funerals for murdered activists. Hundreds gathered to mourn, and each event turned into a rally. There were strikes and burning tyres, round-ups of comrades, reports of the dead and the tortured.

It was a dark and difficult time, yet it was imbued with a spare sort of hope. Our life in Kenya seemed many miles away from South Africa and freedom seemed to be just a faint outline – a sort of hologram we could put our fingers to but couldn't feel.

This Africa held nothing in store for us. Kenya was not Zambia. There was no revolutionary spirit; there was only the sort of crass mobility that would never protect us. So, Mummy and Baba made a plan.

In 1984, as South Africa began its final paroxysms, the last decade before independence when freedom seemed both very far away and impossibly close, we got on a plane headed for Canada. Mummy and Baba left, seeking a place where we might have more secure tenure in the future – where we might have a chance at the kinds of opportunities that accompany the terrain of citizenship and belonging.

We left for yet another country, a place where everything would be clean and new and where Mummy and Baba thought nothing could hurt us.

O! Canada

THE IMPETUS FOR the move to North America was practical. We had a good life in Nairobi, but Baba was technically stateless, which meant that, in time, my sisters and I would be too. In addition, as a woman, Mummy – who wasn't a terrorist and had a perfectly legitimate passport – couldn't pass her Swazi citizenship on to us.

When we were babies, Mummy had managed to wangle favours and talk to Big Men. She would smile sweetly in a waiting room, she would speak softly and not say a word about her accounting diploma or the Toyota Corolla she drove. She would arrive in a *doek* and look down and they would nod brusquely and say, 'Okay *ntombaza-*

na, sizobona.' Not a definitive 'yes' but not a 'no' either. Sometimes they would speak sternly, reminding her that it wasn't their fault that she had married a guerrilla, which they would pronounce 'gorilla'. And in time, Mummy knew, the Big Men would demand more from her than she was prepared to part with, or that someone in the machine would simply say 'no' and her children would be stranded without identities.

Leaving Nairobi to seek a future that could guarantee us documents and a certain stability could only have been Mummy's choice.

Ever the accountant, she was prudent but knew when to champion a short-term venture that would have long-term payoffs. Baba had probably resisted because freedom would one day come; because the kids would be fine; because we would find a way. In the end, her logic and determination would have worn him down. 'Freedom will come,' I can hear her say, 'but in the meantime, there is life.'

We needed to be somewhere, to rest in safety while the drums of war beat elsewhere.

◆ ◆ ◆

In photographs taken in the early weeks after our arrival in Canada, in the muggy summer of 1984, my sisters and I were moon-faced with the trepidation of kids who had just found themselves in an unfamiliar place. We were not Hansel and Gretel in the dark forest but Sally and me in *The Cat in the Hat*, suddenly let loose on a holiday that seemed to have no end. It was liberating but unsettling. We were listless in the heat and the stillness. Mummy and Baba had no work and were with us day and night. There was no way to detach from them. No watchmen teasing and admonishing us when we strayed too far from the motel we found when we arrived.

No one, really, who was all that interested in us.

The days stretched from sunup at six to sundown at ten and each new day was as hot as the last so that you had to forgive everyone for wearing shorts. They had no choice: grannies with their veiny legs, old women with their sun-beaten wrinkled thighs, teenagers firm and lithe and pale in the humid torpor. We learnt not to stare. We learnt to hide our amused glances when a fatty bopped down the street in flip flops and denim shorts. No one batted an eyelid.

Everything was big – larger than it really should be, like the Slurpees at the 7-Eleven and the super-long cars that, for all their length, couldn't carry any extra people. We marvelled at the parking lots. The cars were treated like gods. Unlike in Nairobi, where the roads were lumpy and you sometimes had to squint to see how a parking bay was marked out, here, the lines on the ground in parking lots were immaculate and each space was well lit and spotlessly clean. We arrived in the wheat belt of Canada, the Prairies, in June. At the Canadian High Commission in Nairobi, Mummy and Baba had asked the portly middle-aged man behind the counter if he had any suggestions for where they should settle our family. He said Saskatoon was a great place to raise children and they took his advice. Upon arrival it was immediately evident that there were very few prospects for work or for making the kind of life they wanted in Saskatoon. So, Baba got busy applying for jobs in Toronto and Ottawa. He scoured the papers and got on the phone with recruiters. It didn't take long. He found a job at a place called World University Service of Canada (WUSC) and, just six weeks after we had landed in Saskatoon, we packed up again and made our way east across the country. It took us a week to reach Ottawa in our tiny little brown Datsun that held most of our belongings.

Staying in the Prairies hadn't been an option. In small, quiet towns where getting along is everything, Baba's pride would have hampered our progress. We girls would have been fine in the way that one must be fine in the end, even if bruised and somewhat broken on the inside, but Baba would have been like a caged bull. He would have become angry and frustrated and not like our father at all, only a shadow of himself, crippled by rage. So, we forestalled the drama we might have endured and slipped out of that place that was too small for such a big man and his wife. We left as quietly as we had arrived.

Baba had been hired by the team that planned and delivered humanitarian assistance to some of the poorest places in Africa. In Lusaka, Baba had worked at the World Food Programme and knew the ins and outs of food distribution, and then, at the UN in Nairobi, he had spent a lot of time assisting with Ugandan refugees. So, his experience was tailor-made for the drought that hit Ethiopia in 1984.

There was no place as bad as Ethiopia in the terrible years that followed. The famine killed so many and in such heartbreaking ways that even pop singers noticed. 'We Are the World' was our anthem the following year. Whenever it played, we would think of Baba, far away feeding skeletal babies with vacant eyes and distended bellies.

Although Ottawa had more colour than Saskatoon, we were still one of only a handful of African families that had settled in the suburbs of the capital city. Our presence was as conspicuous here as that of the Rhodesians we had seen striding across Independence Avenue in Lusaka in our childhood. We stuck out like those white NGO workers in downtown Nairobi.

In Canada the whites were just as confident as all the whites I had known but, here, I noticed that the few black people we came across were much less certain of themselves. We seemed to shrink; all of us were trying to fit in and do things the way Canadians did things.

We were cautious and wary of everything. Late that summer, a few weeks after we had unpacked our things in Ottawa, a colleague of Baba's, a woman named Marianne, rang us and offered to take us out. She and her two sons David and Nick had been back in Ottawa for a few years. The boys were the same age as we were and they taught us how to fish and how to not be scared of swimming in the lake.

'No crocodiles here!' Marianne shouted cheerfully from the water. The three of us stood doubtfully on the pier. The water was clear but you couldn't see the bottom. Zeng shook her head and Mandla cried and said she wouldn't do it and I – too proud to admit fear – went in. Slowly.

That first year, Canada was full of these sorts of moments. There was always something unfamiliar around the corner, some neverbefore-imagined circumstance that was suddenly unfolding around me. Sometimes the event would be innocuous and I would stumble but recover quickly. Other times though I felt as though the air was too thin and I would gulp, vertiginous and sick with worrying about fitting in.

That summer I felt it acutely. Between the move to Saskatoon and the move to Ottawa and the swims in Lake Manotick and visits to Zellers, which was the largest department store I had ever seen, I was often overwhelmed by how strange this new place was. I couldn't compare

Canada to anywhere else I had been. The people and their customs and habits were so different from anything I had known.

I lay awake sometimes listening to the rise and fall of Mummy and Baba's voices downstairs, unable to sleep, incapable of even finding a vocabulary for my out-of-depthness.

When school started in September I was anxious. Another new school, another set of few faces. I wondered whether there would be an Ethel here. I wondered when I would stop being the new girl all the time.

On the first day of school I kept my tears in check because I knew Mummy needed me to be strong. If I started crying then Mandla would too. Zeng was still in kindergarten and too small to really understand – she was always fine. But the two of us knew what was going on and we were old enough to worry. That morning we drove to school so that Mummy could take us in. Baba was at work, and Mummy had to get to her office too. So it was a rushed affair – no time for drama. Mandla and I feigned bravery. We waved as she got in the car with Zeng, then stood in front of the building for a while aching with sorrow and desperate with expectation.

That day was hard because first days are always hard, but we managed. And after a few weeks we started to feel more settled. School no longer felt like a foreign place and the streets we crossed to get there every morning no longer seemed indistinct. Even the house – which still smelled a little bit like the last people who had lived there – was starting to feel like home.

Fall came and I liked it. The leaves were not just leaves – they were like little pieces of paper someone had scattered in the air and on the ground as they turned yellow and then red. I began to feel as though I may be okay here. We got into a routine of school and play and home-work and it was still different but no longer seemed like an odd and misshapen life, the way it had at first. And then, one day, in the middle of everything that was becoming mundane and ordinary, on a day just like the ones that had come before it, I was called an African monkey.

The culprit was a boy who had not seemed at all sinister before he said it, so he caught me off guard. The scene remains vivid in my mind mainly because it was brutal and I was the only one who cared. Perhaps it was because I was the one he intended to wound. What mattered then, and still matters now, was that nobody came to my defence. They heard him. They all heard him. There were snickers and there was laughter.

I stood there, frozen. Then someone said, 'Oh! Burn,' as though this were just an ordinary slight, an insult from which I could recover if I thought of a comeback quickly enough. I couldn't, of course and, worse, I began to cry. So that they didn't only see the insult, they also saw, in the big fat tears that fell down my face, that I had been wounded. Then the taunts began. 'Ooh ooh, ahh ahh!' The boy began it and a few others joined in. There was more laughter. They all seemed to join in. And then, as though my inability to respond wasn't bad enough, I lost my nerve and I turned and fled. Mandla trailed after me, too scared to catch up but too worried to stay away. We were both too hurt to speak. I raced ahead, angry with her for having witnessed my humiliation.

I still hate him. I am a grown woman and wouldn't recognise him on the street but there are some hurts we nurture to guard against forgetting. So sometimes, even now, as I watch my own children make their way towards resilience, I sometimes run my fingers over the puncture wounds left by racism's sharp little teeth. I like to remind myself that I was once surprised; that there was a time when I was still young and couldn't recognise malevolence as it walked towards me. I turn these memories over in my mind and refuse to flinch because remembering is a form of preparation; because, one day soon, one of my children will come in crying because their skin will have captured the attention of someone's pink child and I will have to hold them through the awful discovery that something as simple as skin has been perverted by so many.

They will recover and be tougher for having encountered the venom, but in anticipation of that moment, which is as inevitable as the blue skies and cloudy days, I remember that boy and that day and everything that happened afterwards.

I told Mummy. She looked like she was going to cry but didn't. She just said, 'I'll talk to your father,' and when he got home they went into the bedroom and when they came down Baba called me to him.

We sat in what Canadians called 'the den,' which, in our small townhouse, was also the TV room and the dining room. I could hear Mandla and Zeng and Mummy go quiet in the kitchen, straining their ears as Baba started to speak.

He was not gentle. 'What happened today at school?' His voice was already impatient, as though I had done something wrong.

'We were just playing,' I said. I was afraid of something, now, though not quite sure what. 'We were just playing and then this boy just all of a sudden pushed me from the monkey bars.' I began to cry. 'Then he said, "Oh, you're a good African monkey." Then he started making funny noises like a monkey.'

Baba's face darkened but he did not comfort me. 'And what did you say?'

'Nothing. I just walked away because the other kids started laughing and making sounds too. And when I was already leaving he shouted and said I must stay away from the swings.'

Baba was livid. 'You kept quiet? You allowed him to speak to you like that?'

'I didn't know what to say.' Baba was now standing. He was standing and I was sitting and he looked bigger than he ever had before and where usually his size was a consolation – the thing that marked him out in a crowd and allowed me to claim him – in that moment my neck hurt from straining to look up at him and tears crawled out of the sides of my eyes and found solace in my ears.

Mummy came in and said, 'Wally, please, she's a child. What was she supposed to do?'

'What she was supposed to do,' he said, shouting quietly at Mummy the way he did when he was very angry, which was not often, 'what she was supposed to do was to stand up for herself not walk away like some sort of...' His voice trailed off but I knew what he had stopped himself from saying. The word 'coward' stood between us, unspoken. It was always Baba's worst insult. Nothing, in his mind, was lower than a coward.

Mummy looked at him and tried to contain her anger. She always got quiet when she was angry so that she seemed to radiate cold rather than heat.

'You should be angry at them, not her. We should be talking to the school, not shouting at the child.' She was whispering and I could hardly hear her above the roar of shame in my ears. Baba was right. He was always right and he was always strong and I wasn't. Sometimes – especially here in this new place where I was different without trying to be – I didn't know what to do and I didn't know how to be so my words failed me and I became a coward.

My instinct had not been to fight – it had been to turn and leave. Even as I was doing it I knew it wasn't the right thing to do, but still it felt like the only thing I knew for sure how to do. The only place my legs could take me was away and my mouth suddenly did not want to work and everything in me that had ever been scared had been activated. In spite of the brave face I put on for Mummy and the way I shrugged off Mandla and Zeng when they wanted to hold hands on the street, I was still the same child who had hidden in the crowd at Burley Court, the one who had flinched at Mama Tawona's mean face. I knew the lesson that Praisegod had taught me, which was that the safest place was in the middle, but here in this flat country I stuck out. I was an anthill on a prairie. Here, I had to be brave because everybody was always looking at me. They were looking at me, even when I hadn't seen them.

Baba started again. 'Listen to me, Sonke,' he said. 'If anyone ever, ever insults you like that again, you hit them. You hit them there on the spot. You hit them hard and you make sure there is blood. Do you understand? We do not turn the other cheek in this house, not about things like this.'

I nodded, still crying. I understood. I had not made him proud and this was a new and unexpected feeling.

The next day Baba took us to school. Mandla went to her classroom and he took my hand in his and went to the principal's office. I sat next to Baba in a fugue, certain that whatever he was going to say would mark me for life. I would be a target. A tattletale and a baby and, worse, a monkey to boot. Our turn came and Baba rose with the grace of a cat. I came in behind him, the tears already threatening, looking drowned and small. I wished I were Zeng, that I was five and still in playschool and too little to understand the weight of Baba's expectations.

Inside the office, Mr Barry – all the kids called him Mr B – was smiling but his brow was furrowed. He looked curious and kind, the way a principal ought to look. We sat down and before Mr B could even offer a cup of coffee Baba had begun to speak. There were no preliminaries, no soft-pedalling or pussyfooting about.

Baba responded to 'How is Sisonke settling in?' by saying, 'Well, that is why we are here,' and recounting the monkey story in all its shameful detail. I liked Mr B and I wanted him to like me, too. I did not want to be magnified like this, sitting in front of his desk crying. I wanted to see him in the hall and wave the way I had seen some of the girls in my class doing, and for him to tease me and call out in a stern but kind voice, 'If you walk down the hall instead of running you will probably get there without falling, Sisonke – slow down.' But this no longer seemed like a possibility. I would henceforth be the girl who had cried in his office because she had been called a monkey.

Baba didn't care about any of this. He only cared about his anger. He was talking now to Mr B, so I tuned in. He was calm and angry at the same time and his great head was erect with outrage and dignity. His large hands were still in his lap as he spoke. I stared at them when I felt overcome and tried not to look at his face because it only made me sadder.

At the end, before he allowed Mr B to speak, he said, 'I am from South Africa. I think you must understand what that means. I will not allow my child to be bullied.

Do you understand? I will not allow this to happen to her. Not here,' he concluded. 'It won't happen.'

Mr B had listened without interrupting, nodding his head occasionally. At the end, after Baba had issued his ultimatum, Mr B allowed for a beat, a respectable pause to indicate that he understood the gravity of the situation.

'Mr Msimang,' he began, 'what happened is unacceptable. We will bring in the pupil responsible and ask him to apologise. I will also talk to his parents and make sure they understand that we have zero tolerance for this sort of thing. Now, as for the others – the ones who laughed and so on – I mean I think we need to understand that children laugh at all sorts of things without really knowing what they are doing. I mean, we can't punish the entire school for every slight – much as I would like to! I mean, I would spend all my time chasing after bystanders and charging them with criminal offences if we did that.'

Mr B chuckled, trying to lighten the atmosphere. Having given Baba some of what he thought he wanted – in fact, having been reasonable about the whole thing – he felt it would not be a good precedent to let a parent dictate how his school should respond to matters like this.

Mr B exuded confidence. He was clearly good at his job. But general competence was insufficient for this situation and Baba was unimpressed. He would not be charmed or soothed. He refused to be cajoled into concessions that were beneath him. No, he was here for justice. Baba remained calm and angry in a way that always scared me because at any moment the anger threatened to swallow up the calm.

'No.'

Mr B stopped smiling.

'No, they do not laugh at my child and then pretend they don't understand the joke. You are the principal. You are supposed to punish children for their cruelty. You have both the power and the responsibility to do it.'

'I understand that you are upset, Mr Msimang, but the reality is that this is Canada. Not everyone is as enlightened as they should be. The schools can only do so much but unfortunately these things do happen in our society. I can see you are new here and I don't like to say it, but your daughter will have to learn how to deal with these sorts of things.'

The calm was almost fully gone and now the anger had grown and Baba's face became different and his voice was like the elastic on a catapult just before you release the stone and Mr B's eyes got bigger and he looked scared and surprised and also almost as miserable as me.

'And you are happy for my child to be called a monkey on your watch? As a principal, you are proud and comfortable to sit there and say there are lessons a black child must learn? You are happy to say one of the lessons should be that she is deserving of insults? Really?'

The question was rhetorical but Mr B tried to answer it anyway. 'That's not what I mean,' he stammered. 'I'm simply saying that what happened is unfortunate but we can't control every aspect of schooling.'

Baba would not be deterred.

'Those children – all of them – owe my daughter an apology, and if you do not accept this I am not sure how you expect me to trust you to have my child's best interests at heart. So, on this one, sir, we will not agree. On this one, you will not convince me otherwise.'

There was a silence. Not the comfortable type that

Mr B may have been taught in conflict-management or mediation conversations, but the long and awkward one that says, 'I do not know what to say or do now, I am stuck.' Mr B turned red and embarrassed, maybe even – as I had been the day before when Baba had yelled at me – ashamed.

Baba was intimate with the arguments in a way I had never witnessed. It is one thing for freedom fighters to drink and debate the launching of Africans into space, and quite another for a guerrilla to stand at his full height of six feet and five inches in a suburban office that is crammed with Board of Education memos and books on curriculum development and trophies and yearbooks. Mr B looked small and confused because he didn't know that Baba was fighting the arrogance of John Cecil Rhodes and David Livingstone, of Henry Morton Stanley and the wonderful nuns of Inkamana Abbey who had taught him well in high school but never lost their sense of slight superiority in the eyes of God and man.

Baba spoke again, his anger still potent, his indignation righteous. 'You realise, sir, that you are supposed to be on her side – on our side, in fact. You are aware of this, am I correct? That's your job.'

Mr B looked up. He was getting angry. It seemed he wanted to accuse the tall man in front of him of insolence. But he was also scared, perhaps physically. Baba was larger and angrier and blacker than him and so he conceded, but just barely.

'Of course,' he said. 'I will speak with the teacher and Sisonke can identify the students and we will make sure that they apologise.'

He spoke as though this capitulation was the result of his reasonableness rather than because of the moral weight of what Baba had said and Baba looked too weary to fight any more. He was done with history and only wanted the matter resolved so that I could get back to learning and the children in the class could be sorted out and he could go back to the office. Suddenly, he was Baba again and not the puffed-up guerrilla whose spectre had filled the room.

'Good, very good,' he said, deciding that this was the best he could expect. He stood abruptly and Mr B, surprised the worst was over so swiftly, also rose.

'Come, Sonke, I'll accompany you,' Baba said, before turning to the principal. 'It will happen now, correct?'

The man nodded slowly and said, too tersely I suspected for Baba's liking, 'It will.'

We walked together down the hall, my hand in Baba's. The principal walked half a pace ahead of us. When we got to my classroom door, Baba touched his arm.

'You will do this properly,' he said. 'She is not to blame for whatever it is you are feeling about me. You?'

Mr B nodded brusquely: more shame.

Then we went in. Baba stayed behind, standing just outside the classroom watching through the glass. The principal had a word with my teacher while I stood alone in the corner just next to the blackboard. Then Mr B walked back towards me and began to speak. 'Class,' he said, 'we have something important to discuss.'

He turned and looked at Baba over his shoulder. He was still standing there outside the door. Mr B hesitated slightly. Then he reached for my hand and I took it and we stood together in front of everyone as he said, 'Yesterday some of you were mean to Sisonke. It has come to my attention that she was called a monkey.'

Silence.

'You all know this is wrong. Now, I know that not all of

you were there but we will be speaking to everyone who was present on a one-on-one basis. In the meantime, I wanted to start off today by making sure that you all understand that what happened out there was not okay. More than that, I think we all owe Sisonke a big apology. All of us do. Now I'd like to hear you all say it together. I don't want anything like this to ever happen again.'

And he led them all in a mass, sing-songy 'Sor-ry Si-son-ke,' which did nothing to make me feel better about them, but everything to restore my faith in the system and in Baba's ability to be courageous even when I was afraid.

That evening, in the den as I was doing my homework through tears because it had been that kind of day, Baba pulled me close. I was stiff in his arms; still bruised. He smiled at me from deep inside his eyes and said, in the same sing-songy voice they had all used in the morning, 'Sor-ry Si-son-ke.'

Then he hugged me and said, 'Really. I am. I am very sorry, big girl. I shouldn't have been so angry with you. It wasn't your fault that they called you a monkey. I want you to learn how to fight for yourself. You understand? You will be braver next time.'

That sorry meant more to me than the one from the pasty-faced children who had only said it because Mr B made them. It told me that Baba loved me enough to show me what bravery looked like. I belonged to him, after all, and so I ought to be brave. That is what he was saying. And he was right: the next time I was braver, and every time after I have been braver still. I am my father's daughter.

❖ ❖ ❖

By Grade Six, life in Canada had fallen into a rhythm. Because Baba was away a lot and Mummy worked a full-time job, we were latchkey kids. For the first time in our lives there was no social infrastructure. There was no Aunty Angela and Uncle Stan, no Lindi and Dumi, no domestic helper we called Aunty, telling us what to do and where to go.

Instead, we had a strict regimen. Mummy was our only boss and she laid out a clear set of rules. We dared not disobey her. She wrote them all out and went over them with us. She enforced them with a ferocity that made it seem as though our lives depended on them. I suppose they did. We knew which of the neighbourhood kids were allowed to come over and which ones weren't welcome. There were rules about food and homework and playing in the basement and watching TV and the temperature of the heater and playing outside and taking off shoes and putting on boots. We followed her every command because the immigrant child knows that outside is one thing but home is another country.

Outside, in the big bad world, I had learnt to fit in. I dressed like all the other girls – in OP T-shirts and denim shorts in the warm weather and in flannel lumberjack shirts and tight jeans in the winter. I was beginning to sound like a Canadian too – with a nasal tone to my voice and a sharpness in my As that had not been there when we had arrived.

I even found myself in the 'cool group' alongside Shelley and Candy and Joyce. Someone had decided that Shelley was the pretty one in the group. All groups must have one, and often her position as The Pretty One is self-designated. Shelley's prettiness made her the leader of our circle, which entitled her to pilot us through daily conversations organised around her prettiness. She had strawberryblonde hair and blonde eyebrows and eyelashes and a generous lashing of brown freckles all over her face, arms and legs.

They were everywhere, copiously spread across her forehead, spattered across her cheeks, generously dolloped across her small upturned nose, and smudged across a chin so pointy it could have been used to good effect in battle.

She anointed herself our queen and we believed her. Perhaps it was because of the force of her personality and the stubborn way she insisted on being the centre of all discussion. Likely it was because she was mean and confident so she ruled with an iron fist. Joyce was tall and lanky and wore her hair cut short like a boy's with a long heavy fringe sweeping across her face that she constantly needed to blow out of her eyes. It was a style she had made up herself and because her parents were much, much older (her mother was fifty and her father must have been close to sixty) they weren't paying that much attention to her any more so they let her be.

When I started at R. Byrnes Curry in Grade Five, Joyce was assigned to show me around the school, so she became my best friend. We had sleepovers and she knew all my secrets. So desperate was I to be her friend that I even forgave her when she put her big sister on the phone to listen to my accent. We had been talking endlessly about nothing when I heard a muffled sound. It sounded like a giggle and a snort. Then the extension dropped clumsily.

'What was that?' I asked.

'My sister,' she responded sheepishly. 'I told her how you talk and she wanted to hear it for herself.'

I was quietly mortified.

Candy was petite and slender and in truth she was far prettier than Shelley. She had dark-brown hair and an even, just-so mouth and a nose that would never bother anybody. But she was anxious and prone to laughing unexpectedly and often too loudly. She confessed to me – before ties were severed – that she had wet her bed every night until the year before, but didn't answer me when I asked, 'How come?'

◆ ◆ ◆

The last few months of Grade Six didn't go so well. For weeks I felt picked on and insecure. Shelley turned her meanness on me and Joyce and Candy seemed incapable of defending me. I took to eating lunch on my own.

So, I was surprised when Joyce marched towards me at morning recess one spring day. She stood in front of me. The sun was behind her and her hair was flopping in her face as usual so I could barely see her eyes. I stayed sitting and half-heartedly offered her a fruit rollup. She declined. She was here on business. I shrugged. 'Suit yourself,' I said. 'I will,' she responded with equal aggression. Then she said it. In a big rush through spittle and bravado and nerves, she said, 'Shelley says you aren't part of the group any more.'

'What?' I looked up. I was mad at myself for even asking. 'Shelley says you aren't part of the group any more. You can't hang out with us. You've been talking bad about all of us,' she said, sounding unconvinced. 'You're trying to get everyone to hate everyone else, and Shelley knows it. We all know it. I mean if you want to be back in, you'll have to come and say sorry to everyone and promise never to do it again.'

I blinked back tears.

Joyce continued, in a slightly more contrite tone, 'I'm not sure that she'll say yes, but even if she doesn't, if you promise not to tell her, you can still sleep over at my house sometimes.'

I looked at Joyce's hairy arms and gangly legs and thought of her telling me that her parents loved her sister more than they loved her. I thought of her saying that she hated her sister and how I had thought at the time I would never say that about my sisters and then I remembered that stifled giggle on the telephone extension and was immensely sad because it was all suddenly very clear that Joyce had betrayed me long before Shelley showed up and so I just shook my head and said, 'It's okay,' and I stood up and walked away.

Joyce had her own reasons for agreeing to be the executioner. No doubt these were tied up in her not wanting to be seen as the nerd with the braces and the ageing parents, but I didn't care about that. As far as I was concerned she was Brutus and I was Caesar lying prone on the playground.

◆ ◆ ◆

For weeks before this final message was delivered, Shelley had greeted my every word with a sneer. Every story I told led to eyerolls and unexplained titters. Candy and Joyce had often joined in, albeit uncomfortably. They never seemed to know what they were laughing at, but they needed to signal their support to Shelley.

The jibes had begun on a sludgy March afternoon as we walked home through melting snow. I mused about the Loch Ness monster, which we had been studying for the last few days. 'Imagine if there was one in the Rideau Canal?' I said out loud. I had been seized with the creature since I was seven, when Baba brought home a book about it. The idea that something ancient and secret had somehow survived modernity and was trapped in a lake in Scotland intrigued me. Here was a mystery that should be easy to solve, a riddle just beyond reach. Shelley fired back insolently, 'The only monster swimming around here is from Africa.'

She wasn't as clever as me, so she wasn't very good at sarcasm. Her slow-wittedness meant statements like this were easy to shred. You could always see her coming. I read so many books and had memorised so many scenes of witty repartee that comebacks were easy for me. But with Shelley I felt frozen like Piggy in *Lord of the Flies*. I had been reading it at night when Mummy was busy with doing tax files and it had got into my head. I was certain that soon Shelley would be leading the mob, yelling, 'Kill the pig! Cut his throat! Kill the pig! Bash him in!'

I had even scribbled her name into the margin when I first encountered Jack. And when Simon made his entrance, I had written 'Joyce. Definitely Joyce.'

I could feel that I was about to be kicked out and there was nothing I could do about it. Dread had made its home in my veins. The others looked down. In ordinary times I would have retorted, 'Oh big words, Shelley. Can you spell "monster"? I'll give you extra points if you can.' Given how abysmally she was doing in school, I knew this would sting, but I held my tongue. I had learnt to deal with playground bullies, but this was different. Shelley was supposed to be my friend. Hurt trapped me and swallowed my tongue. 'Ha ha!' I said sarcastically, wanting to move on to another topic. I put my head down and kept walking. Shelley smirked; she had tasted blood.

Two days before, Shelley had come to our house after school. She had never come over before so I was surprised and pleased, if a little nervous. Mummy was at work and I hadn't asked her permission to have a visitor after school because Shelley's visit was impromptu. That day, instead of waving us goodbye and going into her house, Shelley had offered to walk me all the way to our housing units. Mandla and Zeng lagged, aware that when I was with my friends their job was to disappear and to act like we only vaguely knew each other.

When we got to our house I unlocked the door and let her in. She dropped her bag at the entrance and didn't bother to take off her boots. She walked straight to the small sitting room where we never played, trailing in mud and dirty snow.

She ignored Mandla and Zeng as they dutifully started to carry out our after-school routine, set out in elaborate detail by Mummy. As usual, we washed our hands because the world was dirty and home was clean. Mandla turned on the heater in the kitchen, swirling the thermostat to twenty-eight to warm the place up like Mummy had shown us, then reducing it to twenty-four after a few minutes. Normally this was my task.

Usually we fixed ourselves sandwiches before going down to the basement to watch TV. Mandla and Zeng went down and I stayed upstairs, watching Shelley's back warily, wondering whether I should disturb Mummy at work to tell her that Shelley had invited herself over and was it okay for her to be here? I decided not to and then thought about how quickly I might get the dirt out of the light-grey carpet Mummy had warned us only to walk on in stockinged feet.

I could see that Shelley didn't care how we did things in our house and I could tell that she was here to discover something, I just didn't know what. I stood in the hallway and watched as – with her back to me – she traced her fingers over Mummy's framed Heidi Lange batik. It had come all the way from Nairobi with us and it hung in a similar position here as it had in our house in Nairobi: just above the couch, facing the television. The hooded eyes and dangling hoops of the jet-black woman in the frame surveyed us haughtily.

Shelley turned her attention to our mantelpiece. It was crammed full of photos of yellow-eyed grannies who had paid a great deal of money to have themselves posed and well-fed black men (Mummy's and Baba's fathers) whose eyes spoke of hard times despite their tight waistcoats and spotless white shirts. Next to them Lindi and Dumi kept straight faces in their school uniforms. And then there were the informal ones: a light-brown woman (Mummy's sister Aunt Thandi) standing in a garden somewhere in Botswana holding a flower close to her face. And my favourite, taken at a picnic at Munda Wanga Gardens in Lusaka – a picture of Uncle Stan and Aunty Angela and Aunt Pulane and Uncle Zola and Mummy and Baba and Kholi and Yoli and Khaya and Vuyo and my sisters and me. We were all laughing and looking into the camera. But now I saw us through her eyes. We were just a group of longlimbed Africans sprawled out on a lawn somewhere foreign.

She turned to me and wrinkled her nose as though she had encountered something noxious: 'Don't you like even know anyone who isn't from Africa?' she had asked. The question was dangerous, each word a missile trained at my heart. I had never even thought about it, but now, looking at the house, at our art and our photos, through her eyes, we were different. We didn't know very many people who weren't Africans.

Shelley looked as though she had just discovered a dirty secret. I was an African, a girl who came from a far-away place filled with black people. I was not a solitary, affable exception: I had a tribe.

In the context of Shelley's small but grand plan of middle-school domination, my difference was a problem. It was cruel and simple and completely within the logic of vanilla-white adolescent girlhood in mid-1980s Ottawa.

What it boiled down to was that we were almost twelve and soon we would be playing spin the bottle and obsessing about boys and in this context it was no longer enough for me to be fun, I also had to be pretty. In Shelley's view the flatness of my nose and the breadth of my face and the Nguni heritage stamped onto my posterior meant that I wasn't. I became a liability.

◆ ◆ ◆

When Shelley and Joyce and Candy discarded the dark girl, they were playing out a ritual that is as old as contact between native women and the masters and mistresses who had conquered them. Much more was at stake than a little fight among girls.

The fight was existential. Their very own identities were on the line, forged as they had been in opposition to everything that I represented. White femininity is constructed as the polar opposite of a femininity which itself revolves around concepts that aren't very feminine at all. Shelley's knight in shining armour would also be fair of skin and hair and he would not be interested in her if she was hanging out with a bunch of other girls who were too hairy, or too large or too dark or God forbid in a wheelchair or fat. If Shelley herself stopped being the epitome of white-blonde petite beauty, the knight in shining armour might keep riding past her. Worse, he might decide to poke her with his bayonet or get his posse and come back and burn down the village of misfits.

That long-ago spring all this was just under the surface so I couldn't see it. All I knew was that I was in trouble and that this situation was not of my own making but that nonetheless it would impact me deeply, perhaps forever, if I allowed it to. I saw it but did not yet know what to do about it. I was strong though. I kept my head up and held my tears back and I saw out the last two weeks of school without friends. I survived, you see, because Mandla played with me at break and ate lunch with me every day and – finally – I let her.

◆ ◆ ◆

The immigrant child knows that the key to survival is in the inflection points. It is in the way the head is cocked or the ease with which the foot pushes off the pavement before the first pedal on your bike. The key to survival is in blending in first, in learning how to be just like everyone else as a first step to freedom. You have to know how the inside works before you can stand outside and make everybody laugh.

My sisters and I learnt that we could only be individuals, that we could only make jokes and be funny – which was the key to popularity and social success – once we understood the rules. Until then, like all immigrant children we were quiet and observant.

The immigrant child doesn't make any noise. She watches closely and sometimes she smiles to herself not because she is without humour – she is only keeping to herself so that she may one day be the one who dances on the table and tells the stories. She is preparing for the day when she will have mastered the art of being normal so that she can stand out.

We could have worn our hair in short natural afros like Mummy did, but with the sensitivity of immigrant children we soon realised that this only highlighted the fact that we were different. We knew that being different signalled inferiority, so minimising the parts of ourselves that stuck out took on outsized meaning. Being like everyone else is important to all children. But to immigrant children, the words 'the other kids don't do that' becomes a mantra. The immigrant child learns to understand that danger lurks in everyday interactions.

Until we went to Canada we had never given a second thought to what we looked like. We were as brown and braided as the next children. We had spent our childhoods flaunting our idiosyncrasies, revelling in a community that embraced peculiarity because it was premised on the rejection of the totalitarian society we were fighting in South Africa. To be yourself was to be free. The adults would watch us streak past them in Nairobi and remark, 'Oh these children are so free.'

So, we were marinated in this milieu, and it was intoxicating. We had been indulged not in the usual way that one spoils a child, but in the way that only a community of exiles can do. We weren't just children – we were representatives of ideals. We were a clean slate and a fair go and a new breed and everything our parents wished for in South Africa. And now, here we were – far away for the sake of freedom, but no more special than anyone else. We learnt quickly that here we would survive by being not peacocks, but turtles. Heads down, we moved forward, one foot slowly in front of the other. When the snows came and the ice froze, we joined the neighbourhood kids, running to the tops of hills and sliding down on our magic carpets. We gobbled up BeaverTails pastries and learnt how to cross-country ski and on weekends we skated on the Rideau Canal and Mummy pretended that she did not hate all of it – the cold and the ice and the absent husband and the patronising Canadians who didn't quite believe that he was off in Ethiopia fighting famine – what kind of an African was that? – and the aching anonymity of being nobody special in a large and flat society.

In the midst of it all Mandla and Zeng became my friends. I learnt to need them. In our old life in Nairobi they had just been in the background, two lumpy pieces of furniture I occasionally bumped into as I ran around with my friends doing big-girl things. In Canada they were suddenly old enough to have personalities and, in the face of so much change, they finally felt solid and important. Their eyes were intelligent and their noses weren't just replicas of mine – Mandla's looked like Baba's and Zeng's was just her own. They were differentiated beings, no longer babies. With its glorious whites – from its winter snow to its pale inhabitants – Canada made us sisters.

❖ ❖ ❖

One Friday Mummy met us at the school gates. It was late spring and she was standing next to the second-hand gold-coloured car she and Baba had bought just before he left for Ethiopia at the end of last summer. Baba was an aid worker – one of very few black people in a management role in a humanitarian mission. He had been gone for six long months working in a camp in Dire Dawa in Ethiopia and some days I didn't even miss him any more. Mummy said we should be grateful and not complain because yes, work took him away, but it also put food on the table and clothes on our backs, so unless we wanted to be hungry and walk naked on the streets we should keep quiet and accept the life we had been given.

We hopped into the car and she said in a voice that was far too soft to be happy, 'Surprise. We're going camping.' Mummy was intrepid in many ways, but she was not a camper. I was old enough to have asked her why she wasn't at work but for some reason I didn't. Maybe I sensed that her voice might disappear altogether if we asked any questions. Or maybe I was just too taken by the surprise; by the gift of her, sitting there holding time on her lap like a blanket.

Giddy with excitement, we buckled up and hit the road. She had packed a bag with our things. She had bought a tent. She had consulted a map. We drove for two hours and did not get lost. All of us were surprised by this, not least Mummy. Eventually we saw the sign after a wooded area that said WELCOME TO CAMP GATINEAU: CAMP-ING SITE.

We had sung and wriggled and fought in the back seat the whole way up without thinking much about what this all meant. But as we neared the site it occurred to all of us that this may not be as simple as it seemed. How would we pitch the tent on our own? Where exactly would we put it? What would happen if wild animals were prowling about?

Mummy parked and we got out of the car. Zeng was too small to be worried, but Mandla and I knew better. We found a spot and began a farcical attempt at pitching the tent. There were a few other small groups around – within shouting distance – but everyone left well enough alone. In Canada nobody pries. Still, we must have been quite a sight: Mummy in her smart jeans and inappropriate shoes, ordering us about in her oddly posh and low voice. Mummy had no idea what she was doing, but, fortified by African pride and the immigrant's commitment to blending in, she wasn't going to go ask for help.

Twenty minutes into our surprise adventure it started to rain. It was a heavy downpour and soon our faces were slick with the curl activator we sprayed on our hair so prodigiously every morning to maintain our Jheri curls.

Mummy looked up at the sky and then she looked at the unerected tent. Then she looked at us with our oily faces and our eyes that were starting to sting and she started to laugh. We did too. We were getting soaked. She raised her voice over the sound of the rain and said, 'This isn't going to work, is it?' We shook our heads. 'Should we try camping another day, girls?' We nodded quickly and started to gather our stuff.

We collected the metal bits and bobs we had strewn across the ground, and unscrewed the poles we had just managed to sandwich together. We lifted the tent's tarpaulin carcass and, as lightning started, we made a dash for the car.

We were not disappointed. Driving back we were little chatterboxes, full of stories of school we would not ordinarily tell Mummy because by the time she got home they would have lost their urgency. That Friday was different. We were with Mummy and the sun was setting and the rain was pouring and the world felt right.

Camping had been a glorious failure but it had given us a chance to be with Mummy outside the structure of all the rules that made life easier for her and safer for us. That trip was an unexpected affirmation we hadn't known we'd needed. It reminded us that Mummy loved us and it told us that we weren't simply a burden – three mouths to feed and three growing bodies to clothe. She loved us enough to leave work early to try something new; something Canadian. We were strangers in a strange land and somehow Mummy understood that we needed to belong not simply to her, but to the world as well.

The bike

MUMMY WANTS US to learn how to be responsible, so every month she gives us five dollars and takes us to the bank to deposit it ourselves. Mandla and I are very neat, our handwriting steady and firm on the page. Zeng is only six so she has to write and rewrite and we sigh and sigh because the bank is quiet and boring and no other kids are ever there except us with our little books that have rainbows across them at the top saying 'Future Account'

When I decide to save up for a bike Mummy is proud and says, 'This is exactly what your savings account is for.'

I complain to her that Canadian kids all have bikes, but she does not see a bike as a basic need – she sees it as a luxury. I disagree: a bike is a necessity like food and water. Canadian parents don't tell their children to save up for basics. Mummy says no: 'A bike is a nice-to-have, not a must-have.' This is a cultural gap that we will not breach.

All my friends have ten-speeds and ride their bikes to school but I walk even though, as Mummy says, I have a 'perfectly good bike at home'. Mummy and Baba purchased it when we arrived in Canada, so I have had it since I was ten. Its brakes squeak, it has handlebars that turn up on either side and worst of all it has a banana seat. I am thirteen years old and my mother sees no problem with me riding around the neighbourhood looking like Fat Albert's broke little sister.

I zip up my disappointment and focus on earning money so I can buy myself a new bike. I put up signs at the supermarket offering babysitting services with our house number on it and calling myself Sissy so that people aren't put off by the name. I volunteer to do odd jobs around the house and needle Mummy into paying for them. I even charge Mandla for helping her with her homework but Mummy finds out and makes me give it back. I am desperate for this new bike.

My progress towards saving for the bike is accelerated when Uncle Glen comes to visit. He lives in Abidjan, which I know is the capital city of the Ivory Coast because Félix Houphouët-Boigny is the life president and happens to be one of Baba's favourite dictators. Uncle Glen lives in the country Boigny rules. He works there in a fancy job at the African Development Bank and he is in Ottawa for a conference.

He comes over for dinner and as he greets us he gives

us each fifty dollars. Fifty dollars. Queen Elizabeth stares at each of us serenely from the middle of each of the clean rose-coloured notes. The Canadian parliament, which I visited on a school trip, looms behind the Queen, ominous and even more regal than she is. I look over at Mandla and Zeng and see they are just as dumbfounded as me. Mummy has to remind us to say thank you and to close our mouths.

Normally, Mummy would refuse to accept the money, but Uncle Glen is her older brother so Baba will not complain that he might have An Agenda. Uncle Glen brings news of Swaziland, and Mummy is happy. The two of them sit on the couch like small owls remembering home. Their faces are puffed like feathers and their shoulders rise and their feet barely touch the ground and their voices are like hoots, low and pitched only at one another.

When the timer on the oven goes off, we move to the table. Mummy and I bring plates from the kitchen, and Uncle Glen keeps up a steady stream of chatter. He tells her about the latest escapades by the young nieces and nephews whose schooling they are both supporting. He tells her about deaths and car accidents and mysterious illnesses and they both shake their heads at a new disease that seems to be targeting young people. 'It turns them into skeletons and they die quickly,' he tells her and she only shakes her head and wonders what it could be.

Uncle Glen turns to us as he dishes up his lasagne. He asks us about school and what we want to be when we grow up and, as we answer, our eyes linger on him for longer than they should. We are inspecting him, taking in the details of his face and the set of his shoulders and the sound of his voice. When he turns to Mummy and they begin their chatter again, we continue to steal looks at him, peeking at him furtively.

He notices and asks, 'So what is it about your uncle that is so interesting to you girls?'

We are surprised that he has noticed. We giggle in embarrassment. Mummy casts an amused eye over her children and asks – 'Zeng?' – because she knows her baby will tell some charming version of the truth.

Singled out and in the limelight, Zeng looks at Uncle Glen and shrieks, 'You look like Mummy!'

There is such amazement and delight in her voice that we all burst out laughing. Rewarded by our response, she continues, 'You do! I didn't know that adults had brothers and sisters.'

'Don't you remember Aunt Thandi and Aunt Zanele?' asks Mummy.

Mandla and Zeng shake their heads but I nod and say, 'I do!'

Mummy folds up her sadness and tucks her loneliness under her plate. Then she smiles. 'Well, we better get out the albums, then.'

We spend the evening flipping through satin-covered photo albums and Mummy and Uncle Glen roar with laughter until, as I have seen so many times, Mummy's face is wet with tears. She laughs so much that it makes us laugh too even though they are speaking in siSwati that is far too fast and complicated for us to understand. It rushes over us, a stream of Ts and Ds and soft Ls.

We stay up later than normal, but eventually it is time to sleep. We say good night and Uncle Glen gives us three tight squeezes and each of us wish that he could stay or that we could go or that he could transport the stories and the laughter here but we have no words for this feeling; it is just warm and a little bit sad and when I am grown I will know that the word for this feeling is nostalgia.

A week after he leaves, I deposit Uncle Glen's money. At the bank, Mummy gives me the last thirty dollars I need and adds forty extra so that there is something left in my account after I have withdrawn the amount to pay for the bike.

The next weekend we go to the bike shop. Mummy is smiling a lot and she mentions more than once to the salesman that she wants to make sure that this is a good bike because I saved up for it myself. I am embarrassed. Her accent is too thick and she thinks he will care about some kid and her savings plan. I am wrong. The man warms to Mummy and he is impressed. He says he has been trying to teach his kids about saving but they won't listen. He gives me a free pump and three extra months on the warranty.

I ride my bike to school the next morning, hunched over like a professional. I move faster than I ever have before with the wind on my face and the morning sun on my shoulders. I wait at the busy corner for Mandla and Zeng to catch up, then I speed off and wait again at the stop sign. When they get to me I tell them to hurry up and I'm off again.

At school I act like it's no big deal. I add my bike to the rack alongside the others, and fiddle with the lock. Everyone notices, though, just as I have been hoping they will. Belonging thrums in my veins.

In October it snows and we pack our bikes away. The cold months have barely begun but I am eager for winter to end. 'It's okay,' I tell myself 'In the spring I will ride further and faster than anyone. I might even make it to the Rideau Canal.'

◆ ◆ ◆

Spring never arrives. In November, Baba returns from one of his trips. Whenever he comes back his presence irritates me as much as his absence saddens me when he is gone. I understand that he has to travel but the stints are long: five months then three then six. When Baba is away we develop a rhythm and when he comes back we have to readjust and we all act odd.

When it is homework time in the days after he returns he always wants to help us. Mandla is perfect at everything so they don't fight. She is good at maths and just as good at English and she gets everything right in science.

Zeng just smiles her way out of everything and he forgets to ask her if she needs to practise reading. She is too busy telling him stories about her day and making him laugh.

He tries to help me with my maths but I don't want his help. I want to show him my essays instead because they are good and he is always proud when he reads my stories. Maths is always a fight. 'Can't you see?' he always says, even when it is clear that I can't see. 'You just carry the eight and round up.' Numbers swim in front of my eyes and confuse me. Words are different. They fall into place neatly, ideas stacked like LEGO pieces. I know how to arrange them.

Mummy is happy, though. She smiles when she comes home and finds our heads bowed and his bending in close to ours. Then, when we ask her permission for something because we are used to not having him around, she says, 'Ask your father,' as if she doesn't know what to do. We are out of sync and it's not as easy as just being happy that he is home.

Within a few days of his arrival, they make the

announcement: we are moving back to Nairobi. They don't tell us that we should start preparing mentally, the way Canadian parents would. They just say it, the way you might say, 'Oh, I'm going to get an ice cream – I'll be back in ten minutes.'

Mandla and Zeng are happy. 'Yay!' As if they are proposing some little adventure. Clueless.

Mummy can see that I am upset so after the announcement she tells the girls to go upstairs and asks me to stay. Mandla and Zeng are a pair, their names always said in a breath and a sentence. I am not jealous. They are younger than me and don't remember as much as I do and I don't need them the way they need each other.

We listen to them brushing their teeth and then Mummy begins. She explains to me that this is an excellent opportunity for Baba and the timing works very well. She says that we will get our citizenship in December, which is great because that is a big achievement for us but Baba's work wants him to start in Nairobi in January so we will be in Kenya in time to celebrate Christmas with the Sangwenis. Baba is quiet. He looks impatient, as though he doesn't understand why Mummy is speaking to me as though I am owed some sort of explanation. He only got back a few days ago and he has not yet adjusted to the fact that I am growing up and that none of us stands still when he is gone.

I am devastated. It's bad enough that we are leaving, but so soon? I don't say much; I just look down and fight back the tears and then ask if I can go upstairs now. I would prefer to storm upstairs and scream 'I hate you!' like they do on TV but I can't. Instead I leave the living room quietly, barely saying good night so that they know how unhappy I am. I sit in my room, staring at my Corey Hart poster and looking at my signed Richard

Marx album, and I'm too sad to even cry.

I look at my homework desk and at the neatly stacked books and at my backpack sitting on the chair and my eye wanders to my side table, surveying all the things I own, which I will soon have to pack up. Then I see the bike receipt.

The thought of the bike breaks the dam and I cry and cry the way I wish I had cried downstairs so that they would know that this hurts and I am tired of always being the one who has just arrived, tired of leaving just when I am starting to feel like I finally belong.

◆ ◆ ◆

The airport smells like sweat and striving and is busy but still has the air of something that is fading and becoming obsolete. I am angry, but as we head into the city past the huge faux elephant tusks that stand like sentries on either side of the road leaving the airport, the rage lessens. The familiarity of the sun and the morning heat and the jangle of traffic and seeing faces that are as brown as mine everywhere make me feel like I belong here in a way that was impossible in Canada.

When our shipment arrives six weeks later I am interested in only one thing. I see it standing in the driveway of our house, gleaming in the sun, and it reminds me of Canada. The bike assumes new importance in Nairobi because it looks as though it comes from overseas, from a place where factories soundlessly churn out spokes and chains and bells that are assembled in wordless concentration by lumbering, well-fed men in light-blue overalls.

I ignore the fact that it is hard to navigate the potholed road in front of our house. I pretend not to notice the way Mummy purses her lips smugly when she tells me to stay away from the main road because I will get killed if a *matatu* decides to ram into me and my posh bike. I don't care. Instead, I insist on riding it around the bumpy streets of our neighbourhood. Even after my third puncture I persist because the bike has become my personal rebellion, a totem I refuse to stop worshipping even if we are in Loresho which is in Nairobi which is thirteen thousand kilometres away from Hunt Club which is in Ottawa which was never home even when I was desperate for it to be.

Loresho Crescent is a beautiful but simple street where Bougainvillea tumbles across hedges and creeps along archways atop wrought-iron gates. Long, wide bungalows peer out at the road from behind fat verandas cluttered with chairs and hammocks and an assorted bricolage of easy and good living. In front of each house there is an askari's box. It is tiny and silly: a wooden structure just large enough for a watchman to sit or stand in. In contrast to the well-thought-out and rambling homes, in which size seems not to be a consideration, the askaris' boxes are a crude vestige of the past. Yet they don't stand empty. Each of them has a man sitting in it, or pacing around it. At night all the askaris retreat into their guard-boxes to keep warm. The askari set-up does not shock me. It is one of the many facts of life that should be alarming but require no comment and so I see it but I don't.

Because we have just secured our Canadian citizenship, we are in Kenya as expatriates. Baba is a big boss, the country director for a large international humanitarian agency. He helps people to make it out of poverty and one of the perks is that we attend the most expensive school in the country and live a carefree life as if the misery he seeks to eradicate each day does not exist.

On Saturdays we go to Silver Springs Hotel, where Mummy goes to the sauna and we splash around in the pool with the children of Kenyan professors and bankers and managing directors and on Sundays the South African students and the people from The Movement come over for lunch. Baba travels but for shorter stints than he did when we were in Ottawa and Mummy is more re-laxed and we have a maid called Edith who helps with the housework and there is a driver so that Mummy does the coordinating, but not all the doing, and suddenly life is crowded again and it is no longer just the five of us. Here with our busy lives and our social status no one will call us monkeys or come snooping in our house looking for evidence that we don't belong.

At school, I make friends quickly and easily. The knot in my tummy eases and I swallow my fears. Soon, it is as if I have always been here and Canada was a nice dream that gave me a passport and an accent and a place to go every summer holiday.

◆ ◆ ◆

My best friend in Nairobi is Patience the Zimbabwean ambassador's daughter. She lives in a hollow soulless mansion with a sweeping staircase just ten minutes away from my house. Patience is boy-crazy and this irri-tates Mummy so Patience and I hardly ever hang out at our house. Mummy doesn't say anything specific – she just finds a way of making her disdain known.

This particular Sunday we agree to meet halfway and hang out at her house. I walk my bike up Loresho Cres-cent and take a shortcut across the big field on the other side of Loresho Avenue. I use the small dirt path that bisects the unused land. Most of the domestic workers who would ordinarily be around are at church or visiting their families in the bursting slums, so it is quiet. Even the kiosks are hardly selling.

I do not know it, but I am a prime target. I am a slow-moving shiny rich girl on a shiny bike, virtually alone in the middle of an urban field. I am blissfully unaware that anyone is watching me as I gleam down a brown path. There I am, bumping lazily along the path, looking at my feet, at the tracks in the mud, at the dryness of the maize, wondering why I didn't carry a few shillings so that I could buy some toast *mahindi* when suddenly I am being pulled and then pushed and there is blood on my ankle and the bike is being yanked from right under me where I am lying all of a sudden on the muddy path.

The person who yanked me is moving too, so fast that at first he is just a blur. He is single-minded and his feet are whirring around the pedals and his tiny buttocks are working hard to get away and then he is gone, leaving me lying there, gleaming alone in the mud on the path.

'My bike. My precious Canadian bike!' I think this or something like it and I start to cry and shout at the same time because I saved up for it and it is mine and no one can just steal it like that. Then my fight instinct kicks in – late but potent – and the Swahili word for 'thief' pops into my head and I yell it as loud as I can.

'*Mwizi! Mwizi! Mwizi!*'

An old woman in front of me, who is ragged and colourless and who just moments before had looked as though she had no will to live, jolts into an upright position – her walking stick forgotten momentarily in the face of danger, excitement, and the possibility of vengeance. She adds her voice to mine, and it comes out in a remarkably sturdy and rich baritone. Our cries carry across the field and together we wail, 'Mwizi! Mwizi!'

People heed the call. All sorts of people emerge. They come from the edges of the field and from the area I have just passed, running from the kiosks at the main road towards me to hear what has happened and to assist in capturing the culprit. A thief is on the prowl and no one will rest until he has been apprehended.

We point in the direction he went and soon there is a chase. The rogue hits the tar road on my shiny bike and I lose sight of them as they go over the hill. Since he is on wheels and those chasing him are on foot, I give up hope and begin to sniff and cry in shock and self-pity. The old lady looks at me pitifully. 'Pole,' she says.

'Aya, asante mama,' I thank her, smiling through tears of foolishness and humiliation.

I am angry. Wasps surge at my temples and swarm my chest. Does he have any idea that that bike cannot be replaced? The little vermin doesn't know how hard I worked. He hasn't a clue of its value. He will not know how to take care of it, or ride it carefully. It will end up on some scrapheap somewhere, sold for a pittance. I am livid. Outraged. I am apoplectic.

I crest the hill, fuming – and there he is! My assailant has been caught. The little cockroach has been caught. He is squirming but he is firmly in the grip of an angry Good Samaritan and a small crowd throngs around him. They have mobilised in my defence. The Good Samaritan had been driving when he saw the Thief cycling away with a growing crowd billowing out behind him. If the boy had made it to another nearby shortcut he would have got away but the Good Samaritan had given chase in his new pickup truck and had railroaded the little crook into the side of the road.

Now here he stands being manhandled before my very eyes. The crowd is intent on teaching him a lesson. As I approach, the Good Samaritan tightens his hold on the Thief. I stand just inside the circle and he greets me. 'Hello, Young Madam,' he says. 'Is this your bicycle?'

Yes, I nod. 'Yes, it is.'

The Samaritan has the meaty face of prosperity and a paunch to match.

'And was it he who stole it just now?' He asks me this authoritatively and I nod and say yes again. The boy is very small. His shoulder blades are wings and he has a long sensitive face, with large eyes and a twitchy nose; he is less a cockroach than he is a mosquito.

The Good Samaritan has the air of a self-appointed prosecutor and judge. He is well rehearsed in thundering accusation and solemn deliberation, so he comfortably wears both hats. Meanwhile, the crowd stands like a chorus in a Greek tragedy, seeing no conflict in serving as both witness to a crime and a jury of my peers.

'So, you stole this bike from this young girl. Did you not?' the Good Samaritan bellows, partly to scare the boy but mainly to amp up the crowd. He is so large and the Thief is so small that, at a purely physical level, it seems unfair that they be pitted against each other.

There are shouts among the people gathered to witness the deliverance of justice. 'Eh! Eh. It was him!' they affirm, even though I hadn't seen any of them until I started screaming so it is likely that most of them didn't actually observe the crime.

The boy – who cannot be older than me – nods in fear. His T-shirt is torn and so threadbare it isn't clear whether it had already been torn before or whether the holes were the consequence of the manhandling by the Prosecutor-cum-judge and others in the crowd who caught him. His wings flutter helplessly, and one looks slightly broken. He is far too thin and he is wearing a sagging pair of shorts and no shoes and his feet look as though they've been dirty a long time and now they are beyond the redemption of washing. I feel sorry for him but I am also still angry, and my ankle is still bleeding, which reminds me to be indignant.

The Prosecutor continues. 'Speak! We do not understand those useless gestures. Do you not have a mouth to speak?'

'Yes *bwana*, I did. I took it.' The boy's voice is quiet and high. Hearing him I think he might be as young as eleven and I regret squealing like a spoilt little piglet. I should have left him to pedal away but it is too late now.

I can see myself reflected in his eyes. My thighs are distorted and look larger than they should in these shorts. I am well fed and adolescent; no longer a child, but not yet a woman; not fat, but far from thin. I am standing on my hind legs looking down my snout at him. Entitled, imperious. Some animals.

The Good Samaritan does not see me this way. He is on my side because I am the victim and the Thief is a lowly poor street urchin – a born criminal.

'Do you admit that you committed this crime on a Sunday? On the day on which the Good Lord our saviour Jesus Christ in heaven tells us that man must worship and rest?'

The Thief speaks up. 'Yes sir.'

'Eh heh!' says the Prosecutor. 'There is no rest for thieves, even on a Sunday, eh?'

The crowd laughs and jeers and it is kind of funny and if this teaches the silly little thing a lesson never to steal again then maybe others will be spared the same fate as me and so I find myself laughing. Then I hear myself in my own ears. I am snorting and I become ashamed and so I stop. I am still annoyed at the Thief but I am starting to wonder why he has to be so small and why his voice is so squeaky and quiet.

The boy does not respond to the Good Samaritan's question so the big man shoves him and he falls and once he is down something is unloosed in the crowd; a certain permission is given and they set upon him.

The boy tries to get up and a young man pushes him down and when he tries again another pushes him back down again and then someone slaps him and I am no longer laughing and the thrill of being vindicated feels like bile pushing against the back of my throat and I bend over and try to steady myself. It would be so easy for someone to hurt him under their rubber sandals. It would be easy for them to smush him as though he were really only a meaningless mosquito and he is not that, he is a boy, a very little one. I begin to panic and say 'Stop' but no one is listening. I waited too long to say something and now it's too late: they are about to tear him apart.

I turn to look for help because the Good Samaritan seems to have lost control of the situation and I see Patience. She peers at me from under her glasses and smiles worriedly. 'Are you okay?' she asks and because the presence of someone who knows me in a situation of stress always makes me cry, I begin to cry.

The Samaritan notices my distress and calls the crowd to order. 'Stop,' he says to them all, and they listen because he is a man and speaks in a manly voice. He turns to me. 'Are you okay, Young Madam?'

'Yes,' I answer, trying to look calm and collected in the

hopes that this might make things easier for the Thief. 'Yes, but I think he has learnt his lesson. Please let him go now.'

'Are you sure?' he asks, turning back to the boy.

I nod.

'Okay, but these guys must be punished otherwise they will never learn. You can't be too easy. It doesn't help – even them in their own hearts they know this.'

'It's fine,' I say.

'Okay, okay. Now, you boy, you must apologise to her.'

'I'm sorry,' says the boy, cowering and crying and looking like he wishes he had never seen my shiny black bike or my gleaming brown skin.

He doesn't mean it. He is saying it because he has been caught and because he has been forced to, but he hates me. It cannot have escaped his attention that the Good Samaritan called me madam. I am indeed a small madam because I am dressed like a junior madam, wearing shorts I bought at Zellers last summer and a T-shirt from Le Chateau that is not fancy but looks as though it was *Made in Canada*. I cannot pretend to be anything else with my well-oiled legs and my expensive but now dusty bicycle. All of this gave me away as a small madam to the Thief long before the Good Samaritan intervened.

He stares at me with naked rage. He is sorry that I am rich and that he is poor and he is not moved by my tears or my vulnerability. This shocks me and then it irks me. How dare he? He stole from me! I shoot him back the hatred he has just thrown at me and the hairs on my back bristle. How dare he look at me like that when he is the one who owes me a clean apology?

'It's okay,' I say, but I am shaken. There is nothing that can be done about his hatred because he is right. People like me own the world and it is all an accident of birth and circumstance. It is all pure dumb luck. Why shouldn't he be outraged?

The looks have been exchanged and the *sorry* has been issued and it is time for this trial to come to an end. Patience says, in a soft voice as though she too is afraid of the Thief and his burning eyes, 'Let's get out of here. Take your bike, we go.'

I am relieved to have someone telling me what to do and I wonder – without sentiment, because the reality of his life is too disturbing for crocodile tears and our exchange has forced me to snap out of my pretensions – what is going to happen to the Thief once we go. The crowd still looks intent on teaching him a lesson.

Now that he has forced an apology, the Good Samaritan is going in for the kill, showing the court how heinous this crime really is. He asks the suspect a few pointed questions.

'This is what you do to foreigners? You do this to people who are in our country as our guests? Instead of hospitality you take from her? What is she supposed to think about us?'

He has figured out from my broken Swahili and my polished accent that I am not Kenyan so I have given him fuel to add to the fire.

'It's fine, sir,' I say to him. 'He has said sorry. Thank you for helping me. I need to get home now, my parents will be worried.'

Mention of my parents seems to remind the Good Samaritan – in all his prosecutorial splendour – that there is a world beyond the temporary scene that is playing out here. It breaks the spell. We are only children after all.

'Of course,' he says, suddenly gentle, perhaps remembering that he is a father himself. 'Do you want a lift? I can put your bike into the back and take you home. Is this your friend?'

We thank him and climb into the cab of the truck while a few of the guys who had been shoving the boy around help us by loading my bike into the pickup. Then, as he squeezes himself behind the steering wheel, the Samaritan issues a stern and final warning to the boy. Wagging his finger in his direction and casting his eye around the crowd he says, 'Wewe! Ebu, you must watch yourself. Take your dirty body back to Mathare where you belong. If I ever see you on this street again – if anyone here ever sees you – you will see my cane. You will see it and you will feel its fire and wish that you had never walked on the streets of Loresho.'

The boy nods and looks at the ground, his toe boring a hole into the ground. Then the Samaritan tells him to scram. 'Go! Are you waiting for us to leave so that you can steal again? Go!'

With that the Thief scrambles away. I see him disappear into the bush with his cracked wing whirring uselessly. The strong one propels him and soon he is a speck among many on the dirt path and he is gone just as quickly as he had appeared next to me in the field.

The Good Samaritan drives us chirpily back to my house, regaling us with stories about other perps he has caught. He is an amiable sort, inquiring about where we are from and what our families are doing in Kenya. When I tell him I am South African, he smiles with recognition. 'Ah! That Nelson Mandela is a brave man. I hope those mzungus do not kill him there in that place.'

He tells me that he knows a South African family. He supplies paper to the University of Nairobi and the administrator in the office of the vice chancellor is a South African woman who is married to a Kenyan. 'Beautiful lady,' he says, 'very, very beautiful because you people you have that brown colour. Like us Kikuyus. Not too dark like the Luos.'

Patience prods me in the thigh and I give her a gentle push with my elbow: file under To Be Discussed.

When we get home the Good Samaritan helps us to offload the bike. He comes in to meet Mummy and Baba. He comes in to be thanked. He accepts the bottle of Tusker and swaps jokes with Baba. They talk about Kenya's economy. They stay away from politics. He is glowing with the satisfaction of having been of use. This has been a good day and he is a good man. He has helped somebody's child, and he has taught a lesson to a criminal. Justice has been done.

Mummy cleans my palms with disinfectant, picking out tiny pieces of stone. She looks at my ankle. Keep it dry, she says, otherwise it won't heal. She clucks and coos and I feel like I am nine years old again. She is triumphant, pleased that I emerged from the battle victorious and with my bike back, happy that the criminal was given a taste of mob justice, and that I kept my wits about me.

In the weeks that follow Mummy and Baba repeat the story to anyone who will listen. They delight in the retelling of it: the growling crowd, the Good Samaritan. It is a quintessentially African story and having just arrived from Canada they relish its contours and hold onto what its outcomes say about the choice they have made to bring us back. 'We made the right choice,' the story says. 'Here there is life and joy even if it is set against a backdrop of misery. This is Africa.'

Often, they call on me, asking me to come and tell the story properly. Families are nothing without the stories they tell.

'Sonke!' Mummy will call out. 'Come and tell Aunty and Uncle the story of the bike.' And I will leave my playmates and come to the sitting room to tell the story. I will add my voice and take the stage, embellishing and honing and hamming it up until each character is filled out. The biggest laughs come when I describe the Good Samaritan and his belly. There are always gleeful chuckles when I describe the tiny old lady with the big voice. In the story's retelling it was she who called the mob, not me. I always tell them that she shouted 'Mwizi!' before I did. She was the one who cast the first stone.

I say nothing about the look that passed between us. I don't tell them that he judged me and did not ask for forgiveness because none was needed. I don't say that in his eyes I could see that I was pathetic, and silly for blubbering when I had only fallen on my well-padded rear while he – a mere boy of twelve or so – had been chased by a car and beaten about the head and had probably endured more in the eight hours since waking than I could imagine with my Canadian accent and my Canadian bike. How could I tell them that he looked at me as if to say, 'Maybe another time we will meet and you won't get off so lightly'?

None of this could be relayed in the stories I was called upon to tell. No matter how many times I stood to re-enact the stealing of the bike I could never say that he made no apologies for himself or that he blamed me for being a certain kind of girl and occupying the world with a certain kind of obliviousness that was not acceptable. I could not tell anyone he wasn't just a thief, though I wanted him to be. He was an exploited urchin, a fully human little monster waiting to grow into something impossible to control and even harder to kill than the cockroach we insisted he was. He was Kenya's future:

desperate and poor and needlessly malnourished.

I never include the most important part of the story, which is that he was the first person who didn't pretend. He stole my bike and he wasn't sorry because he understood he had just as much right to happiness as I did.

The return to South Africa

IN FEBRUARY 1990, Nelson Mandela is freed. I am sixteen years old, and I am staying with Uncle Stan and Aunty Angela in Nairobi. Dumi and Lindi are studying in America, and Mummy and Baba and the girls have moved to Ethiopia because Baba has yet another job that requires us to move.

Uncle and Aunty and I sit in front of the TV as CNN teleports South Africa into the room. Nelson and Winnie Mandela are walking hand in hand. His fist is raised in the air and she is beautiful and they seem like strangers to each other. We are crying. Aunty keeps shaking her head in disbelief. Uncle keeps standing up and pretending he is not crying. I stay still, transfixed.

I watch the scene on a loop, combing the background for details. I am looking at the sky and the faces in the crowd and what everyone is wearing. I am imagining the smell of the place and wondering whether it is cold. I am trying to imagine myself into the moment. I watch the old man who is walking slowly and stiffly. This is not the Mandela of the T-shirts. This man is so lean, so old. He is relying on his wife more than he ought to. I watch and I watch and I watch, as though somehow the screen might suck me in.

Baba is cagey about going back. He wants to be sure that the unbanning of all political organisations is real, that this is not a trap. But it will be safe for me: I am a child who has never been linked to any terrorist activity and I have a foreign passport. Uncle Stan is coming back as an academic and it is different for him too. He is offered a job at the University of Natal. He accepts and in December that year, as the Sangweni family boards a flight to Johannesburg, I am with them. We are headed home.

◆ ◆ ◆

Jan Smuts Airport is bathed in a dirty fluorescent light, the kind that makes even perfect skin look pitted. The ceilings are low and there is too much brown brick. The airport is a fascist fortress, designed to withstand attack. The interlocking buildings all have small windows – air holes rather than features really. Jan Smuts is modern if you consider the 1970s modern. I do not.

Our passports are stamped by a row of stern-looking immigration officials who ask what we are doing here. Each of them seems to have a moustache and I have an urge to giggle, but I sense this would irritate them. I say I am here to visit family and they ask no further questions. Mandela has guaranteed us safe entry into South Africa, even though apartheid is still alive. They do not smile or welcome us but they let us in.

Outside, my cousins Slumko and Mandisa are waiting. Slumko is the glamorous big brother: fifteen years older than me and already a grown man. Mandi is his excitable younger sister, only five years my senior, which is old enough to be far cooler. They grew up in neighbouring Swaziland so they are already connected to what is happening 'inside'.

Slumko studied in America and moved to Johannesburg a few weeks before Mandela was released. He is massive – two metres tall – and good-looking, and everywhere we go people look at him as though he is a superstar. The white women's eyes linger the longest. When you meet their gaze and smile because you have noticed them noticing him, they seem surprised at themselves, and embarrassed.

Mandi still lives in Swaziland but she is in Joburg a lot because that is where all the action is, and her personality is too big for sleepy Swaziland. We hear her high-pitched squealing before we see her face. She too is long and lean and, like her brother, she turns heads. She preens and purrs and dresses so that any woman within ten metres walks in her shadow. In the week-long sojourn, Lindi and I will be pale grey egrets to her peacock hues.

But now we hug noisily and dramatically. This is our first trip home and we sense that our actions will be scrutinised. We are on a stage, unsure exactly who will be watching but knowing nonetheless that we will draw attention. We want to be worthy of the surveillance.

We don't all fit into Slumko's sleek German car so we split up. Lindi and Dumi and I take the shuttle to the Airport Holiday Inn while Uncle and Aunty get into Slumko's car. We are only in Joburg for a night. In the morning we will head off to Pietermaritzburg. We are in South Africa to begin the process of settling Uncle at the University of Natal and have combined this with the business of meeting our family members for the first time.

Uncle and Aunty go to sleep. They are tired and want to stay in, so they release us. Go and see Joburg, they say, and we do. We have only seen the city through Brenda Fassie videos smuggled out by comrades. In all her songs Brenda is glamorous in a way that makes her seem beautiful even though she is not. In the videos, her city looks big and fast and so shiny it cannot possibly be real. I have never seen an African city whose buildings are so heavily concentrated.

Slumko says he knows exactly where to take us, so we turn up the music and ease into the darkness and then hit the highway in search of trouble.

Hillbrow is awash with neon and urine and when I roll the windows down there is the faint smell of vomit. Hillbrow is not yet seedy, though it is slouching towards disrepute; its dodginess is hidden around the corner, just out of view. Cars crawl along Kotze Street, flanked by long-limbed black girls who've come in search of fresh starts. Many of them are jittery. Between the police and the coke it is hard for them to stay still. Paunchy white men leer, here to satisfy a hunger apartheid's laws cannot sate.

We end up at a café where everyone looks chic and is sitting on Parisian-style sidewalk chairs. It is busy inside so we sit outside in the warm evening. The city of gold glitters around us like a madam's box of jewels. Somewhere someone is smoking weed and the smell of it eases us somehow and our laughter is more pronounced, our sense of our own bodies grows, our smiles are punctuation marks, our sighs languorous and revelatory. This country is already ours and we know it so we are basking in one of those moments kissed by the gods: it sparkles and shines and so do we. We are young and freedom is in front of us and heartbreak and pain are yesterday's heroes.

A man appears. It is as though he was sent to remind us that the world is made not only for the young and beautiful but also for the old and the grey. He is shrunken and mottled so that he looks like something discarded, a paper bag lying on the side of the road or a can crushed on the pavement. But he is not nothing. He is a man. At first we only notice him moving at the edge of the frame but soon he is centre stage and rising. He opens his mouth and sings, 'Mona Lisa, Mona Lisa, men have named you. You're so like the lady with the mystic smile.' He croons as though he were born for the stage. 'Do you smile to tempt a lover, Mona Lisa?' he continues and a silence settles on us. 'Or is this your way to hide a broken heart?' His voice is like velvet but he is singing for his supper. He is literally holding a cup in his hand and we are singing along because he has transformed into Nat King Cole in a dinner jacket and a tie and we are transported into a world his voice has made and in it there is no rancour, only the harmony that has been born for this black and beautiful moment.

Without warning or provocation a waitress with a screaming gash of a mouth is shouting at our debonair crooner. She is standing in front of him – 'Get out of here' – and before he can respond she pours water on him and he is humiliated and cowering in front of her, shivering like a dog.

Ah! Here it is, finally: the moment we anticipated as we packed our bags in Nairobi. We landed in South Africa prepared for this confrontation. Truth be told, our lives in exile as the children of revolutionaries were one long rehearsal for this scene.

Here is the villain and she is barely a woman, still a child really, smashing the dignity of a man who could have been our father.

And he is taking it. 'Sorry, please, I'm sorry, forgive me, I'm only looking for bread.' His voice is no longer velvet. Now it is cracked stones, gravelly and ruined by drink. But still each word is enunciated perfectly as though he were educated at Eton and the contrast between what he once was and where he kneels now, wet and trembling on the street, should be too much for anyone to bear.

We are up on our feet and Slumko is roaring and Mandi is hissing and I am shouting and Lindi is stabbing her finger into the waitress's face and the girl who is almost a woman is white as a sheet and backing slowly inside, edging her way towards the safety of the restaurant. We are following her and we are seething and rage boils in our veins and we are so outraged that we forget the old man. We forget to ask if he is okay. Instead, we give the perpetrator our full attention.

'What are you doing?' Slumko thunders. 'That man is old enough to be your father!'

'You have no respect. What kind of behaviour is that?' Mandi chimes in.

'Where is your manager?' says Slumko. 'This is simply not on.'

The waitress gulps. She looks shaken but she is defiant.

'You don't work here,' she says. 'Every day he's here. Every day asking, begging, bothering the customers.'

'We are customers,' Slumko retorts. 'We are paying customers and we didn't complain.' Then it is her turn to look towards the ground, chastened.

I go in for the kill. 'You're racist. That's your problem. You're racist and you think you can talk to him any way you like because he's black.' My objective is to maim, not to reconcile or elicit understanding.

The waitress's eyes snap into focus and she wants to cry but she is stubborn and entitled to express herself and she has never ever been spoken to like this by black people and she cannot allow this travesty to unfold in such a way. 'Don't tell me I'm a racist. You foreigners think you know everything about this country but you know nothing. This isn't America, this is South Africa.'

The word 'racist' is like a dog whistle and the other patrons are now paying attention. A pack has formed.

A white man at a nearby table pipes up, 'She's right. I come here all the time, that old man is a pest. Tell me something? Have you ever been here before?' he asks, looking me dead in the eye. 'Have you ever walked into this place before tonight? Because if you had, you would know we are all nice here. There's no racialism. This one here' – he motions at the waitress – 'is just doing her job.'

The kinship of skin is deep.

They think we are strangers; they have assumed we are black Americans and this makes us even angrier, so Lindi says in her British accent, 'You think we're from America? You think that because we speak English we aren't from here? Don't try those tricks, you have nothing to teach us about our own country.'

An old white woman, who looks as though she may not have a place where she can lay her head every night, wanders into the conversation. She is thinner than an old woman should be, so thin she must not have children to feed her. She takes us all in and hisses in our general direction, 'Don't bother about them. It's obviously a case of bad breeding.'

Mandi loses it. 'Breeding is for horses,' she says in her highpitched voice. 'If you haven't noticed, there are no animals here, just black people who happen to be human.'

The restaurant manager makes an entrance. He introduces himself and tries to assert an authority we do not respect. We don't care about restaurant decorum. We have flown across the length of a continent and travelled decades in anticipation of this moment. A supervisor will not stop this collision course with a confrontation we see as our birthright. We are here to confront the apartheid whites whose boots have been on our necks. We are unruly and ungovernable. We have not been exiles only to return and capitulate with the politeness expected of us by unrepentant whites. We have found the racism our parents fled and we intend to mine it for all it is worth.

We respect the manager only insofar as he is capable of moving our agenda forward. So we demand that he instruct his waitress to apologise.

She refuses.

We insist.

He prevaricates, does not know what to do with blacks like us. We smell blood.

'What are you waiting for? We have demanded an apology for the racist actions of your employee and you seem to be thinking about it. Don't you know that the customer is always right? Where exactly did you get your training?"

We sneer.

He stutters something incoherent.

'Listen, this is not about us,' Slumko says. 'We don't give a damn if she apologises to us or not. An old man has been offended here and he is the one she should be saying sorry to. Not us. She says it, and we let it go. She doesn't, and you'll be hearing about this for a long time to come. You have no idea what kind of connections we have.'

We are steeped in the rules of middle-class combat and far more cosmopolitan than he can imagine. It has been many years since we last suffered any kind of indignity, yet we know all about the moral high ground. We have been raised to fight on behalf of those who cannot speak for themselves. We have the articulate outrage of the entitled and we have the advantage of surprise. We are brown and that should not mean we are afraid or uneducated or polite. We are none of these.

The waitress senses she has been outwitted. She is confused – she had not known that a group of uppity black Americans would sabotage her shift. How could she have known? She looks at Slumko with his hulking muscles and his movie-star looks, and then at Lindi and Mandi and me – tall and elegant in our jeans and our high-heel sandals and made-up eyes – and she knows she must relent.

Her manager – frightened and equally confused – accompanies us back outside. The rest of the café clientele looks on. They have chosen sides – a small number are with us but the bulk are shocked by our cheek. Even here, in the most liberal of Johannesburg's streets, no one has really begun to imagine the future. And yet here it is: brazen and unrelenting and demanding. Everything is tense and frozen and the neon street no longer looks glamorous. We are in a seedy part of town and the whites here are only sitting next to blacks because their choices are constrained.

He is gone. The old Bojangles has vanished and all our remonstrations have come to naught.

The waitress looks at us triumphantly, as if to say, 'So much for that.' But she quickly rearranges her face when she realises that, even though the victim we were championing has slunk off, we still hold the balance of power. We are angrier and more articulate than she is, and his absence does not change that, although it does sting. He is not there to celebrate our eloquence and bravery; he has gone somewhere to find the meal he was seeking. He has disavowed us.

'I'm sorry,' says the manager. He avoids eye contact with the rest of us, as though the fight was caused by too much oestrogen. Then he gives Slumko a look that says, 'Man to man, let's let this go now.' He continues, still talking to our fearless leader. 'I think we have learnt a lesson today and we will make sure it never happens again.' He looks Slumko in the eye as though he hopes that sense will prevail. Slumko is seduced: the inclusiveness of the male gaze is so hard to resist.

'It's fine, man, it's okay. We understand.'

The waitress is released and she scampers away. We stare at her back as she retreats. The manager walks us to our car, intent on making sure we leave his establishment and don't cause any more trouble.

'Next time you are here, please swing by, it will be a free drink. On us!' says the manager to Slumko. The rest of us are invisible. We brought the trouble and now we are being ushered into the car. Slumko is the man of the hour because there is nothing else the manager can hold onto. We are not ordinary blacks he can threaten; we are loud-mouthed women led by a man who surely must be open to some sort of reason.

Slumko gets behind the wheel and the rest of us pile into the car. The car impresses the manager. In years to come he will see many more blacks like us but on this night we are singular and so his disquiet grows.

He reaches in to shake Slumko's hand and then we pull off. After a few minutes of silence we burst into laughter. We retell the story of our heroism, we cheer one another on for standing up to the rabid racists and we dub Slumko the sell-out for forging a pact to bundle us out of there without causing further chaos. We laugh and we feel full although we haven't eaten.

We will dine on the story for years to come and over time we will end the story with Mandi's words as the punchline: 'Breeding is for horses. We. Are. Human.' Sometimes when we are together we will say the line in unison, cackling and giving one another high fives at this part, gloating about how clever we all were.

The old man and his vanishing act will become less and less important. We will forget whether he was singing 'Mona Lisa' or 'Mr Bojangles'. The story we will tell in the weeks and then years after this scene will be about our own chutzpah. It will be about our encounter with the racism we have been told about our whole lives.

❖ ❖ ❖

We rent a car and travel by road to Pietermaritzburg. The trip is lush. We drive on immaculate roads that slice through cane fields. The hills are a Van Gogh and we are sunflowers – soaking in the air and the curves of this new place we have never seen before, which Aunty and Uncle remember as though it were only yesterday. Uncle's job is on the Pietermaritzburg campus, so we are going to settle him in – to buy crockery and linen and make sure the temporary house is spick and span. Our first destination though – before anything else – is Mkhulu's house. We are on our way to meet my grandfather, Baba's father.

As we get out of the car, an old man appears at the top of the stairs. He is grey and short, much shorter than Baba. He is plump and has the air of someone who is well taken care of – perhaps so well cared for that he has grown too soft. Standing looks difficult. The old man leans heavily on a cane and rests for a moment, then he shuffles forward and looks up. I shiver: I am peering into the future, looking at Baba in thirty years' time. The old man does not attempt the steps. There are too many and they are too steep. Instead he stops and looks across the road at the car as we get out with our long legs and our eager faces. As he sees me he puts his arms out, forgetting the cane momentarily. He stands erect and steady, with his arms outstretched, waiting for me. His voice is strained, but I can hear him clearly. He is calling my name, the way one does a lost animal. His voice is old and slightly breathless but it is thrilling in its unmistakable resemblance to Baba's. 'Sisonke!' he shouts. 'Sisonke!'

I move quickly, running across the road and then up the stairs and into his arms. He slumps heavily against me and for a moment I feel off-balance as though we might topple over. But I regain my footing and hold onto him. We cry into one another's jerseys. His is plush and new and still smells like the shop, but his neck and face are those of an old man, stale with a hint of sourness.

'Aiii. Aiii, *mtanami*,' he says. The cracked veranda of the house heaves beneath us. The street looks on, tired and fading. My cousins smile up at us from the steps, and the mountains watch us with heavy-lidded knowing.

This landscape has seen the old man on this porch each and every day of his life. It knew him when he was a young man and before that when he was only a toddler. Those mountains watched him take his first steps on this very walkway and, later, they saw his son born. The sun, hanging low in the sky where it sits now, watched the old man's son close the door one last time and never come back. It waited like the old man. The sun and the trees and the mountains and the sky waited and eventually they all began to see that the boy would not return. They saw too that the man did not give up. And now the sun and the trees and the sky are observing our embrace. They are watching in anticipation of another reunion yet to come. They know I am a mere harbinger, an augury sent in advance of the warrior who will soon return home.

We walk into the dark living room, both of us in tears. I am helping Mkhulu to walk, so he leans on me – the energy it took to stand properly on the veranda now depleted. We stand shoulder to shoulder. His other children – my aunt and uncle who are younger than me and dressed in their Sunday best – are already seated. They stand and greet us and I am surprised that they are so young. His wife is Mummy's age so I suppose it makes sense. Technically they are my aunt and uncle but they are just kids. Strangers. Strange teenagers.

I try not to look disappointed at their presence. Fleetingly, I want them to disappear. A childish jealousy passes through me. Mkhulu doesn't need me – he doesn't need grandchildren at all. He already has children who are younger than my sisters and me. What kind of love can we give him that he does not already have? I feel robbed somehow. All these years spent waiting to meet my grandfather and here he is, beautiful in his old age and also a complete stranger whose life is already full – full of children.

The children look like him and so they look like me. I shake my head as though this is a weird dream sequence rather than the end of one part of my life and the beginning of another. I have only known him for five minutes but I am already greedy for his affection. Exile has been like a blanket – it protected us from ordinary hurts just as it provided a sheen for the loved ones we longed for and made them seem heroic. In my dreams they were all perfect, just as in their dreams we were too.

There is no time for processing these sorts of emotions. We are in the deep end already. Mkhulu has a lot to say and all of it must be said quickly because he wants to make up for lost time.

Over the next few hours, he regales me with stories. He talks about what it is like to lose a son to the mist and what it feels like to be left behind. He says vanishing is an act of cruelty but seems to recognise that it was also an act of love. I don't understand it all, of course. Baba has never spoken about his father and so to me he has been only an absence.

I know small pieces of the story, gleaned over years and told piecemeal and guardedly. In Baba's version one particular school holiday he said his usual goodbyes to his father and to his step-mother (there was another wife back then – Mkhulu has had four in total over the years) and hugged his favourite cousin, Gugu, goodbye. He walked out the door and went back to school. There was a protest at Fort Hare within a few weeks and that was when the M-Plan kicked into action. A few of them went underground. They took a train from Alice to Johannesburg and made their way through a line of police dogs outside Park Station. They did not have the hated dompasses that all 'natives' were supposed to carry and which gave them permission to live and work in the city, so their plan could have collapsed at that stage, but luck was on their side. They hid in Alexandra and then followed instructions from comrades who would emerge from here or there with packages and money and notes.

He was under strict instructions from the movement not to tell anyone he was leaving. All he knew was that he was part of a group of recruits who would take up arms in the new military wing of the people's party. He wasn't sure where he was going. That detail would only be revealed once they crossed the border, his destination kept from him to protect his own safety. This much I had known when I was growing up. Now, all these years later, Mkhulu picks up the story from there, telling me what happened on the other side of the border Baba crossed a lifetime ago.

After a few weeks, a police officer knocked on Mkhulu's door. It was a Saturday, so Mkhulu was home. The officer took a seat in the kitchen, rather than in the formal lounge, which made Mkhulu extremely uncomfortable. He assumed he was here to tell him that his son had been found dead in a ditch on the way to Fort Hare, where he had been studying before he disappeared. That was not the purpose of the visit. The officer was looking for his son. The man was stern in his eyes, even though his mouth was friendly and spoke politely.

Mkhulu told the truth, which was that he had no idea where his son was. The officer leaned in close and told him that he had better cooperate. Mkhulu was alarmed because he *was* cooperating. The officer said fine and leaned back.

Mkhulu pauses in his story and stands up stiffly. He walks to a cabinet standing against the wall and picks up a frame. 'Here she is. My wife at the time. So she offered him some tea and he graciously accepted. You know because of the apartheid laws and so on, technically he shouldn't have said yes, but he was showing his human side. Du Toit and I became somewhat friendly over the years.'

Mkhulu's story continues, taking turns here and there. Remembering how miserable the weather seemed that first winter that his son was gone. He speaks about how his first wife – my father's mother – was so distressed that she came all the way from her village to suggest that they go to Johannesburg to find him. She was convinced that her son had been waylaid by a gang and abducted. 'It was a fanciful theory,' he says now in his polished English. Something about the way he speaks answers questions about my father that I did not know I had.

He continues, getting comfortable on the couch as he lists the milestones that marked the years; the times when they despaired and moments in which they were certain he would soon be home. Then after a decade had passed – the first of three – Du Toit showed up for his weekly visit with a file full of photos. He spread them in front of Mkhulu and said, 'We've found him and it is confirmed. Your son is a terrorist. There he is.'

Mkhulu looked at the photos and indeed there he was, all six foot five of him getting out of the back of a plane. Another picture shows him walking on a crude runway next to Denis Goldberg. He was thin and young. I cannot imagine this because I have never seen a photo of my father in his childhood or in his youth. Growing up in exile, you have to imagine what your parents looked like. There is no space for mementos when you are running. It is as though he did not exist until he became my father. While there are lots of pictures of Mummy in high school, Baba only appears in our family photo albums when we are born, and even then, he is usually behind the camera.

Mkhulu was ecstatic: this was the first sign of life he'd had since his son's disappearance. But he knew better than to confirm his son's identity. So he held his joy in and he shook his head. Slowly, and without a hint of recognition, he said, 'I have no idea who that person is.'

His heart was pounding and his mind was bursting with questions. Finally he had news that his boy was alive. But he stayed ramrod straight. His face betrayed nothing.

I cry now because Mkhulu has motioned for my baby uncle to get the photo. There he is, looking out at me from the past. It never crossed my mind that they took out his pictures and looked at them. That they cried when they thought about him and prayed for him to be safe. I was too busy wondering about them and mourning their absence in my life.

Mkhulu pats my hand, just as a grandfather should, and he gives me a bit of time to recover. He passes the photo around – hands it over to Dumi who is sitting on the couch. And Dumi passes it over to Lindi and they both exclaim excitedly and there is much talk about how different he looks now, about how young he was then. I am profoundly sad but Mkhulu is moving on. He has another story to tell and his eyes are twinkling and his cheeks are rounding out into a smile and he is already launching into it.

After three hours, the old man's energy is flagging. He needs to rest but he has made arrangements for me to sleep in Edendale, with some relatives. I freeze. The afternoon has been wonderful but they are all strangers. I will not be parted from Uncle Stan and Aunty Angie and from Lindi and Dumi. They are my family – more so than the kind-faced strangers I am told are my aunt and uncle.

I look at Aunty Angela with desperation. I will cry soon if this situation is not resolved. What will I say to them in their house tonight over dinner? How will I make sense of it all without Lindi and Dumi? Without Aunty Angela to make the connections for me – to remind me that this is Mkhulu's third wife, that he divorced Gogo Sonke and then married Mam' So and So and then after that they also separated, then there was an illicit child no one knew about and so after that matter was resolved then he married again. This one – the wife who buzzed around us sweetly – is the latest and it seems she is good for him.

Aunty intervenes on my behalf. She says sweetly, in her quiet voice, 'We have a long drive tomorrow and Sonke needs to stay with us, otherwise we will be disorganised in the morning.' I nod appreciatively and exhale. I blink back my tears, disappointed in myself for not being able to just immerse myself, but so grateful to have avoided being among strangers I am supposed to love.

We file out of the living room and stand on the veranda looking back out onto the street. Mkhulu is behind me, looking over my shoulder at the hills. They are purplish and orange in the fading light. I want to lean back as I might if it were Baba standing behind me, but I don't. I am not sure if he is strong enough to bear my weight, and I am still unsure of how to be with him. I do not yet understand the ways of my country and when to move closer and when to stand back. I am still awkward, the daughter who has been too long estranged.

We are all still and quiet. We are full of the events of the afternoon. Then Mkhulu breaks the silence.

'The last time I saw your father,' he says, 'he was on that veranda, with his back to me. He was standing there, exactly as you are now and he was about your age.'

The tears are back and I don't know what I am feeling. I experience a moment of panic and imagine something awful happening to Baba. He has been waiting for clearance and to be sure that he will not be arrested when he arrives in the country. He plans on coming in May – five long months from now. What if he never makes it home?

Mkhulu consoles me. He is gentle and elegant in a way that is distinct to his generation and his era. He puts his hand on my shoulder and whispers in my ear.

'Don't cry for me, *mtanam*'. In the final analysis it has all turned out rather well.'

It is generous of him to think that I am crying for him. In fact, with the self-indulgence of the young, I am crying mostly for myself. I am mourning my ignorance and my losses. I am grieving the grandparents and uncles and aunts I never got to know. I am crying because I am overwhelmed by all that has been lost and grateful that all has not been lost. I am frightened that we will never have enough time to make it right and that if we are given the time we need we still might squander it. I am crying, I suppose, because finally, I am home.

◆ ◆ ◆

The trip lasts three weeks. We go to the rural homestead where Baba and Uncle Stan were raised, to Jobstown, outside Newcastle. We are greeted like royalty. We eat plenty of sheep and a great many plates of tripe. We are stuffed with *mqushu* and *dombolo* and *amasi*. We hear stories about the two of them growing up – about how Uncle Stan memorised the dictionary and how Baba's grandfather owned the dipping station for the cattle. I see, for the first time, where Baba was formed, where he gets his sense of pride and his confidence. The struggle wasn't the crucible in which he was formed. Baba's self-belief was forged among these people who have never doubted their own abilities, never questioned their fortitude and intelligence, nor their determination and ability to plant and grow vegetables, and to rear animals and fence land and water it. I find myself among rural folk – which is new because I have been raised as a distinctly urban child – and I realise how much I have not known about what it means to be from the places on our continent that are wide open and large. It has never fully occurred to me that there are lives unfolding in villages that are pulsing with ambition and energy and passion, just like those in cities. I giggle with my cousins and listen to my aunties and chastise myself for believing for even a minute that I might be bored; that I might be too worldly to find connections here. My cousins are not worldly at all, but they are funny and observant and smart. They are also far more grounded, comfortable in who they are and where they are from, because it is all they have ever known and it has been – in spite of the world outside – a good place to them. My family is not wealthy but it is comfortable. The comfort derives from the fact that, like a few other local families, we never lost our land. This – I will find out in the decades to come – has made all the difference to who we are and what we are able to become.

At the end of the trip we fly away – back to school in

America for Dumi and Lindi and back to Nairobi for Aunty Angela and me. We leave Uncle Stan in Natal. Over the next while, as I finish high school, Aunty will begin to pack up life in Kenya, and then she will join him for a new start back in South Africa. Years of exile are finally ending for them. Similarly, Lindi and Dumi are now beginning to make plans for moving home after their degrees are finished – to a South Africa they have only just visited for the first time. The rest of my family are all in Addis Ababa. Mummy and Baba haven't committed to moving back. Baba hasn't even gone to visit yet. They are waiting to see whether the transition is reversible.

◆ ◆ ◆

I have a few months left of high school and then I will be off to university and so for me the decision is about whether I apply to study in South Africa, or whether I set my sights on America or Canada where I have citizenship and may, therefore, be able to access better financial aid packages.

I am a good student. I excel in English and History and Social Studies. I love French. I take accelerated classes. I navigate the International Baccalaureate programme without involving my parents or asking their advice on this or that; and they expect the same when it comes to university. They don't know the ins and outs of applying to university – they simply expect I will be admitted to a good one.

I sit with the guidance counsellor at school. We talk about the costs and financial aid and scholarships. While South Africa is finally within reach for me, it is also a big unknown. I look at Rhodes University's journalism programme and I am tempted to apply. I phone South Africa and speak to someone in an office somewhere in Grahamstown. She is neither helpful nor nice. She finds my story confusing. Are you Kenyan? she asks. No, I explain, I am an exile, I just live in Kenya. So your high school exam will be Kenyan? she asks. No, I explain, I have done the International Baccalaureate. She doesn't know how to deal with me. We go around in circles. I am transferred to someone else. The questions begin again.

I give up. The American universities to which I have applied are all so much easier. They have either accepted or declined and they have indicated whether they have scholarships available. One of them has offered me a particularly good deal: Macalester College. I call Mummy in Addis. What should I do? 'You are going to America,' she says firmly and quietly. 'There is no option. South Africa will be waiting for you when you finish.'

While no one is surprised at the achievement, there is great excitement. Macalester is in St Paul, which is next to Minneapolis. Together the two cities are called the Twin Cities. When Gogo Lindi hears that I have been accepted at a college in the Twin Cities, she picks up the phone and rings me, all the way from Washington DC. It's a few weeks before my high school graduation, and about two months before my departure.

Gogo calls early, before school, so that she can be sure to catch me. Aunt Angela passes me the phone with a hurried smile.

'It's your Gogo Lindi,' she says. 'Don't stay on the phone too long or you'll miss the bus.'

Gogo is calling to congratulate me on my university acceptance. The adults in the family expect us to be high achievers and when our hard work pays off appropriate amounts of praise are lavished upon us. It is my turn now but before me there was Lindi who attended a prestigious hotel school and Dumi who left for Florida two years ago where he is learning how to be a pilot in a place called Boca Raton. A year after me, Mandla will crack the Ivy League and attend Cornell and she too will get a call from Gogo, confirming her pride and pleasure.

Over the years Gogo has only become more like herself, so that now her every word is predictable, her every tone and inflection mimic-worthy. She has matured into a genuine all-star diva. Nothing she says lacks accent or ceremony. Her turbans have grown more immense and complex by the year and the machinations required to produce each outfit have become more labyrinthine. Her commitment to the continent as a whole and her exposure to its many splendours allow her to order the finest Ankara fabric from Nigeria, and use the most intricate lace to overlay her dresses. Her boubous are made of the best Senegalese cotton, stitched with elaborate brocades by a tailor who lives in Maryland, or sent from friends in Dakar and Cotonou.

Gogo's yellow skin glows radiantly and her eyebrows are always arched to perfection. I can't see her but I am picturing her as I hear her voice on the line, purring her pride. She cannot believe, she says, that I am following in her footsteps. She insists that I must acquaint myself with the University of Minnesota campus and says that I must reach out to dear friends who have been comrades in arms: Vusimusi and Nothando Zulu.

There are black South Africans in Minnesota? I exclaim. No. She clarifies: 'They had different names when I met them, but they needed proper African names and it was the era to do that sort of thing so we did. We abandoned those slave names and created something new.'

I am half-smiling at my madcap revolutionary Gogo.

Since our time in Lusaka she has moved from country to country for the ANC. She is now the Chief Representative of the African National Congress in America – one of our most important diplomats. Her weeks are a blur of speaking engagements and appointments. She meets with people like Charlayne Hunter-Gault and lunches with Maya Angelou and she holds court with Jesse Jackson and Randall Jackson who she says are not related although both are dashing men of a certain age. She dines with senators from states with names that are not English and which remind me that America itself is older than the four hundred years it pretends to be. South Africa is not quite free yet but we are close and Gogo behaves accordingly. She does all her coordinating and delegating and cajoling and impressing from a well-appointed townhouse just off 16th Street and U Street.

In a few years' time she will be conferred with the official status of ambassador by our first president, Nelson Rolihlahla Mandela. He will dispatch her to Malaysia to serve as the High Commissioner for the Republic of South Africa in 1994. But that is still to come and neither of us knows this so today on the phone she is still a freedom fighter of a sort. She is also a gracefully ageing woman who is calling to congratulate her favourite grandchild and tell her to look up old friends when she gets to America.

She mentions Mahmoud El-Kati whom she worked with in her black and proud days. She thinks he is still living in Minnesota. 'He will take you under his wing. You will find that he is a man of great wisdom, and a man who cares deeply, so very deeply, about his people.'

Aunt Angela begins to flit around me now, worrying about the cost of the call, and wanting to say a few words to Gogo before we hang up. I am getting restless and really do need to go if I am going to catch the bus that picks me up at the top of the hill. At eighteen I have begun to endure her stories and recollections rather than revel in them the way I used to as a child and so I say, as delicately as I can, 'Gogo, I'm going to be late to school.'

'Okay dearest,' she continues slowly as though my rush and her pace of speech have nothing to do with each other.

'Now in terms of Mahmoud, I am not sure where he is based these days. I haven't spoken to him in a long time, so I will need to try to trace him. I think he is attached to the university. I will find him. It's wonderful to know that you will be in his keep and under his wing. And you will soar my darling Sisonke, you will soar as you always have.'

This is classic Gogo, always the drama and the poetic flourish and always at her own speed. I smile and hand the phone over to Aunty with a glint in my eye. We will have a good giggle afterwards and I will tell her about Gogo's parting flourish: 'Sooooaaarr!' I will intone and we will sip our afternoon tea and cackle about Gogo Lindi whom Uncle Stan refers to as The Eighth Wonder of the World.

Soon enough it is time to leave. College awaits. I fly to Addis to spend a few weeks with Mummy and Baba and Mandla and Zeng then I head off to America. Another country.

College Girl

MY STUDIES BEGIN in what they call the fall semester of 1992. It is late summer when I arrive, just before autumn splashes her reds and yellows and oranges across the trees and sends in the wind to blow the leaves so they fall in delicate pirouettes and lie in drying heaps. Everything is green – the freshly mowed lawns and the trees along the sides of the streets have an unnatural look to them, a Technicolor movie rather than real life.

The airport in Minnesota is clean and new and expensive – nothing like the yellowing-brown Jomo Kenyatta International Airport with its grey floors and stale air. At the carousel I am met by a young man holding a sign with my name on it. He is a chipper American student not unlike many I will meet in the next few years. Once my luggage arrives he pulls my bag behind him and begins to talk. He keeps talking until we reach a grey minivan that has the college logo on the side. He keeps at it, talking the whole drive into the city. The sheer friendliness of him overwhelms me. I feel like an allergy-prone child who has been accosted by a friendly Labrador.

He speaks to me in a slightly loud and slow way and after a few attempts to engage him in a way that demonstrates my fluency in English, I stop trying because it is apparent that his idea of me isn't contingent on the reality of who I am. Still, he is well-meaning in a way that makes me feel sympathetic towards him, in spite of my irritation.

I look out of the window and occasionally, when his tone demands it, I feign interest. I have been brought up to keep my thoughts to myself until I can trust that the person to whom I am speaking is interested in what I have to say. Mummy views saying too much too soon as uncouth: the product of bad upbringing. My silence is no deterrent, however. My guide talks about everything from the weather to sports. He points out landmarks and tells me uninteresting 'facts' about the Twin Cities. I try to keep my eyes open, fighting sleep.

After about twenty minutes in the air-conditioned stillness of the car we pull up to a sidewalk a few metres behind the dormitory where I will live for my first American year. He issues a set of carefully worded instructions about campus security, the laundry room and places to 'grab a coffee,' and gives me a 'coupla tips' on taking the bus, but it is all too much information to process. I'm tired.

Somewhere in the tornado of words is a suggestion

that I go for a walk along the Mississippi, which we crossed on a large bridge as we made our way on the sturdy Minnesota roads which, I will discover in the coming winter, are impervious to winter blizzards and late summer rains.

'If you keep on Summit you'll walk straight into it,' he says. At first this confuses me because I wonder what I might be keeping. I am not yet used to that peculiar way Americans have of saying certain phrases: 'keep left,' rather than 'stay to your left'. 'Walk straight into it.' I imagine myself walking into the river humming 'Wade in the Water'. As the image pops up in my head I smile – America will indeed be an adventure.

I am on campus a week early for an international student orientation that is scheduled to begin in two days' time. This means there are very few people around. My room is on the third floor of Doty so I lug my suitcase to the lift and wait. Then I notice a sign saying 'Elevator not operational until 9/1/1992.'

As my chipper guide had said, 'the troops' will only begin to arrive in the next few days and so I realise I have to trudge up the three flights of stairs. I do so feeling suddenly very alone. And very annoyed. At home there would have been three random guys hanging around in the foyer, offering to help me with my bag – expecting a tip, of course, but available and friendly nonetheless. Here – nothing. Just a quiet, sterile building with no one around. The lack of people was a bit spooky.

The chipper American also gave me detailed notes on getting to Target where I would be able to buy bed linen but, having read my share of Mark Twain, and after inspecting the room which is sunny and exactly what a college room is supposed to look like, I decide to go and look for the northern shores of the great river that Huck and Tom had once navigated.

I set off down Summit Avenue looking for the Missis-sippi River. He was right about walking straight into it. I walk right to the shore and I could keep going if I want to, straight into the river's wide muddy body. It is disap-pointingly river-like and uninspiring and this worsens my mood. It looks nothing like I had imagined when I thought of Mark Twain and to make things worse it is a hot, sticky day – far hotter than it ever gets in Kenya and it reminds me of that first summer in Canada and how much we suffered in the sun and how intemperate North America can get with its swinging seasons. I look again at the brown water, feeling underwhelmed about this big adventure and, as often happens when boredom sets in, I make a note in my head to do some things that I forgot to write down like buy a hat and some shorts be-cause Nairobi is always a civilised temperature and the days are mostly mild and perfect and here it is so bloody hot.

I am eighteen and I think I know everything, especial-ly about America. I have watched enough movies and met enough Americans abroad so I think I am prepared to settle right away into the land of the brave and the home of the free. Or is it the home of the brave and the land of the free?

On TV America looks clean and in real life it smells clean and so – ridiculous as this may sound – I assume it is safe. In my mind I have always made a correlation between how a place looks and smells and whether or not it is safe. Perhaps it is because the parts of Nairobi where you need to be vigilant normally announce them-selves: they are unkempt and have muddy tracks and good places for people to hide, or they are full of sweaty crowds in which fingers can sneak into your pockets or hands can slide anonymously across your bum. In quiet neighbourhoods where askaris are on hand, Nairobi feels as safe as safe can be.

So, because the geography feels familiar – I have seen white picket fences a thousand times on TV – and because it is America, the greatest country on Earth, which I don't really believe but kind of do because Americans say it so much themselves – on my first day in America, I make the grave error of starting to feel comfortable in my surroundings.

It is late August so it is hot and humid and the houses on Summit Avenue are quiet – almost as though this is a set for a movie rather than a real place where people laugh and dance and actually live. The street is especially quiet, I will soon be told, because so many people are at their lake houses for the end of summer before the academic year starts. I am wearing shorts, because that's what Americans do. They walk in shorts and they drink Slurpees or iced coffees and they do not mind if African girls do the same. Who cares? I love that Americans say this all the time. In our house the phrase has always been banned. 'Your family cares,' Mummy says the first time she overhears me say this to Mandla after I have picked it up at school in Canada. Mandla was sharing an exciting piece of news and I was at the age where being an asshole was fun. 'Who cares?' I said, squashing her story and killing her joy. I was ashamed then and never said it again, but something in me thrilled to its use by others. It signalled an emotional freedom I was never allowed.

I walk down the street with my mind in overdrive, thinking about Kenya and Canada and all the places I have lived. I smirk at the thought of drinking a Slurpee and am swept up for a moment in memories of that maiden summer in Canada all those years ago. I make a note to myself to say something about this to my sisters when I call home later. I walk a bit faster, realising I still have a lot to do. I am getting a bit nervous about exchanging my travellers' cheques as well.

So, I am walking and thinking and feeling not-too-tired but sort of anxious on my way back from the river which has been so unmomentous. I pass a local school, which is just a block away from campus. I am struck again by how quiet it is and how well kept. I wonder if in America they have groundskeepers like we do at ISK or whether they contract companies to do it. I am about to remind myself to take the travellers' cheques out of my backpack when I get back to the room when I see him.

He is in the driver's seat of a parked car and the door is wide open. He has long black hair and a milky chest, which becomes a pale stomach, which slides into a tumble of black hair which is thatched at his crotch, where his penis is standing bolt upright. He is masturbating, stroking himself and looking at me without a hint of embarrassment in a way that makes me want to vomit and also makes me feel as though he has just vomited on me, and then he smiles which breaks the odd spell I have been under since seeing him and I turn and run. He doesn't chase me but that doesn't really matter because even though it is only a matter of seconds I am petrified.

I am startled – Bambi with her big eyes in the forest. I have never seen one of those uncloaked and standing upright in the stillness of the afternoon sun. I run with the full reach of my Zulu legs propelling me towards my dorm and I only stop when I see that I am on campus again, in front of a building that says 'Doty' in practical brown lettering, which is exactly the spot where the chipper American dropped me off only an hour and a half before.

It will soon be late but the sun is still up and the day is fading and washed in that orange prettiness that settles on North American summer evenings, and makes them look so good you want to remember them forever, even if nothing in particular has happened to make the day special.

Something about the apricot evening and the smell of the overly watered grass and the immaculately kept and professorial homes makes the exhibitionist masturbation incident feel sort of surreal and I begin to imagine myself telling Mandla and Zeng the story and saying, 'Now how's that for a first day in America?'

The idea of their laughter makes it seem like the whole thing has happened just so I can tell it and I start half-smiling and picturing Mummy asking what is so funny as my sisters gasp for breath on the other end of the line and them saying, 'Oh, it's just something you wouldn't be interested in,' and laughing harder and her insisting and then grabbing the phone and me finally telling her and her being appalled and this reminds me that I need to get a phone card at Target which I still want to get to before it closes and that makes me wonder whether the bank will still be open but everything in America has a drive-through and is open twenty-four hours – even banks – so hopefully it will be fine and I am about to make another mental note about that when trouble taps me on the shoulder.

Trouble – especially when you are not looking for it – is usually nondescript. He looks too old to be a student, although not by much. He is short and slight and dressed immaculately in a white linen jacket and white linen pants as though he has just strolled off the set of *Miami Vice*. He is even the same colour as the black guy on the show whom everyone loves because he looks like he is a pointfive, which is our slang way of saying half-caste in Nairobi, which I will soon learn is not a term that anyone in America uses – they say 'biracial'. Anyway, so Trouble is short and light and dressed like a Cubano and when he speaks he has a voice like Fred Sanford. I am tall and, a long time ago, I decided not to like point-five guys because it's so predictable. I decided to only fall in love with very dark-skinned guys because of black is beautiful and predictability. Plus I have never liked guys who are shorter than me even though that is very predictable but I am eighteen and can't be expected to think everything through thoroughly. All this is to say that nothing about this situation seems conducive to a love match.

His opening line comes as no surprise and as soon as I hear it I am irritated and want to move on so that I can get to my banking drive-through.

'Hey, girl, heaven must be looking for you 'cause...' I am gobsmacked by the actual real-life use of a line my friends and I have laughed at for the last two years.

I wonder whether this is a trick, whether he isn't some sort of joke my Nairobi friends are playing on me – sending me the exact opposite of my type to come and drop tired lines on me on my first day in America.

I respond with a terse hello – the kind that is supposed to say, 'I'm not really interested and I am just saying hello because I don't want to be rude.'

He doesn't notice my frostiness.

'Where you from, Angel? You go to school here?'

My well-raised African girl politeness problem rears its timid head again and so, instead of rolling my eyes and walking away, I respond.

'Yes, I'm a student here but I'm in a bit of a hurry so I can't really speak with you right now.' I am starting to move even as I say this but he falls in step with me.

'Listen to you. You sound like some kinda uppity girl.'

He does a poor imitation of my accent, 'I caaan't speak.' He laughs at his own joke then continues, 'You from Connecticut or somethin'?'

'Sorry,' I say, 'I really am in a hurry.'

By this time we are standing in front of the lift that will take me to the third floor, which is where my room is: 309 Doty. I try to move past him to press the button for the lift but he moves faster than me and blocks my way.

'C'mon girl. You haven't even told me your name.' This is said in a half-whisper that may have worked on a Hollywood film set, or even on someone who was not tired and irritable. It is not going to work on someone unattracted to the sayer of those words.

I start to worry a bit, though, because in Nairobi whenever I am walking along the street, if a man is too persistent, saying 'ssst, sst' for too long, I just keep going and eventually he gets tired and directs his attention elsewhere. By then his eyes have already tasted you and his mouth is a big O with his jaw dropping on purpose so that you and everyone else watching his performance on the street know he wants whatever is inside your jeans or under your shirt neatly tucked into your school uniform and his body turns as you swish past him and if you glance over your shoulder to make sure he isn't following, you'll see him looking with eyes bulging like the wolf in bed pretending to be Little Red Riding Hood's granny and you just shake your head and get annoyed but it is always fine because you are moving in a crowd and he disappears quickly.

But here – right now – there is nowhere to hide. I can't barge past him because this is not a crowded street and there are no blaring cars and exhaust fumes and no small shops to duck into to pretend I need to buy something. There is no one here except me and him and the worst part is that I am so painfully close to the peace of my room but not close enough and I can't figure out what might work to make him disappear.

So, I capitulate and tell him a made-up name. I tell him that my name is Sarah because telling him that my name is Sisonke will make him say, 'Huh? That's a pretty name. How you say that?' or something similar and it will prolong the conversation unnecessarily.

Then I tell him I have to go because I am late, and I turn away from him because I remember I had made a note to self earlier that the lift is not working and to use the stairs when I come back from my walk.

He follows me.

We are in the stairwell now and I feel so dumb for not anticipating this. I just thought he would get it and be gone. But he hasn't been getting it and now I don't know what to do in an empty stairwell with a strange man harassing me. I have nowhere to go but up, though, nowhere else but forward, so I climb stiffly and stupidly until we reach the third floor. He is still behind me making silly talk about how it is hotter than hot and damn it was like this in Charlotte but he hadn't expected it in Minnesota and I push the door open into the reception area and then stop walking and turn to face him.

'Damn, girl, don't you know not to stop short like that? I almost knocked you over.'

If I weren't so scared I think I would be able to laugh.

'Listen,' I say, 'I'm really tired, I have had a very long day. I need you to leave please.' I am still saying 'please' because everyone knows that being rude to strange men is just asking for trouble.

'I just want your number,' he says.

I am now freaking out so if I knew my number I would give it to him just to get rid of him, but I don't yet know what the numbers are in the rooms because I only arrived two hours ago. I tell him this but he thinks I am lying.

'Okay. I'll take yours,' I finally concede.

I am worn down and rattled. I have just seen a strange penis in broad daylight and am now having to deal with Trouble in a white suit.

'Nah, you ain't gonna call me, College Girl. What's your room number? I'm around here a lot. I'll pay you a visit.'

I keep quiet.

'I ain't gonna hurt you, College Girl.' He says it in a voice that is very low and immediately the word MENACING pops up like an air bubble over his head like in a cartoon and I want to cry but I just say, 'I didn't say you would hurt me. I told you, I don't know the phone number here on campus. I just got here.'

'College Girl. Listen to that pretty voice. You tell me your room number and I can figure it out.'

It dawns on me that I am trapped and in danger and my best option is to be downstairs where there might be more people around. The campus is still pretty empty because I'm here early for international student orientation, which someone told me was just being told things like, 'Picking your nose in public is considered impolite,' and 'Americans generally respect time.' Also, I remember the chipper guy telling me that the residence coordinator had an apartment on the ground floor so I think to myself maybe he'll be in and I can knock on his door if Trouble lets me get back downstairs and I am suddenly very thankful for the chipper chatter in the car – it had not been mindless after all.

'I need to go back downstairs,' I tell him and I slide past him, hoping he won't physically block me again.

'Whoa, whoa, okay, okay, College Girl. Okay. I can see you scared and I'm not a scary kinda guy. I just wanna talk a little. I ain't gonna do a thing, pretty girl.'

'Good,' I say as I start to move more quickly, heading down the stairs with him right behind me, a shadow I haven't asked for. I feel like a hostage but I am not sure I have a right to feel this way yet.

I write instructions in my mind, a note to remember to tell my sisters. Rule number 1: *When you are in America, do not think the rules are different. It's exactly the same as anywhere. Do not allow yourself to be alone with the strange guy. If he is following you, turn around and stay in the light.*

I get down the stairs and push the door out into the green and almost bump into two girl giants walking their bikes up the path a few feet from the staircase. Trouble is a few steps behind me, still coming out of the building and so I follow my instinct, which is to rush towards them. I feel slightly hysterical and I know I sound desperate, which seems odd on a college campus in America where everything is so neat and manicured and normal looking.

'Hi, can you please help me get to my room, this guy is kind of bothering me,' I say in a half-whispered rush.

They don't hesitate. 'Of course,' they both say as though they were twins. They look like Viking women with long legs and strong backs and blonde hair and worried eyes and just like that there are three of us and only one of him and I can breathe properly again because even though I am still a bit scared I am not alone any more.

I can tell they are a little bit frightened – like maybe they are wondering whether this is some sort of domestic dispute and he isn't just a random guy – but, actually, who cares because before they appeared his attention was starting to feel like way more than just another attempt to pick up a girl he just happened past on the street. And what was he doing in the heart of campus right next to Doty residence anyway?

Once I am certain they are with me and our circle of belonging is strong because we are all women – which counts for everything when you are in danger from a man – I turn to him and he suddenly shrinks and seems not so menacing and somewhat deflated as he watches them protect me and he also looks surprised and has an expression of betrayal on his face that almost makes me feel sorry for him – as though I have overreacted in front of people who have no business in our business. Before the Vikings came he thought he was protected by our shared brownness – as though our skin colour was some sort of a cloak – and I can see that I haven't played by the rules of the game but I don't care about that. Right now I need to feel safe. But funny, isn't it, how, even after his antics have put my heart in my throat and scared the crap out of me, even after all of that, as we walk past him I feel the need to apologise to him – to say over my shoulder, 'I'm really sorry, I have to go.'

Never mind that he should be the one saying sorry to me. It's okay though because I have a team now and our legs are young and strong and we are walking away and in two strides we disappear into the stairwell.

The Vikings look over their shoulders as the door closes behind us and one of them puts an arm around me then drops it as we hit the first step once it is clear that he isn't following us. We walk in an awkward silence and in the absence of danger we are no longer clever and I am aware that I am not as lithe and chiselled as them and we are unlikely to ever be friends, so that when we reach the third floor and they offer to keep me company, I say, 'No, I'll be fine.'

They deposit me at my door and after they leave and I am firmly inside I bolt it and sit on the bed, and cry stupidly. The story I am going to tell Mandla and Zeng about the masturbator and then the guy from *Miami Vice* isn't so funny any more so I curl up under the Ethiopian shawl that Mummy gave me at the airport in Addis two long days before, and I worry myself into a jumbled sleep.

◆ ◆ ◆

I am woken up by the sound of a fist banging on a door.

A man is yelling, 'Open up. Open the fuck up!' It isn't my door but it is somewhere on the floor – too close for comfort.

One by one, door by door, the banging and the yelling continue. He is making his way down the hall, pounding and screaming. 'Hey, I know you in there, College Girl!'

It is Trouble and he is outraged. I am not even sure I am fully awake, but it doesn't stop and soon I start to worry that his anger might knock the door down. I wonder if I will survive. I wonder if he will rape me or kill me or both. I wonder – if I live – how I will cope with four years of studying in America.

I am the sort of eighteen-year-old who has always known better than to adore America, but underneath the irony I was as convinced as everyone else that it was the greatest country on Earth, because actually I am only eighteen and even when you pretend you don't believe something like that, all you really want to do *is* believe.

When he reaches my door I freeze on the bed and I

breathe in as slowly and quietly as possible. I am sure he knows this is my room. 'Open. The. Fuck. Up!' Bang. Bang. Bang.

I start to pray as he hits the door the way the three little pigs must have prayed when the big bad wolf was huffing and puffing and getting ready to blow their house down. My lips move and I throw some panic-stricken words at God and I do a side prayer asking Him/Her to forgive me for not believing in Him/Her before and by the time the prayer is done Trouble has moved on. He is banging on the next door and then the next and I exhale and I can't believe it and I say, 'Thank you,' out loud looking up at the ceiling towards the place I think God might be, then I think, 'Oh shit, that was too loud.'

He hasn't heard me though. He keeps on banging and when he is finished with the left side of the hall he pounds on the doors on the other side of the corridor then he stands in the foyer and yells, 'I will fucking see you again, College Girl. You hear me? I'm gonna get that number.' Then he is gone. I do not sleep for a long, long time. Instead, I lie on the sheetless bed clutching the shawl and smelling Mummy and hoping he does not come back.

In the morning I make a mental note to remember that just because one crazy thing has already happened to you it doesn't mean another won't come your way on the same day. The universe was supposed to know that I had just seen an unwanted penis so it shouldn't have given me a whole separate other person hell-bent on raping me just minutes later.

I sit up in bed and think about how I really need to go to the bank first and then get to Target, but before everything I need to get a phone card so everyone at home will know that I got in okay, which makes me wonder what I will say to Mandla and Zeng when they ask me what America is like in their ironic but still expectant voices. Mandla will say, 'Like dude, is it like totally excellent party time?' and we will keep the *Wayne's World* references going for a little while, but then she'll still be waiting for an answer and I am not sure I can tell her the truth, which is that America is just like Kenya which is just like Canada which is just like Zambia which means there is nowhere in the world any of us can go to be safe because America – the home of the brave and the land of the free – has just proven to me that, when you are a girl, Trouble is always just around the corner and you never know what he is going to look like. I am not sure how to explain to my sisters on a scratchy telephone line that they shouldn't worry about me, they should just keep their guards up and their fists ready.

Black girl in America

AMERICA GIVES ME anonymity and, also, it gives me love. In that order. The two are intertwined forever in my heart and both belong in that place inside me that belongs to America.

Anonymity comes first and then – in the terrain of the unknown, in this landscape where I am nobody special, in the crevices and dark shadows of places where I have no birthright – I find love.

Until now, I have always been at the centre of the universe. I was born into an Africa that was waiting for me and into a movement that needed children as emblems of the future. We were totems, all of us – grand experiments who were testament not just to our parents' love, but to the ability of the struggle to regenerate, to sustain itself. It wasn't just us, the ANC kids. All across the continent, we were Africa's promise, middle-class children who were birthed with the sole purpose of walking away from the past with determination and absolute confidence. The post-colonial children of the elite – those whose parents' hearts were filled with dreams – we carried the vision of a decolonised future in our smiles.

In America I am given a new meaning. I am not the centre of any universe. I am just a black girl.

In America I learn quickly that to be black is to be both unknown and unknowable. As an outsider I see almost immediately that this society deliberately misrecognises black people and the effect of this is to diminish them individually and as a group.

At first I marvel at the stories of mistaken identity. My friends were the best and brightest in their schools. That's why they got plucked – pulled up into a private four-year college. They are shining stars – known and seen by everyone in their communities. The minute they step beyond their shattered drooping blocks into the cities that gleam and glitter grandly, they become invisible.

It's like a superpower they didn't ask for but know how to use to their advantage. Sometimes their luck runs out. They'll be there, doing very little – just walking, just shooting the breeze – and suddenly they attract attention, like glow-in-the-dark figures.

They learn to creep, to walk close to walls, to put their hoodies up and keep their heads slouched; to shrink so they aren't noticed. Attention aimed at ghetto children is rarely positive.

In my first year I am assigned a room with a girl named Katie. She is half-white, half-Sri Lankan. Everyone hangs out in our room a lot. We party in Darius's room and he raps. Rob and the football guys dominate the TV at Cultural House – the space designated as safe for Hispanic and black students. We watch Martin Lawrence and crack up. After he goes on *Arsenio*, everyone agrees Bill Clinton will be the first black president.

Someone says, 'They thought my cousin was a guy on *America's Most Wanted* so they shot at him.'

Someone else says, 'The clerk said I looked like a lady who had been in the store last week and stolen a watch so she kicked me out.' And another one: 'That landlady said she forgot what I looked like. I just met you last week and you supposed to be tryin' to rent me an apartment! How are you gonna forget what a client looks like? My money's the same colour as everyone else's money.'

I learn very quickly that to be black in America is to be looked through, passed over, ignored or locked away. It is to be constantly misrecognised.

Everyone has a story about the police frisking them. Everyone has a strategy. No one questions it. This is not a matter for political intervention. When I volunteer at the Minneapolis Urban League the project I work on focuses on training teenagers to know their rights and respond politely and respectfully when the cops stop them. Every lesson begins and ends with, 'Put your hands up and don't run or you will get shot.'

None of these experiences would be new to my compatriots who grew up in South Africa. They are not entirely new to me either. The years in Canada took their toll. Still, I have not grown up in the belly of the beast. When your individuality is denied, when you are constantly thought to be someone other than who you are, you either die or you blossom. America shows me how this feels. I am grateful that it's already too late for my soul to be killed by my encounter with American racism. I am even more grateful that, by the time I go back to South Africa, its worst edges will have been blunted.

So, because I am already almost grown up, and have been raised to believe I am the centre of the universe, America does not threaten who I am. I meet it with a sort of gratitude. It makes me a soldier in a way I may not otherwise have been. And it creates for me the sort of kinship with African-Americans that is only possible when you have struggled alongside another human being.

◆ ◆ ◆

Before I went to America I was as politically aware as a high school student can be. I was enrolled at the International School of Kenya and I was on the student council and I wrote for the school paper. My favourite classes were Social Studies and English and French because we read real books and grappled with ideas and our French teacher was a renegade and he plucked his eyebrows and we didn't know yet what gay was but he wore kikoi pants and was anti-authoritarian. And the carefully crafted multinational bubble made us feel as though we were special and loved and also part of the politics of the country, even though we weren't.

In the last semester of our studies, my friends and I decided one day to skip school. CNN was reporting that Kenya's one-party state would soon end and the students would be the ones who would bring Moi to his knees after decades of corruption and violent clampdowns on those who dared to dissent. And so we went downtown to watch. We wanted to see the students throwing stones at the police. We felt we were expressing solidarity doing this, and we even believed that we were part of history knowing we had been there. We were scared though and we just hung around the edges of the crowd, worried. We were never in any danger and, had anything happened, we would have been too precious to hurt. The embassies with which we were all registered would have intervened or someone would have called someone who knew someone and everything would have been fixed. But it never even came close to that because we watched from far away – outsiders, voyeurs, kids watching the world unfold before our eyes.

So, it is only in America, in the fall of 1992, that I begin to understand the difference between being politically aware and being politically active. I have grown up politically aware but, because Mummy and Baba allowed us to be children, I have – until now – done nothing in my own name. It is time for me to get active. I do not decide on this randomly. Living in America makes me think about myself in new ways. More importantly, it provides outlets, gives me ways to try on these new constructions of myself.

It begins of course with being made to feel small. In the first few weeks after my arrival, I am followed wordlessly in shops in the Mall of America. One night, as I'm coming home on a bus from the University of Minnesota where there had been an event hosted by the black studies department, an old man sidles up to me as he gets off and says softly in my ear – almost lyrically – 'Nigger bitch.' His breath is hot and stale.

This feeling is novel, maybe because I have spent eighteen years mainly protected from the psychological harm that comes of being looked through or past or over. Canada punctured but did not manage to deflate my self-esteem and Nairobi put the air back in my tyres, puffed me up again. So now, each time someone dismisses me, every story I hear in which, purely because of the levels of melanin in their skin, one of my friends was abused, I grow stronger. The abuse becomes a source of pride rather than shame. I am no longer that wide-eyed ten-year-old girl in Canada and I am beginning to understand, for myself, the power of having an analysis – a lens through which to interpret the world. It signals the difference between drowning and swimming to safety.

America makes me brave because it forces me to fight for myself. It makes me brave because it makes me seek out love on my own terms, not on the basis of what is expected of me.

Over time, I make friends. There is LaKeesha who comes from Gary, Indiana, Michael Jackson's home town. She is short and petite and wiry and so intense our friendship is like a love affair. We talk through long nights, we cry, we become fused to each other: an inseparable and incongruous-looking pair. I am tall with a big butt and a teeny chest, and she is short and petite, but with boobs enough for both of us. We laugh about sharing our assets. Physical differences aside, we occupy space in the same way – we fill every room with our preoccupations. When I am reading *Sula* (for the umpteenth time) everyone knows it. When we discover *for colored girls who have considered suicide / when the rainbow is enuf*, there isn't a table we sit down at that isn't informed about it. We read out loud. We read together. Our sisterhood is intense and instant – kinetic. Then, there is Sharon – a year ahead of me. Sharon is from Natchez, Mississippi, but went to high school in Minneapolis. Her mother came up north, following the river, looking for freedom for her kids, like so many other black people before her. Sharon is the hope of her family – hard-working, diligent, strait-laced. Yet all Sharon wants to do is act. When she is on a stage, nothing else matters. But good college-educated black women with strong family ties don't become actors: they become accountants or lawyers or doctors. Sharon struggles with the decision, wedded both to the joy performing brings and to her commitment to being a good daughter.

And there is Simone. A Caribbean version of Twiggy, Simone is from St Vincent originally. She too has been raised by a single mother and, like the rest of us, she cannot afford to mess up. Simone isn't prone to smiling. Hers is not a heart that is won over easily, but she is protective and loyal and as good a friend as you can ask for in a hostile environment where you need someone who has your back. There is Katie, my roommate that year; her father is Sri Lankan, her mother white American. There is Marika whose pale skin and freckles belie her African and Native American heritage. The group of us become angry and eloquent spokespersons for diversity. We are intense. We spend our time together becoming new women. We read a lot. We talk a lot. We shed layers – getting rid of the parts of us we didn't like before we came to university – and in the process we grow thick skins.

We form a poetry troupe. At first we call ourselves Sistahs of the Rainbow. A year later we have shed the solidarity and become Sistahs 'n' Struggle. Only the black members of the troupe remain. We scowl often. We stage performances. Sharon and LaKeesha can really act and have talent. The rest of us are passionate but should probably not be on stage. It doesn't matter to us, though; our politics is more important than our art. Our politics is our art. The venues where we perform are always packed. We rehearse earnestly, reciting everything from Margaret Walker to Sonia Sanchez to Ntozake Shange to Nikki Giovanni. White students both love and fear us. We care a lot what they think even as we profess not to. We say we are only speaking to black students and we believe it.

Soon everywhere we go on campus we are recognised and applauded and this makes us even angrier because all the accolades don't change the attrition rate for black students on campus. It doesn't increase enrolment figures either. So, we begin to understand that good intentions are as much our enemy as the nameless suits who we are convinced are orchestrating racism from their lofty heights atop the corporate ladder or the university administration.

We get angrier. We decide acting is not enough. We decide to take on institutional discrimination. We scrawl graffiti on campus in chalk. We put up signs saying white students should 'Be afraid.' This avoids the formal structures – it is the easy way into a system we can tell is designed to trick us. Joining committees and participating in processes seems like a trick. We know our history. We stage a sitin at the president's office, demanding that the university review its policies in relation to hiring black professors, admitting greater numbers of students of colour and addressing the high dropout rate.

We win some concessions and we celebrate. A black professor is given tenure. A new political science hire is made and he is African. We have not yet learnt – because we are so very young – that institutional racism is a wily old beast, and that these are just superficial wins.

We lose a lot too. The casualties of racism on campus stack up. We cry a lot. The numbers of black students who arrived at the same time as we did shrink. One friend – Andre – turns into a shell of himself. He drifts. He acts in odd ways. He was hilarious. We all loved him. Then one day he is incoherent and rambly. Then he is gone: dropped out. Our numbers are too small. Each departure, under circumstances that are unhappy and unplanned, shakes us and confirms what we already know – that certain kinds of black people are not meant to survive systems designed to ensure the progress of certain kinds of whites.

I lose my patience. I find it hard to be friends with the other African students on campus. They titter and cluck about black Americans. They use the usual tropes – they are lazy, they are damaged. They are full of excuses about how different Africans are from African Americans. I get tired of hearing the same old lines, about how whatever happened during slavery severed the connection between blacks in America and those in Africa. At first I simply nod, or sometimes I act like I am not really listening. Like them, I knew the rigours of having a nightly homework routine and not being allowed to play or talk on the phone or watch TV night upon night until physics was mastered or essays were completed so I know what they mean. But, a few months in, their disdain makes me nervous. Intellectually I can see there is little difference between the two campus communities – the small striving African one and the striving black American one – but there is a rift. It isn't ugly or openly antagonistic, but it is there.

As winter begins that first year of college, Spike Lee releases *Malcolm X*. LaKeesha and I see the movie on opening night. Our bellies are filled with fire. We read *The Autobiography of Malcolm X* over and over again. Brother Malcolm comes alive in our dreams. We scream in excitement, reading out passages. 'Listen, listen, listen!' I will squeal, looking up at her. 'This is too good. "I believe in the brotherhood of all men, but I don't believe in wasting brotherhood on anyone who doesn't want to practice it with me." This is what I've been saying.' There is nothing like reading the ideas of someone whose experiences mirror your own, whose intellect speaks to you like a guide. Malcolm X pushes us to say, out loud, what we had feared most in our hearts.

Over the course of that first semester, I decide that neither the Africans nor the 'good whites' are worth spending time with. The Africans are just trying to get their degrees and find jobs so they can hold up the hopes and dreams of their villages or their parents. They are busy with their toothy grins beaming for white Americans who want to talk about their summers spent volunteering in Bujumbura. I am full of the arrogance of youth so I don't want to admit that, for these young minds, being in America is a crucial step towards being a first. I don't want to accept they have every right simply to get through – to survive, to make friends, to use the opportunity of America how they see fit.

I am full of judgement and righteousness. I throw myself into more Malcolm X. I go back to Steve Biko, whom I read in high school and did not really understand until I was in America. I read Stokely Carmichael. I read about the Black Panthers.

The poetry we perform is mainly by women, but the politics – the words that animate our conversations, and that push us to act in the real world – these belong to men. It takes a while before I understand the effect this has on my own political sensibilities.

I move away from the African students. I look at them from a distance and sometimes I try to mask my disdain for their lack of politics, but mostly I don't. I am heading in another direction.

Had I been born into a Black Consciousness family my exposure to American racism at university may not have been so transformative. I was not born into such a family. Instead, in our house, nonracialism has always been the quiet centrepiece of our politics.

Mummy and Baba are proud and dignified and can stand up for themselves when necessary. They understand and appreciate Biko, but they are grounded in a different sensibility. They are part of a Charterist movement, one deeply connected to the idea that Africans are also civilised and intellectual and as worthy of respect as whites. Theirs is not a politics designed to question the very basis of white people's civilisation. They don't wish to tear down the idea of liberalism and traditions of secular democracy and this seems sad to me.

For the first time, I see my parents not as revolutionary heroes, but as slightly naive. They have been duped by whiteness. Like Christopher Columbus, my friends and I believe that, with the help of the guiding spirits of Steve Biko and Malcolm X, we have discovered blackness.

It is years before I understand Bell Hooks' ideas about radical love and discover Audre Lorde. The words of these particular black men – the way they express anger – is so seductive. I ignore the ways in which their blackness seems to have little space for my woman-ness. It takes time for me to discover it is possible to embrace radicalism that looks and feels different from the radical ideas of men. And so it takes me longer than I would have liked to see that there are ways of being tough and angry and confrontational without being judgemental about the choices of others. It takes me even longer to realise that those with more moderate politics than mine were making choices that weren't necessarily based on being compromised or constrained. Mummy and Baba weren't ignorant of Biko. They had considered his point of view and differed – not on the basis of weakness, but on the legitimate basis of intellectual and strategic disagreement. I couldn't see that then, though it is plain now.

The fire before freedom

IN 1993, MUMMY and Baba move back to South Africa. They are based in Natal, in the economic hub of Durban. Like many of the other exiles, they head to the cities closest to where they left, where family is. Within a few short years, they will move again – following the money and the elite opportunities available in Pretoria and Johannesburg. In 1993, though, everyone is scattered across Port Elizabeth and Umtata and Durban and Cape Town.

In the early 1990s, there are murders every week in Natal. The IFP and the ANC are involved in a proxy war. It is evident that, although the last white leader of South Africa, Frederik Willem De Klerk, professes to be on a path to peace and a negotiated settlement, there is a dirty-tricks campaign designed to derail the process. It seems the news is never good. Mandela is beginning to look old and his comrade and lifelong friend, Walter Sisulu, is too. Still, there are others who can lead us. Among them is Chris Hani.

He is fiery and radical and all the things that the white people fear. He is immensely popular.

Mummy and Hani's wife Limpho studied together at school in Lusaka, and Baba knows Hani from his MK days, and so whenever I read his name I automatically put 'Uncle' in front of it. Baba and Uncle Chris were to-gether in the camps. Where Baba and Mummy chose us over the revolution, the Hanis chose the struggle. They paid a very heavy price for their commitment. Like us, they moved from country to country. But unlike us, their father was a specific target – one of the highest-priority targets of the apartheid regime. They under-stood mortal danger in a way my sisters and I had never had to imagine.

Uncle Chris has this incredible capacity to both stir the pot and calm emotions. He is deeply suspicious of white South Africans, yet he is totally committed to the notion of non-racialism. He is the first person I come across who can articulate this so precisely without look-ing hypocritical. Chris Hani has survived assassination attempt after assassination attempt. He has every reason to mistrust the white minority regime. Yet he has also waged long and hard battles within and outside the ANC – to make the party fairer, to make justice part of the core values of the communist party of which he is the leader. His Marxist analysis makes it impossible for him to privilege race over class. So he doesn't – he refuses to make a false choice, but he does not use this as a crutch.

He does not hide behind nice words about whites simply because some of his comrades in the ANC and SACP are white.

Uncle Chris is a key voice in calling for cautious optimism. He is not convinced that the whites are ready to relinquish power but he is convinced the path of negotiations is important for the moment.

By the winter of 1993, there is talk about who will succeed Mandela. But we do not have freedom yet. I wonder, all the way from Minnesota, whether we celebrated too soon – whether Mummy and Baba should have gone back. Perhaps we got caught up in the frenzy, in the excitement of picket signs and pop songs and tightlipped UN officials and Scandinavian prime ministers and the referendum. We should have known that white people would never give up power so easily.

◆ ◆ ◆

In spite of my worries about what is happening at home, I settle in on campus. Winter break comes and I go to DC to see Gogo Lindi. Lindi – my big-sister idol from childhood – is there and Mandi comes too and for Christmas we are joined by a host of others – South African students from up and down the East Coast, as well as a few strays from the rest of the region.

Gogo is thrilled to have us all around to take care of her and to dote on her two small grandchildren. I am doing well at school and adjusting to life in America, but I miss the variability of life at home. I miss interacting with children and old people. Everyone on campus is the same age and, maybe because I never went to boarding school, the environment feels manufactured sometimes.

We talk a lot about South Africa and what is going to

happen next. The negotiations between the white minority regime and the ANC have fallen apart. A new process is slated to start in the coming months. The atmosphere is tense at home. In Washington I regale everyone with stories of what we are going to do with whites when we take over. 'Teach them how to wash their own dishes!' 'Hand over all their diamond rings and use the proceeds to educate black children!' Gogo delights in my playful radicalism.

In February, as the semester begins, I am excited to be back on campus. LaKeesha and I hug and catch up and I fill her in on the time in DC and she – as usual – is full of tight anger, worried about her brother and her mother and her sister. A looming sense of disaster always hangs over our conversations about her family, something brooding and explosive about the community where she was raised. I, on the other hand, am upbeat after the trip. In spite of my scepticism, and everything my black analysis tells me about the bleakness of prospects for genuine change where white people are concerned, I can't help believing that South Africa will soon be free.

❖ ❖ ❖

Then, the unspeakable happens. On the morning of 10 April 1993, Uncle Chris is gunned down in his driveway. He lies in the driveway, dying. His thirteen-year-old daughter Khwezi runs out. It is too late. Chris Hani, the people's hero, is dead.

It is hard to express how painful this is. I want to go home, but it is expensive. Mummy asks what good it will do to fly into the storm. I don't argue. My whole life has been spent in the calm, avoiding the storms in South Africa. Circumstance seems always to conspire to keep me away, safe and far and disconnected.

In the days that follow nine people are killed. None of them are white because black people in South Africa have internalised selfhate to the point where we can only contemplate hurting ourselves. Still, there is something about black anger – even when it is selfdirected – that frightens whites.

Mandela knows that the youth, the ones who adored this great man who had the heart of a lion, may very well say they have no faith in whites, or in the peace process, that they only have faith in fire and violence and an immediate end to apartheid without the niceties of negotiation.

So, he gives a speech, an important and powerful statement full of rage and moral authority. He goes on television and cements his place as a peacemaker. He says:

> Chris Hani is irreplaceable in the heart of our nation and people. When he first returned to South Africa after three decades in exile, he said: 'I have lived with death most of my life. I want to live in a free South Africa even if I have to lay down my life for it.' The body of Chris Hani will lie in state at the fnb Stadium, Soweto, from 12 noon on Sunday 18 April until the start of the vigil at 6pm. The funeral service will commence at 9am on Monday, 19 April. The cortege will leave for Boksburg Cemetery, where the burial is scheduled for 1pm. The funeral service and rallies must be conducted with dignity.

With this, Mandela becomes the de facto president of South Africa. He takes the hard road and we follow him. Whites – who once feared him – can't help respecting him. Blacks – who have always admired him – recognise the depth of his leadership. It seems the old man was worth waiting for.

Two men – a black man named Cyril Ramaphosa and a white one named Roelf Meyer – step out into the middle of the battlefield. They touch hands, reaching across a distance that once seemed too great to bridge. They are vulnerable – all eyes are on them – but it is clear in the wake of the assassination that something has to give.

They clasp hands and don't let go. An election date is set. Uncle Chris's death turns into a watershed moment. The ANC averts a war and Meyer and Ramaphosa and those chosen to negotiate a compromise begin again – this time in earnest.

The country lurches forward. The provisional Constitution – guaranteeing one person one vote – is soon agreed. The violence abates then spikes then abates again. We breathe. Again, we begin to think that those slogans about freedom in our lifetime were true. Freedom is on its way but there is no changing the facts of history.

Chris Hani is dead, killed by hateful white men. The days of the dead are not yet behind us.

◆ ◆ ◆

After Uncle Chris's death, my anger boils over. At school things are falling apart. Keesh has decided to transfer – to leave Macalester. She needs to be on a bigger campus, at a school where she doesn't feel so under siege. Having grown up in Gary, in a black city, she has felt the absence of black people keenly in the last few years of living in Minnesota. I feel it too but it is different. I didn't grow up in America, under the shadow of neglect masquerading as autonomy. I understand her decision, but it is devastating. Navigating my anger alone is one thing; surviving on a campus where we have alienated so many people because our sisterhood has sustained us both is another thing altogether.

In May, at the end of the semester, we say goodbye. I sense that everything will be different. The momentum of our shared anger, our reading and writing sessions, the poetry performances – all these were spurred on by Keesh and by who she inspires me to be. Without her, I am not sure what I will do.

◆ ◆ ◆

I head home for the summer holidays. I am looking forward to seeing everyone – especially Mandla and Zeng. But I am also anxious about how I will manage my emotions. America has emboldened me and quickened my temper. I have no time for racists – indeed, my identity now hinges on this impatience. Before everything else, I am black and I have little energy for those who don't understand or respect that. Over the course of the past semester I have done a lot of soul searching. I love my parents but I am convinced they simply don't understand race and racism. They continue to be naive, to have hope in people and systems that have never been concerned about the well-being of black people. I anticipate the trip will be frustrating in many ways.

Mandla has started her studies at Cornell University in New York state and we talk on the phone every week. Mummy and Baba and Zeng are living in La Lucia. Their neighbours are all white. Their house has a tiny sliver of a view to the ocean. Mummy is working and so is Baba and Zeng is enrolled in a prestigious girls' school in the city, where her uniform includes a bonnet. The bonnet – indeed, the entire uniform – is ridiculous and colonial and emblematic of the enduring character of the strange new society into which we have just been transplanted.

I am unbearable.

I brandish my new radical politics like a sword. I am impatient with Mummy and Baba, and I have absolutely no time for whites.

Mummy takes deep breaths and tries to ignore me. My sisters treat me with a combination of awe and amusement. I am both hilarious and utterly mad.

In the aftermath of Uncle Chris's death a timetable has been put in place for the transition to be finalised. Elections have been scheduled. So, here we are, together for the first time in a while, in South Africa, on the eve of liberation.

Mummy and Baba want us to understand the history and geography of our new country and to understand the clashes between the British, the Boers and the Zulus in particular. They want us to be familiar with the Battle of Isandlwana and the Battle of Blood River and to have an image in our minds of how they played out on the landscape itself. For us to face the future, they want us to know our history.

So Mummy plans a family holiday in the Drakensberg. We load into the car. The three of us are in the back seat, crammed in. I am in a mood. I get why they want us to do this, but I am not so convinced of the modus operandi.

I ask Mummy what we will do if the white owners of the guesthouses she has booked don't let us sleep on their sheets and in their beds. Mummy is irritated.

She takes the bait. 'Stop it Sonke. This attitude is too much now. This racism thing is an obsession. We didn't send you to America to develop an attitude problem.'

I am in no mood to be lectured about racism.

'It's not an attitude Mummy, it's just the facts. We can't wish racism away, and we can't pretend these people are just going to change overnight, so I'm just saying if we are going to be sleeping in their houses we should be aware they might not want us there.'

Mummy has created a file with brochures and details about the trip. At the top, there is a flyer for the first place we will stay, a farmhouse called Penny Farthing. I flick through it, looking for more ammunition. 'So we're staying at Penny Farthing. What does "penny farthing" mean anyway?' I ask. Scorn drips from my mouth. 'It sounds extremely colonial.'

Baba explains that a farthing is a British coin from a long time ago. 'Classic,' I retort. 'This is going to be interesting.'

I read the brochure aloud, informing the family in my best David Attenborough voice that the farm is 'three thousand hectares, strategically placed near the KwaZulu-Natal battlefields – near Rorke's Drift, Isandlwana and Blood River.' Hmmn. 'The owners have been on the property since 1847,' I add with a flourish.

I am disgusted. 'White people steal our land and decimate our people and we go and sleep in their houses?'

'Decimate' is a word I use often.

Baba is slightly amused by my disgust. 'The Zulu were never decimated,' he says. 'They routed us, but "decimated" would imply we were virtually extinguished. That was certainly the experience of the San but it wasn't the case with the Zulu nation. If you are going to be angry, that is one thing, but do so on the basis of facts,' he says.

Mandla and Zeng are tense, sensing a serious confrontation looming.

This is a mere technicality but I bite my tongue. I judge Baba silently, but I am still African child enough to hold my fire when it comes to my father.

We pull up to the house after the long drive from Durban and the old woman who comes out to greet us seems both pleased to see us and slightly bewildered. She is faced with an African family of five. Three tall teenage girls, a short mother and an imposing father.

Immediately, Mummy charms the old lady with some little chatter about the drive. Baba impresses her with his knowledge of the region. The three of us are gangly and quiet – but we greet her politely and in impeccable English so she seems pleased. She walks us into the house and shows us around wearing an air of indulgent befuddlement.

We settle into our rooms and rest a bit before dinner. Over dinner I am surly and I excuse myself early. I tell Mummy and Baba I am not feeling well but the truth is my rage will not allow me to sit at the table with the other guests and pretend this house isn't haunted by the ghosts of colonialists.

In the morning I am ravenous so there is no avoiding breakfast. We sit at the table and the smell of *mdogo* wafts through the house. My favourite – sour porridge. I dig in. 'You are enjoying your porridge, young lady?' says our host. 'I am,' I say.

'It's wonderful, isn't it? My Zulu made it.'

I am stunned. Mummy and Baba are stunned. Mandla and Zeng are stunned. I put my spoon down.

'Who made it?' I ask, giving her a chance to self-correct. 'My Zulu made it,' she says oblivious to her racism.

'Is she yours?' I begin to ask. 'Like, as in, you own—' Mummy cuts me off. 'Sonke...' she warns.

I look from her face to Baba's. He looks amused – as if

he is prepared to let the chips fall where they may.

I decide to go for it. Mummy's warning lingers in the air, though; it has succeeded in slowing me down.

'I am just wondering,' I continue, 'whether she has a name. The person who makes the porridge. Because she isn't *your* Zulu. She is a person.'

I am angry that I have not been direct enough. If I were at school, in Minnesota with my friends, cloaked in the anonymity of not having Mummy and Baba around, I would simply say, 'This is racist bullshit.'

But I am not in Minnesota. I am in South Africa and my parents are watching me so I go easy on the old lady and berate myself internally for it.

She does not see it the same way.

'Yes, I know she has a name but there is nothing wrong with me calling her my Zulu. That is what we do here and nobody minds.'

'How do you know?' I am seething now.

'No one has ever said a word about it,' she continues blithely. 'Well that's that then,' I say evenly. I look at her with contempt.

She looks slightly scared, though she isn't sure why she is scared.

The table is silent for a long uncomfortable moment. No one chews or swallows. We do not touch our food. Mummy breaks the silence.

'Well, I think it's time for us to start our day,' she says in an upbeat and cheery way. 'We have a lot of walking to do today.'

The old lady's Zulu bustles in the background, collecting plates and washing dishes.

We gather our things from the bedrooms. We load them into the car in silence. We get in the car and Baba drives. We sit in silence.

Finally Baba says, 'We shall have to make sure there is a Zulu to cook us some porridge at the next place we stay, guys.'

We burst into laughter – relieved and angry all at once. 'Wowowowowow,' says Mandla deadpan but with characteristic wryness.

'Wow,' agrees Mummy – also deadpan. 'Wow,' says Zeng. 'Wow,' I add.

'What a wow,' says Baba.

We drive to the battlefield of Rorke's Drift, to hear about how our people fought bravely but were defeated.

Years later, I discover a penny-farthing is an odd-shaped bike – the ones with an enormous front wheel and a tiny rear one. I Google it and Wikipedia throws me a gem: 'An attribute of the penny-farthing is that the rider sits high and nearly over the front axle. When the wheel strikes rocks and ruts, or under hard braking, the rider can be pitched forward off the bicycle head-first. Headers were relatively common and a significant, sometimes fatal, hazard.'

I wish I had known then – I would have had even more biting fodder for Mummy. With the passage of time and everything I now know about what South Africa has become, it seems apt that our attempt to get to know our history better was launched in a farmhouse named after an obsolete British invention.

I imagine the old lady as she was twenty years ago. In my daydream, instead of riding in a bakkie in keeping with her local circumstances, she is sitting atop a high-wheeler bicycle. She is bumping along, propelling herself towards a future in which she no longer understands the landscape. She rides over the fields where Zulu fought Brit and lost. Suddenly she looks down and realises she is riding over the bones of the dead. She loses control. The penny-farthing begins a slow sideways fall. In the process she is hurled off it and into the air. I see her frail frame suspended midflight – a grey blot in a blue Midlands sky. Can you see her? She is up in the air like so many of her time and her generation. If you listen closely, you may just hear her calling out for *her* Zulu.

Freedom

SUDDENLY, FREEDOM IS no longer coming: it has arrived. The date is 27 April. The year is 1994. On this day, black South Africans gain full citizenship rights and white South Africans begin to put the stain of racist shame behind them. The occasion is momentous.

In countless acts across the country, as the day unfolds, white and black South Africans move towards one another like newlyweds about to take a vow.

Until this point, whites have collectively been skittish about the impending day. They are afraid of how their lives will change. For so long they have understood the world in terms that are either black or white. Oversimplification has been a key ingredient in apartheid's success. Now they are thrust into a world of grey – of doubt and anxiety and exhilaration.

Despite their full participation in the steps that have led them here, many whites remain fearful of what this new era might bring. On this bright autumn day, they let go.

The letting go has been months in the making. Jingles have played on the radio and television every day imploring us all to respect one another, to give peace a chance. Brenda Fassie's 'Black President' has been on heavy rotation in shebeens and nightclubs across the country, getting us ready for Nelson Mandela's confirmation as president of the Republic of South Africa. Posters in the green, black and gold of the ANC and the orange, blue and white of the National Party (NP) adorn streets in every city. Political rallies fill stadia, crowds roar their jubilation, singing, 'Viva the ANC, viva! Long live the spirit of the UDF, long live!' We race towards our destiny.

When the day finally comes it is both climactic and oddly underwhelming. On one hand there is joy and noise and celebration. On the other is a barely audible sound; it is apartheid's long slow hiss into obsolescence. Quite suddenly apartheid has lost its spectral force. It is a demon defeated, no longer a Klansman on a horse inspiring fear in the hearts of black people. The night rider who terrorised us for so long is revealed for what he is: a little boy in a billowing sheet with cut-out eyes. Sitting perfectly still underneath the uplifted sheet, he is peculiar and sad. He looks like he is trying to disappear.

This revelation of this unveiling is greeted by a surprised moment of silence. But it is only a short pause. Within seconds South Africa is hurtling towards democracy.

In the streets and across great swathes of rural country, the euphoric young rub shoulders with those who are simply grateful that they have lived to see this day. Old women achingly bend and tremblingly mark; they silently cross and dutifully fold.

Even before papers are counted, victory is assured. The authority of those who have for so long been the wretched of this land is unmistakable. 'Lililililili!' Ululation fills town halls and ripples through trees and across valleys, lifting in the wind.

Hands wave, bedecked in white gloves; we are *isicathamiya* and *maskandi* music. We are Hugh Masekela's husky voice, we are the breath in his trumpet, a long purple note of freedom. We are slave quarters rising like hips to greet a lover long lost and now found; we are an embrace where two oceans meet.

On this day, even the weather complies with our wishes. There are no rains, only blue skies and a stillness in the reeds. God has decreed that today nature will not interfere with the triumph of humanity.

And so, with our landscape serving as a steady backdrop, we move and we groove, we sway and we sashay, starting in the fairest Cape and ascending north towards the mighty Limpopo. Watch! See how we shimmy, how we weave our bodies in a timeless *domba*. We are the sacred Venda python sloughing off our old skins as we enter history's gates. We are majestic; glistening into the future, we wind and we wend and we dance ourselves to exhaustion. As the moon rises we know that soon, when the votes are counted and the results are announced, we will finally be free.

◆ ◆ ◆

As South Africans rise to begin their day – to cast their ballots – I am in Minnesota, driving towards Chicago in a rented minivan. In the car with me are two Mandlas, a Kgomotso, a Lunga, a Sbusiso and a Rogene, all of us students at various universities in the Midwestern state of Minnesota. We are on our way to the South African consulate, determined not to miss out on history.

We arrive at the consulate and we are ushered into a small waiting room and then into the area where we will vote. We left very early in the morning; I stand in the sterile booth under dead fluorescent light. Until now, I would have had no cause to be in this building; the consul would have turned me away. In one fell swoop this has changed. The irony of this hits me hard as I look at my identity document.

I am twenty years old, about the same age that Baba was all those years ago when he left South Africa. I mark my ballot with a vote for Nelson Mandela and the African National Congress.

Afterwards, I look for a phone. I have topped up my AT&T calling card in anticipation of the lengthy call. The phone rings in Durban, thousands of kilometres away, and Zeng picks up. I ask excitedly, 'How was it?' At fifteen she is too young to vote, but she has no trouble answering my question. 'Amazing, Sonke. I wish you were here.' She is in high spirits, and her voice has the quality of bubble gum; it carries across the static in the line like pink and blue glitter thrown into a breeze. She describes everything: the exuberance of the crowds, the fear that it might all go wrong; the hilarity of two old white women insisting on jumping the queue even as democratic elections were taking place that sought to put an end to that sort of behaviour.

She laughs and, with her special brand of social

commentary, she does a faux newsreader's voice, saying, 'Here, reporting live from the frontlines we have Mrs Smith. So, Mrs Smith, you want to skip the line because you're white? What are you voting for then, Gogo? I think... yes, Mrs Smith, I can confirm that you get to stand at the back of the queue like everyone else, the old days are over!' We laugh uproariously, grinning at what a long road it will be for some white folk, our missing each other tangible through our laughter.

The phone is passed around. I speak to everyone – cousins and aunties and uncles. The house is full of relatives and friends who have come to share the day with us. Ours is the home where everyone has begun to congregate in the year since the family has 'returned' to Durban.

Finally Baba is on the line. I clutch the telephone receiver as though by force of will it might transport me to Durban. 'So, you are in Chicago?' he asks. 'Yes, Baba,' I respond, trying to pretend that I am not overwhelmed by the sound of his distant voice. 'Well that's good,' he says, 'I am glad you made it.' We are quiet for a while, suddenly unsure what to say. Then he says what I have been waiting for him to say. 'Here we are, Sonke-girls.' He uses his affectionate name for me.

He laughs and then says awkwardly, almost in a whisper, as though he can't believe it himself, 'We did it. We are free.'

That X marked in a voting booth in Chicago marks my spot in history. It marks my place in a new nation at the start of a new era.

Jason

WITH LAKEESHA GONE there is more space in my life for my other relationships. My friend Genevieve moves in with Simone and me. We live off campus in a dingy dive of a place. There are two bedrooms and the landlord tells us a third bedroom can be fashioned out of an 'alcove'. We wedge a bed in there and this becomes Gen's room. Except it is too small and she ends up never using it. She moves into my room where we keep the heat on at full blast and barely ever make it to class on cold days. We are like sisters too – but without the politics. Gen is easy. We talk about boys and I go home with her to Boston over school holidays and there is never a need to preach or read anything aloud. Simone has her own room and she is mending a broken heart so she stays out of our way and we leave her alone. When she breaks from one of her moods and wants to smile we are there with food in the kitchen, or under blankets in front of the TV.

Winter wears us all down. The monotony of school is compounded by the weather. Stiff fingers on the steering wheel in the car. Numb toes at the bus stop. Teary eyes in the wind whipped up between buildings on the way to class.

In the midst of this greyness, Jason appears. We meet at Stairstep, where Simone works. Simone graduated in May and is now working full time, while I still have a year to go. Every morning I drive her to work and most afternoons I pick her up. It's a long drive – a good thirty minutes on the highway from St Paul to North Minneapolis. But we bought the car together. We put in $300 each. She was in good condition when we bought her from a friend who was heading off to Nicaragua to join the Peace Corps. She's a VW Fox so naturally we call her Foxy. Even though Simone is the co-owner, she doesn't have a driver's licence. She keeps failing the test. So I drop her off at work and, on especially cold and miserable days, I pick her up because the wait for the bus is like death.

Stairstep is a church-based initiative in North Minneapolis. It is run by an African-American couple called the Johnsons. They are a fine husband-and-wife team – both tall and willowy and put together in a no-nonsense sort of way. Whenever she is around I feel as though I have to sit up and smooth my dreadlocks. She is that type of woman: always freshly lipsticked yet without ever seeming to be concerned about the freshness of her lipstick. He is about a decade older than her. He doesn't make me as viscerally nervous because he has an easy laugh, but he brooks no nonsense so I am never fully comfortable around him. Their toughness seems to have been forced on them by circumstance. It's not inauthentic, though, just a reflection of the guarded approach they have had to adopt to make it in life.

As it has been for many professional black people of their generation, their middle-class status has been hard won. They are steeped in the respectability of people of faith. They carry the burden of people who have always had to do better and more than their white counterparts, so they have learnt to be conscious of rules and demeanour. Yet they also possess a certain radical agency. They remind me of the 'firsts' who surrounded us in Lusaka. Like ours had been, theirs is a community fired in the hearth of ambition. They, too, are focused on the survival of their people. They have an air of prideful woundedness yet they are generous, in spite of their guardedness.

Stairstep is located in a converted house. It is done up tastefully and is never full of people or noisy or any thing like what you would expect a black community institution to be like. Neither of the Johnsons would have liked that. The office is for arranging events and planning community activities, but it is not for lounging around and making noise.

If I get to the office early, I sit on the couch reading or studying. Mrs Johnson doesn't mind this because it's an activity she feels belongs in the category of constructive behaviour. Still, I have a strange sense that if I put one foot wrong she will have no problem asking me not to return.

One afternoon, I arrive as usual to pick Simone up and there is a guy sprawled out on the couch, where I normally camp with my books. He looks just a bit older than me but strangely he does not seem worried in any way about Mrs Johnson. I am immediately nervous. I want him to sit up, to exercise some decorum in this quiet, respectable room. He is long and lean and has an angular shaven head and a thick broody brow and it is impossible not to notice he is exceptionally handsome. He is the colour of a cougar. I say hi, quietly – because I always speak quietly when I am at Stairstep, as everyone else does, and also because he is very handsome and I do not want him to think I am being friendly just because he is handsome. His eyes flicker with recognition, as though he knows me. His smile is a drawl; it unfurls itself in a slow curl. He is unabashedly interested.

'He-eey...' he says slowly. 'Who are you?'

There is something charming about the fact that he is asking who I am and not what my name is. I fumble around in my head, trying to think of a witty retort. I can't think of anything so instead I flick my head in Simone's direction and say, 'I'm her roommate.'

He nods and says, completely deadpan, 'Oh, you live with Miss Stuck Up here?'

I want to laugh because it's a perfect description of Simone. She is snooty. She carries her disdain for the world on her face. Anyone who spends any time with her knows, though, that under her furrowed and disapproving brow she is protecting her heart from disappointment.

I don't laugh because Simone's wrath is real. She rolls her eyes and huffs, ignoring him. I can see the enmity already, and wonder what happened before I arrived. I wonder how long he has been sprawled on the couch and whether Mrs Johnson is going to walk in any minute and dress him down – telling him to sit up and put his bags away.

I am at the height of my Erykah Badu phase so I've got a large piece of fabric wrapped around my dreadlocks. I am also petrified of the cold and so, as usual, I'm wrapped in a sweater from The Limited. I've got leggings on underneath a pair of baggy jeans and, on top of all of this, I'm wearing a mountain of a coat I bought at the Goodwill store.

Simone – who is always well turned out because that is the type of girl she is and because Mrs Johnson expects her team to maintain a certain standard – hates my Goodwill jacket. She thinks it's appalling. I don't care. It was clean and barely worn when I bought it – even if it is ugly. Most importantly, it is utilitarian. It is warm and when it comes to matters of heat and cold I have absolutely no vanity.

So, in spite of my worries about Mrs Johnson, I settle in next to him on the couch and we flirt. I flirt. Jason – who doesn't know how to flirt, really – is just himself. The charming, best version of himself.

Four o'clock comes and Jason asks to come along. He gathers his things and asks, 'What's for dinner?'

Simone and I exchange looks. She feigns irritation but she can't sustain it because he is very handsome and neither of us can fully believe that he's prepared to just hang out, to just chill with us with all his languid beauty.

As we cook dinner Jason teases Simone. He calls her Nose In The Air. Later, Genevieve – who is like a little sister to us – comes home. He sees her and again his eyes widen. She is curvy and pretty and it is hard not to look at her like that. Something shifts. He is no longer interested in only me. Yet he is not interested only in her. He wants both of us. He is not embarrassed. This is how it will be with him. There are never any games, so our relationship proceeds in this way. His honesty impresses

215

me; the truth hurts me. Jason refuses to be conventionally polite. He doesn't pretend to be a regular guy who plays by regular rules.

There is something about the intensity of his affections that makes me feel as though I am in uncharted territory. Falling for him feels both necessary and reckless.

Jason is unemployed, and unemployable. He tells me this on the first night. He says it without bitterness or pity. It is simply a fact. He doesn't want a job where people tell him what to do and how to be. He collects a disability cheque. He is twenty-seven. He is an open book and yet he is the most mysterious man I have ever met. He is on medication because he is bipolar. He tells me this immediately but of course I have no idea what it means. Even if I had known I wouldn't have chosen any differently.

In the years that follow Jason teaches me about loyalty and love and, yes, about madness and living on the edge of what everyone else thinks is safe and straight and proper.

When Jason moves in Genevieve is displaced. She has to go back to her bed. He occupies me. He settles into my life. From the minute we meet he acts as though he has a right to my love; as if he is entitled to my heart. Gen does not like Jason – but her reasons are deeper than simple displacement.

Suddenly though she is back in the alcove. Suddenly she is the third wheel. She goes from being my best friend and confidante to being an outsider – a little sister watching as her big sister becomes someone she no longer recognises. I hear her unasked questions and listen to her silent admonitions. I keep quiet because I don't know how to answer her. She watches me go deeper and deeper into a relationship that makes little sense.

Jason spends his days writing rhymes and drawing because he is a poet and a rapper. The poems are not as good as I want them to be but he is magnetic and so intense in his delivery that I forgive him his lack of talent. He fills up our lives, talking at us and thinking around us and sometimes brooding but mostly just occupying what had until then been our house with his energy and his constant words. He raps loudly in the shower. He sits on the edge of my bed memorising lyrics and reciting them at a manic pitch. I go out to school or work and come back and he is where I left him: in a trance of rhymes and beats.

He flirts with Gen and tells her as often as he can that he wants to sleep with her. He is not joking. He does this in my presence. She rolls her eyes and I smile because I know it is true but I also know she would not do that to me. He would, but he is unconventional and that is his thing. I am trapped in the logic of his world. This is how it begins.

When I am alone I repeat what he says to me: that I should be happy that he is not lying about his desires, that he is telling the truth unlike other guys. I pretend I am pleased but deep inside in those alone moments (which are rare because he is always there) I wonder why he doesn't simply crave me and only me. My desire for him is singular. Why does his heart have to wander; why can't I be enough?

After a while I tire of Jason always being at home cooped up with the heat turned high. I want him to go out – to be busy, to record his songs.

So when he says one morning, as I am getting ready to leave, that he wants to use the library, I am thrilled. I give him my campus card. I regret it. He looks for me on campus. Then he is on campus every day. On campus, he pages me. He wants to know when my classes will finish. I find myself wanting a bit of peace – a few minutes without him wanting to be with me. I don't realise it at first but this is the beginning of the end of my freedom.

Gen and Simone and Sharon start worrying. 'Everything is moving too fast,' they say, like a chorus in an ancient Greek play. I get angry. You just don't understand, I respond, like some cursed maiden – Persephone abducted by Hades. I am lovesick. The abduction is not against my will. I am not sure if there is a word for this. Some days I resent him but there isn't a single day when I don't want everything he has to give me. His attention, and the long hard talks where he tells me how unevolved I am spiritually, how much I need to grow. 'Why do you need people so much?' he asks. 'Why do you care what people think?' I have never been an especially needy person, never one to be swayed by the crowd. This doesn't matter, though. Compared to Jason, I am vulnerable and tied to convention – to meeting the expectations of my parents and my friends.

So Jason and I spend almost every night crying in each other's arms. I am always the first to cry – big silent tears so Gen and Simone won't hear me. I cry in frustration and hurt. Why does he have to be so critical of me? Why is nothing I do ever enough? And he gets angry. 'You don't have to protect yourself. Don't defend how you are – just change,' he says. 'You're holding onto ego, to how you want to think of yourself, not what is true about yourself. Let the truth in,' he says. And this sets me off even more. I can never win.

It is a cycle. Every night, after berating me, he consoles me. He is never remorseful about what he says. He never retracts. He is moved – by himself mainly but also by my tears – but he is not repentant. And so he cries too, and he holds me and says, 'I love you Booboo. I just want you to get stronger. The world is full of enemies who won't tell you what I'm telling you.'

At first I don't see the enemies. I don't understand what he means. In time, I will. I will learn to see the world through his eyes because that is the only way for us to work: on his terms. Every night I am exhausted, worn down by the emotional energy it takes to be examined like this. Still, I get from Jason what Baba couldn't give me because he was gone so often. I get the undivided attention of a man. I get the scrutiny Baba only applied to homework, but never – once we were adolescents – to our hopes and dreams and to our hearts. He couldn't have given us this, being who he was – a man of a certain time and place who did his best otherwise. But our hearts want what they want. Our hearts sometimes lack logic so they find what they want, regardless of the costs.

Jason gives my heart what it had wanted for so very long: to be examined and engaged. He looks at me and finds me to be flawed. He names every flaw. He wants me to be better or different, to be some version of myself that is impossible for me to become. Still, there is a wondrous, unmistakable truth I cannot escape. Through all the drama, having looked at me and found me wanting, still, he wants me.

❖ ❖ ❖

Mummy and Baba fly to Minnesota for my graduation. It is May and finally Minnesota is warm. I have spent the winter smothered by him, feeling less and less like myself but also oddly safe. I come up for air occasionally but in general we stay in bed. Most days I don't make it to class. My grades are terrible. He raps and draws and I figure out ways to avoid going out too much.

As graduation day looms, I get nervous. I have made arrangements for Mummy and Baba to stay in a hotel close to campus. As usual Mummy has taken care of all the payments. She has been putting money aside for their travels for a few months – planning as she has always taught me to.

I have fallen deeper into the Jason trance. He isn't manipulative with money – he just doesn't really need to think about certain things if I am going to take care of them. So Mummy had taken care of all the deposits – calling the hotel with her credit card details all the way from Durban.

I can hear the growing excitement in our own phone calls as we get closer and closer to the date. Their first-born is about to have a degree from America. I imagine Mummy showing off to her friends – calling Aunt Tutu to say nonchalantly, 'Oh, sorry my dear, I won't be able to phone you next week. Me and Mavuso are just flying to America next week. Yes, Sonke has finished her degree.'

◆ ◆ ◆

We throw our caps in the air and hug. It is over. Simone and Sharon and Genevieve and Mummy and Baba are here. More magically, as a surprise, Uncle Stan has flown in. The sky is blue and the air is moist and America has given me what I came looking for – and more. I have a degree and I have spent four years making friends and learning how to breathe fire and rage and to manage myself and to develop a politics steeped in identity and analysis. I am supposed to be ready for the world.

After the ceremony we drive to dinner. I am proud too – of Mummy and Baba and Uncle Stan. I am amazed they are all here. Jason doesn't join us. He decides to skip my graduation dinner. In fact, he wanted me to stay at home with him; he didn't understand at all why I needed to go out. This sort of thing happens all the time. It made perfect sense to him that I would forgo the dinner, and let my parents down. Who cares that they have travelled around the world to see me and to mark this moment? I am too invested in pleasing people, he says as I walk out the door.

He scrutinises everything I do, forcing me to think about whether I am motivated by desire or convention. It is thrilling and exhausting. No one can understand it but I know I need it. Everyone else sees a bully because Jason is always difficult, always arguing with everyone, always making me choose and I usually choose him.

This time of course I can't choose him. I can't abandon my own graduation dinner and leave Mummy and Baba who have flown all the way from Durban. I can't let them eat with Gen and Simone while I sit in our cramped bedroom and cradle Jason's face and listen to him beatbox and tell him I love him.

When I get home from dinner Jason is still angry. We have another screaming fight. Within the logic of Jason's love, my decision to go out to dinner with Mummy and Baba is a betrayal and he is strangely right. Given what we have become – a cocooned universe unto ourselves – he is right. And this is always the problem. Jason only wants the bubble, is incapable of living by the rules and expectations of the rest of the world. He is not capable of trying to be polite – not even for one night can he sit and smile with my parents and pretend to be happy because he has no idea how to compromise and why should he? He is the yin to my yang. I have smiled and sat when I was told to sit and stood when I was told to stand and moved when I was told to move – this has been my life.

This is what I love most about him: this absolutism, this unstinting refusal to bend. Jason is committed, not just to me, but to himself and his way as the only way. It is selfish, yes, but it is free.

That evening, as crazy as it seems, Jason is at his most lucid.

A few days later, Mummy and Baba and Uncle fly back to South Africa. Before they leave they try to talk about my plans for work, my next steps. I am evasive. I mumble responses and give jumbled-up answers about my visa being extended. I change the subject.

'We'll see,' I keep saying.

The truth is, Jason is tired of Minnesota and he wants to go back to California. We have hatched a plan to move to California. In fact, Jason has not really asked me, he just knows I will come. So I do. I put off South Africa. I am now truly free to move home and I don't. I move to California. No plan. No job. No ticket home to South Africa. Just Jason.

Mummy is flabbergasted when I tell her I'm not coming home. 'What do you mean?' she asks. I am not really sure what I mean so the conversation is awkward.

Baba says that he will speak to me when I come to my senses because he can't understand how, when South Africa is free and Nelson Mandela is the president, I can be in America not even working at a proper job or having a plan.

He asks what my intentions are with 'this person'. He cannot even bring himself to say his name.

'I am not sure,' I respond. Scared, now that it is him on the phone. 'Sonke, there are certain things that we don't do in this family. This is one of them. You do not just live with someone – just like that. Before marriage.'

There is something here, something in the edge in his voice that tells me he is sniffing around me, trying to determine whether I have already fallen from grace, whether I am already a 'certain kind of woman'.

He thinks what I am doing will 'tarnish' me. This is rich given that I was born only five months after he and Mummy married.

So, this is what it feels like. The blood pounding in my ears, my legs slightly wobbly. This is what it feels like to defy him.

After all these years of being the good daughter, my moment of rebellion has come.

There is no screaming. I simply say, 'I'm doing this, Baba.'

He hands the phone to Mummy and I am furious. 'Mummy, tell him to get back on the phone.' I am seething.

'No, my girl. You have made a decision, now you live with it.' We end the call.

I cry and cry. My eyes are red for three days. I am angry that they didn't even give me the benefit of screaming at Baba

Still, my actions are clear and his refusal to engage doubles my resolve. I will not be the one to break the silence. I come out of the tears more resolute. I will do what I want – or, rather, I will do what Baba doesn't want me to do – regardless.

This one long act will make up for all the times I nodded and swallowed my words and bit down on my re-sentment. It will make up for my silences when I should have been crying – from Lusaka to Nairobi to Ottawa and back again.

My heart is a jagged edge but my chest is full of pride. Jason does not understand what the big deal is. He knows how it feels to be forsaken and cast out, but he does not know how it feels to choose yourself over your tribe. He cannot understand what it is to be an African daughter who simply wants to be her own person, to make her own mistakes. He doesn't know what it means finally to be defiant because for him defiance has always come so easy. I envy him this, his natural-born polarity.

Folie à deux

SOME DAYS I wanted to kiss his forehead before he opened his mouth because he was a poem and a love song and a dirge. We used to wrestle on the black carpet in the crazy apartment we rented in Oakland but the fights were always pointless because he was stronger than I was and was only letting me pummel him. He never fought back so eventually I would collapse and hold him as though he hadn't been the source – the very creation – of my pain and it would all be better for a little bit as our tears mingled then disappeared into that overplush shag.

Everyone says it doesn't matter what someone looks like on the outside but you know and I know and every woman on this Earth knows that beauty can be blinding. And when you are the beauty – well, that is fine – but when you see a beautiful man and that man sees you too, that is intoxicating and begins to mean more than it should. And he was that beautiful man who looked back and smiled and he had caramel skin that made my brown look sallow and that brow and a nose slightly too large and straight that seemed both incongruous and sexy on a face so finely drawn. He was an American invention with that long slow sweet smile, that boppety-hoppety-bop that bounced his walk and defined the cadence of his voice and so I loved him like I loved black America.

Jason never lied to me. He told me straight away that he was manic which didn't mean anything to me. I had never heard of it and so I loved him. When I realised that it meant that he was wired differently, that his ups were higher and his downs were lower and that in between he was headstrong and convinced of his own righteousness, I began to love him with a deliberateness and a certainty that was the opposite of blind.

He was meaner to me than any man had ever been although not in a way that was meant to hurt – only in a way that was meant to teach me something that I could only understand through him yelling at and contradicting me. That's what he said and all these years later I still believe he believed that. I believe it too some days, when I remember him in the right way.

Like once he said that I wasn't pretty because my face was lopsided but that I was still nice to look at because the kindness in my heart made up for it and I cried and cried and he was not sorry he said it because it was true.

It sounds worse now than it felt at the time, like some sort of bad movie every girl has seen – a movie smart girls avoid – but it wasn't cliché, it was thrilling and I was never really in any danger since all he did was slap me with rough words and sometimes not even that, just sharp and brutal meanings.

And here's the thing; the thing is that every single one of the seven hundred and thirteen days between our meeting on that winter afternoon in Minneapolis and our parting on that cool Oakland morning when I kissed him goodbye and got on the plane with a one-way ticket Mummy bought me, every, single, day, was, that, intense.

But no one else understood. Mummy didn't care about existentialism, she just wanted her daughter back and Baba was too angry to speak. Angrier than he should have been and his being right fuelled my righteousness and made it harder to leave. I didn't want to be wrong. I wanted to be right. I wanted us. To be right.

Jason was obsessed with us. He was not obsessed with me – that is a different thing. The idea of us captured him because even if I was miserable I was there and that made us something special. No one else had cried so much and bled inside and just stayed. Still, he was incapable of caring about what I had risked to be with him. He demanded sacrifice, but he was never grateful for it.

He wasn't interested in talking to my father and wooing my mother and that was a lesson I needed to learn. But I was only young and there is only one first time. Only one time when you will get lost like that to the point where you have no idea how to come back – until only a scream will get your attention.

He made me wish I was the kind of girl who nursed thoughts of suicide although I had no reason to throw myself off anything. Our love was a centuries-old tale. It was a song sung by mutes – hopelessly doomed and yet so desperately attempted. Our love was a long-burning pyre and if I had ever suggested that we clasp hands and ignite ourselves he would have bellowed at me and twitched his eye and run his tongue over his front teeth the way he did when he was so angry that he didn't know what to do with himself and then he would have said, 'Booboo you have no fuckin' idea what you are talking about and how close I have been to death,' which is why I never told him that some days he made me want to inflict murder on myself.

Jason had good reason to want to jump off something and be suspended in air for a moment before taking flight into nothingness, but I *didn't* and he wasn't trying to die so why should I? And I didn't really want to but everything had this life-changing quality between us. Every word he said, every whisper, every moment felt like it was life and death and so loving him was a kind of murder and a kind of dying and also it was living and breathing and even salvation. And when I came out of it, when I finally came up for air out of the embalming fluid that was our mutual obsession, I was different and not as interesting as I had been when I had been halfcrazy with love.

When Jason talked about the times when he had been hospitalised he was never ashamed. He refused to back down from what he had seen so the voices and the shadows remained real. He unsettled the boundaries between mad and sane, laughed when I couldn't see in other dimensions. He refused to be the problem.

Mania became him. I never saw him off the pills but the memory of the things that lurked and grunted inside and outside him as well as the peace and the absolute mastery of fear that he had had to wrap his arms around when he completely lost his mind were all still with him. They had become a part of him. Madness was a kind of freedom and since I was the opposite of this and had always been sensible and good at drawing inside the lines and making pretty pictures, I needed him to trouble me. So you see? He was my rebellion. But madness has its costs and when those became too high I cut out and saved myself and I am glad because he was the freest person I ever knew but freedom is costly and I was broke. He broke me even as he freed me. It's hard to explain. After a while everyone called me crazy too because I took so long to leave and because it became harder and harder to have real conversations with anyone else – he always needed to listen. 'Shhhh! You hear that?' There were always whispers interrupting our conversations –

strange noises and murmurs coming from the walls and behind them and even if I didn't hear them I believed him that they were there. They call these delusions but I never liked the term: if one of us could hear them then they were real.

When we moved to California I got a job and when I went to work I had peace and, yes, sanity and there I would remember a little bit of who I was, without his ceaseless examinations of God and his suspicions about who might be at the door. He used to call me on the office phone and I would cry after I put the phone down because it meant he was awake and he would show up soon. When he was sleeping at least I knew he wasn't on his way. Coming. With his questions.

Sometimes, the phone would ring as soon as I arrived in the office because he had timed how long it would take me to get there. And when I didn't pick up because I knew it was him and I had work to do and ours was the only real income in the house though his disability cheque helped, then he would come even sooner. So after a while there was no winning and then I started to hate it and I didn't know how to break free from it. Then I got angry, so angry, when really I should have been afraid.

Loving him was an experiment. Until I met Jason I thought I could love someone into being a better version of themselves. Jason taught me that I could not exist to be a balm and a salve for someone else. He didn't want it, but even if he had – what a silly idea. How silly of me to make the oldest mistake in the book of love.

I was clever and independent and coming into a feminist way of seeing the world but still I thought there was something essential in me that balanced something essential in him; that I was the melody and he was the beat.

Then one day my African upbringing reared its

common-sense head because he could not and would not hold down a job because he was not on the right dosage of meds and he was suspicious of everyone and thought he had enemies everywhere and I began to wonder what this would look like once children came along. Still, even then, I stayed, locked in a pose that made no sense because I was afraid that leaving him would make Baba right and also it would make me sensible and boring and dutiful again.

In the end – for all the drama and tears – I only loved him for what I knew he could teach me, and also maybe a little bit because I thought there was something selfless about loving someone who was mad, about seeing through the diagnosis to the man inside. So there I was with my dutiful heart, swapping one obligation for another. There was nothing selfless about how I loved him. I loved him because I wanted to find myself, which is not really proper and deep love at all. So even today when I think about him I want to reach across time and space and touch his beautiful cheek and say sorry to him for that. I did love him though probably less than I would have admitted at the time. I know this now in retrospect because when it was time to go I just left. I stopped worrying about who he would talk to at night and whether he'd end up in a fight because someone looked at him the wrong way. I didn't linger and, in the end, it was not horrible because I wanted to go far more than I wanted to stay.

And then, when I was finally back home on another continent and there were oceans and rivers between us and Lake Merritt was just a vivid memory but no longer a reality I had to walk around to get to work I thought about how he never lied to me and I cursed him and missed him but could not go back to him.

◆ ◆ ◆

In my favourite memory of Jason he is standing in front of me in the cold with frost on the hairs in his nose, and the wind is stinging my cheeks and we have just had another epic fight about God knows what and the Minnesota snow is blinding but also what I need to clear my head and I don't have a jacket on, only boots, and he says to me, 'Booboo I'm the craziest nigga you will ever meet and I'm the only one who will ever love you so it hurts like this. Crazy comes at a price.'

Even now, this very moment as I write this, I am far away and so much time has passed and still I am crying with the remembering of it because Jason was my first love and he taught me that love is not enough and he helped me draw a line in the sand that no one else since has ever crossed. I learnt from him what it looks like to belong to your own self.

Home

WHEN I RETURN from America I am like a love letter that has been torn up and put back together again. There are pieces of me missing. Recognising this, Mummy is gentle with me. Sometimes she speaks to me as though I have just returned from the frontlines of a war. Baba doesn't know what to say and so he avoids me and tries not to look irritated on those rare occasions when we bump into each other in the house. He leaves early most mornings and comes home late. I spend a lot of time crying. I am heartbroken over a man and he doesn't know what to do with this knowledge. He has no idea how to relate to the woman his child is becoming.

I pretend to be busy when he is around and I sense he is grateful. He is still angry about me living in sin and deciding not to come home, and I am still angry at him for behaving like a misogynist patriarch. I am angry for the time he spent ignoring me. There is a heaviness between us that has never existed before and yet it is freeing. I no longer have to labour under the yoke of Baba's approval. I have disappointed him – deeply – and I am not sorry. In fact, I am proud. That he may never understand this only bolsters my resolve and sense of righteousness.

It is left to Mummy to try to patch things up between us. She is reassured by the fact that I have no money; she knows I will live at home for a while and that proximity alone will go a long way towards forcing a reconciliation.

She is right. The fog of lovesickness begins to pass. I am grateful for the peace. Grateful to be home alone in the day when Mummy and Baba and Zeng are gone, so I can cry and eat and have my privacy and aloneness. I am grateful, too, for her cooking. For her unspeaking presence – for what she doesn't say but notices nonetheless. Mummy's mothering is light – it is not always delivered in lectures.

Slowly, I begin to feel my way out of the anger at Baba and the loneliness and rage at Jason. I laugh because of Zeng. She is in her final year of high school and while I was at university she grew up. She is funnier and sharper and more naturally witty than any of us. She is the baby, though, so her heart is wide and it is open.

I whine about Baba. She nods in understanding – they have had their own clashes. Eventually though she is tired of it and she says, 'Talk to him, babe, this is getting boring now.'

So I do. I wait for him to come home from work. It gets later and later but still I wait. When he arrives he sees me in the TV room. He understands immediately that my presence is an invitation and so he joins me. We have not done this since my arrival a month ago. We sit and talk about nothing at all and it feels fine. I see his love and disdain and decide to live with them both because I am tired of fighting. I decide to love Baba in spite of the things he chooses not to understand.

So there is peace again in the house. Mummy is happy, even though she is smart enough not to rejoice too loudly. She smiles more and begins again to tease Baba and me about our bond – about the ways in which we are similar, from our left-handedness to our hard-headedness.

◆ ◆ ◆

I start looking for a job. I fill in applications and busy myself with perfecting my CV. The Australian High Commission is looking for a programme officer. I don't know what this means really but I meet the requirements – an undergraduate degree in international relations or politics, an interest in policy, and experience working on social issues. I write a winning cover letter about how much I want to support the project of building a new non-racial society. I triple-check my CV and fax it off.

Within a week they phone to invite me to interview. I put on my only suit – a maroon blazer with shoulder pads and matching pants. I wear low black heels and carry a shoulder bag as though I am a grown woman. I put on my most serious face and try to look calm.

My American degree and the years spent in many different parts of the world intrigue them. I worry they will hone in on these weaknesses – that the panel will see that my global experience actually distances me from the community projects they fund; that I may find it hard to understand the contexts in which their projects operate.

These worries come to nothing. The panel is only too happy to hire me. I speak English in a way that suits them and yet I am 'local'. Never mind that I am South African in name only – simply because my ID book says so – and that, in reality, there is very little about me, beyond my DNA, that is local.

I get the job.

The night before I start work, Mummy sits me down in the living room. 'Let's talk, my girl.' I know she is going to give me a talk about saving money and how I mustn't use the phone at the office. She surprises me.

'Remember the camping trip?'

I smile and know immediately what she is talking about. 'You mean the camping trip that never happened?'

We both laugh at the memory of it. A decade has passed since she tried to pitch the tent while we stood perplexed and giggly and unsure what had taken over our mother. The rain had come pouring down and saved us from having to spend the night in the woods. We had packed up and gone home to our small duplex in Hunt Club and watched movies, the four of us squeezed onto the couch – three brown girls and their mama. I was thirteen then and aware of my budding breasts and spreading thighs even when nobody was looking at me. That aborted camping trip had made me forget myself for a few hours – had let me put aside my selfconsciousness and self-absorption.

Tonight, sitting in the dim light, I am no longer awkward. I am tall and pretty in that way all women are in those fleeting years when they are no longer girls but have only just become women. I can see in Mummy's eyes she can't quite believe I am now a woman poised to march into the world without her.

'Yes, the camping trip that never was.'

Mummy smiles. I can see she is happy that I still remember that day. I think for the first time about what life must have been like for Mummy in Canada – the loneliness without Baba, and the difficulty of navigating a new and strange place. Mummy always protected us from feeling unstable, from sensing her own anxieties, and so I assumed, as a child, that she had none.

Tonight, as she tells this story, she takes me back; she paints a fuller picture of the woman I never saw because I was too much of a child to worry about anything but my own needs.

She begins.

It is a warm spring day in 1985 and she is happy because she has survived her first winter in Canada. For months she has woken up in the dark day after day after day and pulled on her boots and braced against the cold to shovel overnight snowfall from the driveway. She has made breakfast for her children and then made her way to the office over ice and through storms, month after unending month, alone and tired and lonely.

She works as a junior accountant at a small firm, despite her years of experience. She sits in a cubicle and does basic balance sheets and income and credit statements. The work is mindless and not well paid, but it is work and it matters for the future she is building. On this particular day, when the boss approaches her cubie, her mood is good because finally the sun has decided to shine again. She is humming gently under her breath but when he approaches her she stops. He is querying something minor – as usual. She clarifies quickly and slightly nervously as is her custom, but he does not seem to understand what she is saying. She considers just conceding and saying, yes, you are right, it is my fault. The trouble is that the implications of the error he is implying she made, but which she did not, in fact, make, are significant.

So they go over it again. The third time, he sees that she is correct. He wants to say, 'Oh! I see,' but he doesn't. He is embarrassed because she is contradicting him in front of the others and the mistake he has made will have financial implications. So he stands over her desk and decides to shout. He turns red in the face, and bellows, saying she is in Canada now, not Africa, and here things are done professionally. Then he calls her a bitch. To be precise, he calls her a dumb bitch.

At this point in telling the story, Mummy has raised her hand and is holding out her palm as though the boss is standing right in front of her, as though she still needs to guard against him.

She resumes her story.

After he has spoken these words, Mummy remains silent. SiSwati rushes to her lips, but stays in her mouth, locked just behind her teeth. She feels as though she is skating, like that time she fell after getting off the bus. The ice had surprised her and her legs, in boots that were not sturdy enough, had betrayed her.

The boss hears her silence and knows that he should stop but he does not. He makes it worse. He says, 'This is not a charity, it's a business! Don't come here and tell me how to run my business.' He is screaming and no one else is moving or talking or doing anything, but watching this display although their heads are down and they are pretending not to listen and someone is in the kitchen, frozen, afraid to move even when the microwave beeps.

Then he stops bellowing. He stops and he looks at her and sees that she is only looking and not saying a word and he begins to be afraid and he doesn't know why. So he turns and, with his shoulders slumped in defeat, although you could argue he is the victor, he walks quickly to his office. He slams the door. This is his way of acting, for the sake of the others, as though he is angry and has a right to be.

She knows he is not angry, only frightened because she looked right through him as though he were dead and he is not the sort of man who knows what to do with that. He cowers in his office, afraid that, like some voodoo priestess, she might steal a hair from his jacket or drive a pin through his eye.

She does not, nor would it ever occur to her.

She packs her bags and nods goodbye to her colleagues. The sting of humiliation and the urgency of rage force her to slow down. She does not move quickly, though she wants to. Something in her body tells her to be deliberate and slow. Finally, when she is done, she walks into the corridor and waves at her colleagues. They are aghast. She smiles but says nothing. Then she turns and looks through the window. He is sitting at his desk and senses someone is there and so he looks up. She looks back. She looks at him long and hard. Not mean or even hurt, just clear-eyed and firm as though she is remembering every detail so that the moment never fades from her mind's eye. He flushes and looks down and this satisfies her. Then she puts on her great big coat. She puts it on and walks out and never returns.

No amount of sorry can undo what has been done. Mummy cannot even tell Baba because as usual he is gone. He has a six-month emergency relief assignment in Ethiopia so she cannot confide in him. She cannot ask him – as she might if he was sitting in bed, listening to her story – how it is that this man can speak to her this way. She cannot say, 'Me? Talk to me that way? Does he know who I am?' She cannot fume aloud and say that she did not move her children and fix her eyes on this country only to be called an African bitch. She has no one to say these things to but she thinks them and they keep her strong and she resists the tears because if she allowed them to, they could drown her.

Mummy gets into her car and drives away. She drives steadily and slowly but she drives away, knowing she will never return. The day is bright and the winter is over. She goes to school and fetches her girls. She is there when we come out of the building. She stands there and smiles as though she is a Canadian mom with time on her hands and cookies in the oven at home and we are surprised as she encircles us with her arms and then we are surprised again when she says, 'Let's go camping,' and we giggle in the back seat all the way there.

Once we are in the camping grounds we shout instructions to each other, trying to pitch the tent and when the heavens open up and the rain pours down on us we laugh and are happier still when she says, 'Let's go home, girls.'

The following week the office calls and she says, 'No, I will not consider it. I am not coming back.'

She looks for another job and in the interview the head of HR is surprised when she says in her soft and tired voice, 'I left because my dignity is not for sale,' and something about the way she says it makes that company ny offer her the job.

When the story is over Mummy and I sit with the television light flickering on our faces. I wish I knew this about Mummy when I was in college and heartbroken and looking for answers about racism and fortitude. I think about how often I turned to the words of poets and writers and great thinkers; of the times I ran to the library with its heaving shelves full of books in Minnesota, when all along Mummy has been here.

I see clearly for the first time how much I have taken her for granted, how much I have focused on Baba because he was the freedom fighter and she has always just been our mother – strong and determined but, in my mind at least, apolitical. I see what a mistake it has been to think that, just because she doesn't talk about racism, she has not felt its lash and its sting. I regret this immediately and recognise it as a function of my adoration of Baba. I have loved her, but it has never occurred to me that she ought to be an object of my admiration – a hero just like Gogo Lindi.

I am embarrassed suddenly, even as my chest swells with pride. Like most children, I have only seen my mother as I needed to see her, not as she has always been. I am lucky, though – she has had the grace to wait, to find the perfect moment in which to turn my face towards her, and then to take the time to whisper, 'Listen, my girl, and look at me: this is who I really am.'

New blacks, old whites

I HAVE NOT lived in the same house as my parents for almost six years so it is difficult to get used to them again. Mummy and Baba are awfully busy – more than they ever were when we were growing up. Like everyone else of their age and social class, they are hard at work nation building. Their skills are in demand and now that they are home they want to make up for lost time.

Baba is busy being a First Black CEO and First Black Director General and Mummy is busy making her mark in the community of returnees who are reshaping the business and cultural life of the new South Africa. She is the First Black Woman to Open an African Restaurant, then she becomes the First Black Woman Table Grape Farmer, then she is named Woman of the Year in one category and Runner-Up in Entrepreneurship in another.

Our house is just a stone's throw away from Africa's largest mall. We have no black neighbours. It is only us – these curious black people who seemed unafraid and aloof. When we host braais or social events we are careful not to make too much noise. We presume our neighbours are racist, and that they think black people don't know how to behave in the suburbs. Mummy's strategy is to give them as little opportunity to gossip or complain as possible. She always sends Baba around to each of their houses with a note for their letterbox: 'Dear Neighbour, we are having a small gathering on Saturday. We hope we do not disturb you.' Mummy and Baba are steeped in respectability. My sojourn in America has taught me not to care less – I roll my eyes at their manners.

'Seriously Mummy, are we going to go out of our way to show them how civilised we are? Have they ever given you a note like that? No, they just have their things and they don't even worry about us.'

She always responds calmly. Mummy knows not to get her blood pressure up over her radical daughter's politics.

'You and your militant politics. Do unto others as you would have them do unto you. You can be as rude as you like when you own a house. Until then, this is my house, my girl.'

Zeng and I smirk obnoxiously and saunter off because we have our own ways of dealing with the old whites in the new South Africa. Zeng is another sort of first black. Her generation is an experiment. Her friends reflect the changing face of the country. There is one set who – like us – grew up in exile in Lesotho and Zambia and Uganda and Sweden and Russia and the UK and Canada and America and all sorts of other places. They returned as teenagers in the early 1990s and tried to integrate into South African schools. All of them were South African in their hearts but they had not encountered South Africa until after some pretty fundamental parts of their identities had been formed. So, they became an instant community, made of teenagers we'd known as kids in Lusaka or whose family names we had heard all our lives, whose experiences mirrored ours, but whom we had never met.

She has another set of friends who grew up inside the country and whose parents are doctors and lawyers and professionals who managed to become part of the middle class as the Group Areas Act that kept blacks and whites apart started to be relaxed in certain places. Some of them are the children of activists who never left the country. Their parents were involved in the United Democratic Front. These ones have crazy stories; stories of police raids and political uncertainty.

Their parents had spent months in detention or weeks running from police. These children had attended too many vigils and stood by too many corpses. They knew all the freedom songs and could speak five African languages and the Queen's English so, while they are different from Zeng, they understand what it is like to belong to a movement that is also a family. The liberation struggle is as much in their blood as it is in ours.

Then there are others: the friends Zeng never really made, the ones whose parents aren't anyone special. These are the black kids who are bussed in to the suburbs from Atteridgeville township or Mamelodi to attend the high school down the street from our house where Zeng is initially enrolled in school. These kids can't relate to Zeng and she can't relate to them. They think she is stuck up because her English is perfect and her isiZulu is faltering and her seSotho is non-existent. They think she is stuck up because she lives in a house down the street and doesn't need to wake up at the crack of dawn to catch a bus to be around white children who scorn them and laugh at their hair and their noses and the way they speak.

Like Zeng, they also grew up in the dying days of apartheid. Unlike Zeng, they do not live in middle-class comfort. Stray dogs roam the streets and there are shacks and overcrowded schools in their communities. Nelson Mandela may be sleeping on fine sheets and soft pillows in Pretoria, but life has not changed much for them yet. They know enough about discrimination to have grown thick skins. They are tough kids – they seem like they know how to survive. So in spite of her big mouth sometimes Zeng doesn't have any comebacks for their barbs at school when they start to call her a coconut. She shrugs and acts like she doesn't care. She sticks to herself and for the first time at school she doesn't really know where she fits in. The white kids can't relate to or claim her and the black ones regard her with scepticism.

Mummy and Baba eventually pull her out of the school down the road when she is so unhappy she doesn't want to go any more. In addition to the friction with other students, there is constant harassment by teachers who are not happy with how the black girls dress, with the way they wear their hair, with their 'hygiene'. It's like low-grade warfare.

Before I came back from America Zeng was often alone at home. Mummy was as organised as ever so there was food in the house, but there was little else in terms of structure or attention. When I come back, I notice that, even when they are home, Mummy and Baba are often preoccupied – not even with each other's lives any more but with their individual pursuits.

I don't begrudge Mummy this: she supported Baba her whole adult life and was busy raising us so it's about time she turns inwards to focus on herself. It means, though, that Zeng has been spending weeknights virtually alone because Mummy and Baba are always out. There is either this state dinner or that meeting, or this person who has just returned from overseas.

She is only fifteen so she is old enough to seem fairly selfsufficient. Mummy and Baba assume she can take care of herself. She is the baby of the family, though, and she can't. They let go of her too quickly.

Mandla and I had already done our growing up by the time we came home. Zeng was still incomplete, only an adolescent. She bore the brunt of their busy-ness.

In those early months when I am still living in my parents' house, living under the same roof as them again, I can see that it is hard for her to navigate that line between the freedom that comes from their busy lives, and the quiet neglect it has wrought.

Zeng and I become close. Given the five-year gap between us she has always been a baby. She was only eleven when I left the house at sixteen and, although she was older and funnier every time I came home for holidays, I didn't know her as well as I knew Mandla.

Now, though, we spend a lot of time together. Mandla is still in the States, finishing her degree. Before I start my job, we borrow Mummy's car and cruise around a lot, tooling around the suburbs. We often get thumbs-up signs from black people who have never seen black girls our age driving around in an almost-new Toyota Corolla.

One day we arrive at a small shopping centre near home and when we return to the parked car we find a small group of men in overalls gathered around the vehicle. They pepper us with questions. Where are you from, you children? They ask. We tell them. Our parents have just returned from exile, we say. They want to shake our hands. It is embarrassing to be celebrated for our good luck. We aren't quite sure what to do with their kindness, with their blessings and best wishes for us. We have done nothing to earn it, except to hop into our mother's car. We can't say this, though. To those uncles and fathers gathered around the car with their blessings and their good wishes, our success is a reflection of the future they imagine for their children. We represent progress.

Afterwards, Zeng and I drive in silence. We see, with our eyes wide open, how much we have taken for granted about our lives.

There is a certain kind of innocence among black people – an innocence that will quickly be lost. In those early days, black people are bound together by a pride and a solidarity that underscores everything we have collectively been through. I don't know it yet, but this feeling will eventually fade. A decade later it will all but disappear.

In the future, a new and arrogant black will emerge. This new black will not be interested in the stories of the poor. This new black will see the uncles around my car as a shame and a stain, rather than as part of herself. And the uncles themselves will not trust the new black, so they will no longer look upon her with pride.

But all of this is still some distance away. In these early years of innocence, older people still look at Zeng and me driving around Pretoria with a shine in their eyes and with their hearts bursting with pride and you can practically hear them say, 'If you can win, my child, then I too have won.'

I still think about Jason every day. I have gone from being broke in Oakland – not being able to afford bus fare – to being part of a new elite. I miss him. We speak on the phone a lot. I cry a lot still. But I know I am not going back. There is a new South Africa to build. Jason sidetracked me for a while but now I am back home and I can see the complexity of the task at hand. There is the politics, of course, and there is the economic reality. There is also something social, a rebuilding of the fabric of the society, that I find fascinating.

Among whites, our middle-class status provokes a different set of responses. Unlike the black people who greet us with pride, whites are angry and resentful. We are the enemy. We represent everything whites in Pretoria fear they will lose with the end of apartheid.

By the time Mandela died they all professed to love him, but, in these early years, immediately after the elections, they do not love him at all nor do all of them accept him as their president. They curse him. They throw his name in our faces and hurl him at us like a swear word in traffic.

Once, as I am overtaking a white woman in my car on the road, she turns and spits his name at me in rage: 'MANDELA!' I have no idea what I have done to make her angry – but that doesn't matter. I cackle in my car, alone, relishing her frustration, understanding that she is not angry with me – she is unhappy with the world that has changed without much warning right before her eyes.

Zeng and I often find ourselves clashing with angry men in bakkies or embroiled in screaming matches with tight-faced women wearing shiny tracksuits. Often, the battles are fought in suburban sanctuaries – in malls close to home.

More often than not, the drama takes place at our local supermarket. Zeng starts to call our weekly skirmishes the Pick 'n' Pay Wars.

The battles typically begin in the parking lot. Invariably, one of our white foes swoops in and steals a parking spot for which I have been patiently waiting. It happens so many times it stops being annoying and becomes a running joke. Even if there are plenty of free spaces, somehow the exact bay I want attracts the attention of the owner of a weathered yellow or blue bakkie. If I beat the driver to the spot there is fist-shaking and anger, sometimes a slammed door and a tantrum.

If the other party wins, they shoot us a look of smouldering triumph and get out of their car in a way that demonstrates that their life has new purpose and meaning now. The scenes play themselves out endlessly. It is exhausting and sometimes, because the white righteousness is so powerfully exhibited, it is easy to forget apartheid was a crime against black people. You might find yourself thinking whites were the historical victims of a system of injustice.

◆ ◆ ◆

On the day the permed blonde woman bumps into me in Pick 'n' Pay, I am ready for war. She is talking to her daughter and not paying attention. She bumps into my trolley by mistake. No big deal. I look at her, waiting for an apology though I know none will be forthcoming. That day, knowing that she is not sorry – and is unlikely to say sorry – makes me angrier than usual.

If this were a normal society she would simply have

said, 'I'm sorry,' and moved on. But we are not living in a normal society. So, instead of saying sorry, she sneers and huffs and tells me to get out of her way. Rudely.

I am livid and, of course, amply prepared to fight this fight. I am tired of the endless entitlements and the petty racism that seem designed to make me feel apologetic for taking up any space at all, that make me feel as though I am trespassing when I simply want to get on with the mundane chores to which all members of society are entitled. Something springs loose.

Instead of manoeuvring around her, I stand my ground. I say, 'I will get out of your way when you apologise. You bumped into me.'

It seems she has also been waiting for this moment, for this opportunity to tell off one of these new blacks.

She responds in Afrikaans – a language of which I have absolutely no knowledge and which I have been politically educated to despise. Growing up, Afrikaans was a symbol of apartheid and its place in my consciousness has been cemented by the stories of all the uncles and aunties from the 1976 uprisings who left South Africa in the wake of attempts to force Afrikaans to be the official medium of instruction for black children.

I cut her off. 'Speak in English! I don't understand you.'

My voice is too loud – because her tone had been unacceptable.

I am not Mandela.

She is startled by the intensity of my response. 'What?' she says.

I repeat myself and, for good measure, I add, 'This is our country now. You must leave if you don't like black people!'

She rams her trolley into mine, only this time she does it on purpose. This time I am also ready so I ram mine into hers. She rams back and I ram again and so it goes back and forth. We are like lunatics attacking one another with suburban weaponry.

Finally Zeng shouts, 'Sonke! Stop.'

It breaks the spell and I back off. I stand there heaving and glaring at my opponent, unsure of what to do next. Then Zeng – in her succinct and sarcastic voice – says, 'She's just nonsense babes, not even worth it.'

The Permed One is outraged. What sort of a black person spoke like this? 'That is enough!' She starts looking around because she wants to call for the manager. Zeng will have none of it.

'Let's get out of here,' Zeng says, unhurriedly. 'This is ridiculous.' 'Stay right there,' she shouts. 'You wait. I'm going to complain on you.'

Zeng can't resist. She stops and turns.

'What you mean to say, is that you want to file a complaint *against* her. A-G-A-I-N-S-T.' She spells it out. 'Learn to speak English, lady. Seriously.'

We leave then. The two of us walk through the shop in blazing insolence, performing our discontent. Our slow pace signals our superiority. We are not afraid. We refuse to run. We will not be chased in our own country – not in a free South Africa.

In the car, we drive for a while in silence. Then Zeng punches me on the arm. 'Whoa! That's why you're normally such a scaredycat! When you lose it, you lose it, hey?'

She sighs with the wisdom of someone far older than her seventeen years. 'They really, really aren't worth it, babes.'

She is right, of course, but I have just come from America where whites seldom try that sort of thing any more and where, if they do, black people put them in their place swiftly and with little sentiment. South Africa is not yet that country.

I am aware, however, that much of South Africa's new endeavour as a nation rests on proving Zeng wrong. South Africa is trying to become a place where everyone is worth it, where even the worst among us is worth the time and the effort and the love it will take to explain.

This is the premise of the new deal. The racists aren't nonsense. They are fucked up, but they are not beyond redemption. The compromise required to end apartheid through a negotiated settlement means none of us get to write others off.

That is the theory, of course, but I struggle with it. Having narrowly escaped the need for white approval when I left Canada, and having learnt not to fear hurting white people's feelings in America, when I finally come home I am ambivalent about white people.

Having been raised on the mantra of non-racialism I recognise the push for forgiveness but I find it hard to be patient all the time. It is well past time for black people to dictate the terms of engagement with their white compatriots. I often find myself bristling when whites huff and puff and fling their exasperated entitlement around in queues and in public spaces. They always have something to complain about and I wonder how this is possible, given that they are still here, with their houses untouched and their schools and offices uncharred. It is a constant source of tension – managing my anger and disciplining my agitation, all while figuring out how to be part of this new country I have waited for in a way that is appropriate to the historical moment.

I have a feeling this time will soon pass and that the decisions I make – even the small ones, like whether to extend a hand of friendship – will matter very much in the long run.

◆ ◆ ◆

Night after night on TV, the victims of apartheid are broadcasting their stories. The Truth and Reconciliation Commission (TRC) is South Africa's attempt to reckon with its past even as it is racing headlong into its future.

Most nights the news bulletin carries a small clip of the proceedings of the day – especially if something explosive has been revealed. There is a longer in-depth weekly analysis on one of the national broadcaster's TV stations, in which Max du Preez provides some commentary and a team does additional reporting on the perpetrators or the victims of the crimes under the spotlight.

Night after night we watch as the perpetrators deny having done anything. They don't say they did nothing *wrong* – they deny having done anything at all. It is remarkable, as though apartheid was a series of years that unfolded as white men in uniform twiddled their thumbs and did nothing to cause untold misery and violence. Almost all those called before the Commission deny responsibility, pointing the finger either at higher-ups or at junior-level staff. There was so much bloodshed, such an abundance of lives lost, yet these crimes seem to have been perpetrated by shadows. Ghosts had bludgeoned victims to death and buried them alive. Zombies had done it: the walking dead.

In my new job at AusAID, I identify projects to be funded in South Africa and recommend them to head office in Canberra. I also have to update head office about social and political developments that may affect our funding relationships and our partnership with the South African government. For my first big assignment, I have to report on a special set of hearings of the TRC that focus on the experiences of women activists during the apartheid era. The office is interested in looking at areas where Australian funding may be useful.

I arrive at the venue on the first day and immediately feel out of place. I am in my new work clothes and suddenly the heels that work so well in the office make me look too dressed up. I am attending as an observer and the word suddenly feels like an accurate reflection of who I am: an outsider.

Because the hearings specifically focus on women, the male commissioners and researchers recuse themselves. They recognise that the women who will testify need to feel comfortable to speak in an uninhibited manner. The audience is almost entirely female.

Gcina Mhlophe, the nation's foremost public storyteller, opens the session. She is tall and stately. She looks a little bit like me – and I am still getting used to this feeling, of looking so much like people on the street but knowing nothing about them. Being home means bumping into mirror images of myself everywhere after a lifetime of being in African countries but never quite looking like an archetypal Kenyan or Zambian. Being home, I am acutely aware of the dissonance between being *of* a place by virtue of physiological heritage and being *from* a place by virtue of memory and experience. I look like I belong, but I don't.

Mhlophe's voice is resonant, almost manly in its depths; tailormade for this role. She speaks a poem and very quickly my eyes are filled with tears.

> Watch my eyes, hear my voice, I tell you true, I talk about the bones of memory [...] This is the time of the story-teller and every single person in this room has got a story to tell and more must be told.

◆ ◆ ◆

Over the next two days I listen to many stories. I sit alone because I am not there as a family member or as a victim. Others are clustered together because they have come in groups and across distances. Attending is important. The women have come to speak and to ask questions. They have come to testify.

The women speak of lovers they last saw slipping out of their homes at dawn, of sons and daughters who said goodbye and headed for school and never came back. They have come to ask if anyone has seen them, to check if anyone knows where they went. When Thandi Shezi's testimony begins, I don't know what to do with myself. Shezi tells the commission she was detained by the Security Police in 1988. She spent a year in solitary confinement, under 'suspicion of being a terrorist'. While in detention, she was tortured multiple times. She endured the water torture for which the security branch was notorious – and, in her instance, the bucket of water in which her head was dunked was laced with acid. She had electric shocks applied all over her body. She was gang-raped.

Her tongue swelled massive from the effects of the electrocution.

She sit at the front of the room and says:

Then the four of them started raping me, the four of
them. The whole four of them started raping me whilst
they were insulting me and using vulgar words and said
I must tell them the truth. They said if I don't tell them
the truth about where the guns are and where is this
other person they're looking for, they will do their
utmost worst.

But after they finished raping me, they took me to Sunset Prison, Diepkloof Prison... The way I had been assaulted and had been injured, I couldn't speak for myself, I couldn't talk. When the doctor asked me what had happened, I couldn't even explain to the doctor what has happened to me, because my tongue was swollen in my mouth. I couldn't speak. So they told the doctor that I was a prostitute, that I'd been arrested in Hillbrow and when they were trying to arrest me, I ran away, so that's why I got injured.

At the end of the hearings, on the final day of the week, I drive away in tears. I drive across the long highway and into Pretoria, looking at the perfectly erected streetlights and the immaculately cut grass, at the arcing bridges and the perfectly fading sky. Everything around me is so beautiful and orderly, and yet Thandi Shezi's testimony will not leave my head and nothing could be uglier than what was done to her. The disjuncture between the clean exteriors of both cities, and what happened in their shadows, in the dark places apartheid hid from view, feels overwhelming. I think about Thandi Shezi alone in the police cells and it feels like I might split in half from the tension of it, from trying to hold both the country's history and its tenuous present together in my mind; trying to reconcile what has been done with how we plan a future together.

I can't go home. Instead I go to my office. It is dark but there is a security guard there so I feel safe. I switch on the lights and turn on my computer. I need to write this report while it is still fresh, before the days pass and dull the emotion.

My colleagues on the other side of the Indian Ocean are not expecting such a soulful report from the frontlines. They have no idea what to do with the pieces of my heart that land on their computer screens. It doesn't matter, though: I am writing for myself. Scattered throughout my memo are notes, a blueprint for how I will make myself South African. I report on the TRC thoughtfully, analytically and with an outsider's eye. This is how – in the years to come – I will work my way into the heart of this country. This job will help me to go to places I would not go on my own – to townships where I know no one and to rural parts of the country where I am a stranger. It will be awkward every time I introduce myself, when I appear lost, when I have to tell a long backstory to explain why I don't speak the language, how I am still learning. The TRC makes me want to be South African even as it shows me how lightly I got off – how lucky my childhood was. It eases the longing I had as a child, even as it ignites a curiosity that I know will never fully be satisfied – a longing for answers about how people survived and how they would make it into the future without tearing themselves apart.

South Africa pulls at the parts of me that are the softest, and appeals to my toughest instincts. Like Jason, the country is manic and self-involved and consumed by its own logic. And, like Jason, this only makes me love it more – I want to save South Africa. Of course, like Jason, South Africa doesn't need saving. She only needs to be loved without judgement, to be accepted for who she is. To be cried with and tolerated when she is awful and to be embraced when she is at her best. It takes me twenty years to understand this: South Africa doesn't need heroes; she needs the best type of friends – those who bear witness.

Simon

WE MEET IN my office on a warm winter's morning in 1997.

He is handsome – tall with blue eyes and a slightly floppy haircut and a smile that stays in his eyes just like in the movies. He has a great chin – with a cleft like a character in a Mills & Boon novel. There is something reserved in him, something lovely and kind that seems unaware of or uninterested in the coincidental way in which his mouth and his nose line up on his face. I warm to him immediately. He has none of the white saviour sanctimony I have already encountered in other experts I've been assigned to work with in my new job with the

Australian High Commission, and so we hit it off.

He is in the country to help with the drafting of South Africa's first national youth policy. So we talk shop, and in the context of the discussion, he asks me if I want to attend the launch of the policy in Cape Town. He's flying back to Australia – where he's from – the following evening but I say I'll get back to him about it in a few days over email. As we part he promises to get me a formal invite and I find myself smiling, thinking it would be nice to talk to him again.

A few days after he leaves, South Africa's first national census results are released. It's the first time most black people in the country have been counted and it has been a massive and important undertaking. Over a hundred thousand people have been employed as enumerators; for a year there have been television and radio ads urging people to participate and explaining the importance of the day.

In previous censuses, the townships where black people lived had been ignored. Census gazettes simply hadn't listed townships. Millions of black people had disappeared. They had been real enough to work in white homes and businesses as domestic workers and labourers, but for purposes of planning and infrastructure, they were ghosts.

I go through the census summary closely, cross-checking it against the much larger report that has been sent to the office. There is an incredible amount of detail in there – a lot of which I think might be important for the new youth policy. I get excited when I think about the fact that South Africa is literally remaking itself. Every new policy, every bureaucratic process feels revolutionary because it is done in the name of democracy. This is not a state intent on counting us in to destroy us, it is a state that wants to know its citizens better in order to understand their needs. In my enthusiasm, I fax Simon a summary document that outlines what the census is telling the nation. It's about thirty pages long although, of course, when he tells the story he will insist it was at least fifty pages and it finished the toner in his home fax machine. I stand at the machine late at night after digesting the contents of the census. I am oblivious to the fact that it is 3 a.m. in Perth and the sound of a fax machine whirring in the study has just woken up a man I like, thousands of kilometres and an ocean away.

Still, he is gracious. He sends me a warm and funny thank-you note that teases me about the fax that was so urgent it needed to be sent at 3 a.m. He makes me smile and now I am curious about him. I think about him the whole day, opening the message a few times unnecessarily and finally realising I might like him a bit.

A few weeks later he is back in the country – this time in Cape Town for the national youth policy launch. I don't go but I like the fact that he called to say hi on his way through to Cape Town.

On his next trip, we agree to go out to lunch. I wear a maroon business suit which looks great but I am worried my forehead is breaking out in pimples. Still, I am pleased with the intimidating height of my head wrap. He pretends not to notice the spots and compliments the head wrap. I am impressed he doesn't call it a turban. Over lunch, I wait for an awkward moment, a misstep when he says or does the wrong thing, but it never comes. He's easy and funny and self-deprecating. There's no pathos as there was with Jason.

He goes back and we start to send each other daily e-mails. He writes things like, 'It was good to see you yesterday. I wondered whether you have seen Leunig's cartoons? He expresses vulnerability so well. That whole thing I was telling you about fatal optimism... Here is a scan of one of my favourite illustrations.'

We flirt in those notes, saying more on the computer than we might face to face. Still, we are restrained. These are the days before the widespread use of laptops. I check e-mail only when I am in the office and there is something about being in the company of others when I write to him that keeps me from saying everything I want to.

He is in and out of the country all the time so it feels fun and light despite the fact that he is so clearly perfect for me. His absence helps to slow things down as well. I don't need to see him all the time. I don't have to think about where it is all going. I can hang out with everyone else and not have a boyfriend. We become friends. We are attracted to each other and the attraction makes the hanging out more fun but this is new territory for us both.

Then it happens. We are no longer checking each other out. We go out to dinner at a restaurant in a pretty suburb of Pretoria one evening. The place is called Giovanni's – a converted old house that had been grand and charming and is not a favourite haunt of the diplomatic corps and international NGOs in Pretoria. It is raining and we sit on the veranda. The raindrops are big, the kind that always fall at the end of a humid day during a Highveld summer.

We order and get comfortable. I slip off my shoes and I'm barefoot under the table. We dig into a conversation about his divorce, about his two children; about heartbreak and loneliness. My feet find his and they rest on the tops of his shoes. My hands clasp his and, if I could, I would sit on his lap, curl into him as though we were alone. It's the first time I've ever felt so connected to a man. Everything he says strikes me as poignant. Our fingers twist and play, and I can smell his neck and I want to sit closer to him and it is clear that we are now an us.

Of course, the feeling is one thing. The reality is another.

Simon is a decade older than me and he has kids and he is white and none of these things are part of my game plan. I raged against whiteness in college; I poured my heart into poems about beautiful black love. I am in South Africa, where we have just defeated white supremacy, and I am in love with a white boy It makes no sense.

I want him to be black but he is not and this is South Africa where white people have collectively done some fucked-up shit to black people and he can never ever be angry enough about it to satisfy me. How could he be? He grew up on the beach in Perth, in a city on the other side of the Indian Ocean where it was always sunny. What does he know of suffering?

In my self-righteousness, in my search for a frame to suit the politics I've embraced in the past few years, I don't ask what I know of suffering let alone what love has to do with suffering. I stew and I steam. I rage and, eventually, I decide it can't work.

The conversation is hard, more so because it's not about him, or about me, but about an ideology, an idea of myself I'd like to hold onto as the sort of radical young woman whose politics and life are pure and clean.

'Let's take a break,' I say. 'I can't do this.'

He has seen this coming for weeks. It's been almost a year and he's met my sisters and he's met Mummy once. I have not been able to introduce him yet to Baba. We have had fight after fight about racism. I've snapped at him for smiling too hard at the car guard and for making conversation with waiters. 'Patronising,' I spit out. He can't do anything right. I am starting to dislike myself, and who I become when I am trying to perform my politics.

He is heartbroken and, in a different way, I am too.

I am alone again. Suddenly the self-righteousness that propelled me to break up feels hollow. There is nothing satisfactory about walking into a restaurant without the stares and the titters that used to accompany us. I miss him.

Still, I sustain my position. I date a bit. Nothing serious. I keep the door open to him. I don't want him to disappear completely in spite of my words to the contrary. Something inside me is cleverer than my brain.

His messages are always muted. He doesn't say 'I love you' any more but I know he wants to. Sometimes he still writes me notes the way he used to, brimming with detail – with observations about the weather and the wind and the sun. He was a man who had been a boy who had lived by the sea and these movements, the changes associated with the seasons, matter to him and carry a poignancy I simply hadn't thought about until we met. Other times he just says, 'How are you?' and the brevity of these messages makes me think maybe his love is fading, makes me worry about what might happen if he got fed up and left my life completely.

Mummy asks after him often and I'm always short with her. 'Where is that nice Simon?' My answer is always the same. 'I have no idea, Mummy.' It is none of her business if we are still in touch. I refuse to acknowledge her questions as a subtle signal of acceptance. In her quiet Swazi way Mummy is saying, 'He is as different from you as he is and still you love him, and so will I. If you love him, then I will too.'

It is 1999 and Nelson Mandela is no longer the president and South Africa is still free. Freedom means many things in the new South Africa. For Zeng and me it means sleeping in on a rainy Cape morning. Sheets of rain blow past the little garden flat Zeng is renting in Woodstock. It is grey and foggy and our heads are sore – mine more than hers. We are lying on her bed.

We drank too much last night. I was so drunk I smoked cigarettes and pretended to be French. Zeng holds her liquor better – more practice. So she took care of me. It was a nice role reversal, the little sister guiding her sloppy drunk big sis to the car. She is in her second year at UCT and I've quit my job to pursue a second degree. Baba and Uncle Stan have been adamant I won't progress in my career if I don't get a postgraduate degree. So I have just started my master's in the politics department while working a parttime job.

My stomach is churning. I don't know whether to sit or stand. I don't let myself get drunk often so when it happens there is always a story. I am a hilarious drunk.

Zeng relishes the moment. She's usually the one with a hangover so she is smug and amused. I think I might vomit. I get up and immediately I have to lie down again. I will never drink again, I groan. Zeng laughs. She is sunlight, even when I feel like death. She has no pity but I'm glad we're together. I missed her when she moved to Cape Town. The house in Pretoria wasn't the same without her. Mummy and Baba were rarely there – busy with their projects. So we've reconnected and in Cape Town she has her crew but she makes time for me. She no longer adores me – we are peers now. Something has happened to shift her, to make her capable of dispensing advice, not just of receiving my wisdom.

In spite of my sorry state, she wants to talk. I don't want to listen but I'm too discombobulated to object. She shifts to stand next to the window because she knows cigarettes bug me. I watch the smoke curl and disappear – translucent against the grey sky. I wish vaguely that I could be more like her – unconcerned with what Mummy and Baba think and, so, able to drink and wear their sighs with a shrug. I was too scared of them to experiment with smoking as a teenager and, even now, their disapproval looms large. Even being here is – at least, in part – a function of my desire to make them proud. Zeng seems – at least, on the surface – to suffer no such desires. She is who she is and she does what she likes.

So classically 'first' and 'last' born are we that it binds us. We seem cast in stone. Mandla is still in America but she is as much a middle child as we are first and last. Often, our advice to one another emanates from this knowledge – that our birth order has determined our stance towards Mummy and Baba, but it also plays a role in how we see the world. We may be grown-up but in some ways our parents are still the planets around which we orbit. In so many of my decisions – even when I am not in direct conversation with them – I seek their approval. Mandla, on the other hand, is constantly fighting to be herself – to be recognised and heard – so she is headstrong even in her relative silence. And of course Zeng – the lovely one who lags – manages to appear as though she doesn't care even when she does.

So today I lie in bed and it hurts my head to even breathe, but she's cracking me up, reminding me of last night. Thinking about it in retrospect, the scene – the conversation, the smoke, the nausea – is a marker of how we are becoming women.

She is talking about the French man whose accent I imitated last night. I had blanked that out. We laugh. 'Can I 'ave a cigarette?' she says, reminding me of my ridiculousness. 'Babes, you talked like that all night. To the guy's face.' If it didn't hurt, I would laugh harder. 'Shame, poor Frenchman. He didn't know what hit him. He was cute, though.' I'm about to roll my eyes but she changes the subject again – so quickly I feel dizzy.

'Speaking of cute white boys, babes, can we talk about the shocking hypocrisy of breaking up with someone because he's white?'

My cheeks flush. I am embarrassed and angry. Black Power angry.

'How is that hypocrisy?' I retort.

'It's hypocrisy because you love him.' She is telling the truth.

'I am not sure if I do.' I'm lying.

'Please, babes. You weren't scared off by the fact that he has kids. It doesn't bother you that he is a decade older than you. You aren't disturbed by the existence of an ex wife. You're not worried about the fact that he lives in bloody Australia – Over There or Down Under or whatever they call it. You've got over all these pretty major things. After all that, you break up with him for no real reason? Please. You're just worried about what people will say.'

I am quiet because I know she is right.

'Yup. All your activist radical talk, and look, you've fallen in love with a white guy.' She is not saying this unkindly. She is just stating the obvious.

I stay quiet because she is still right. My silence gives her permission to continue. I keep listening

'And I get it. I mean, I don't really because I'd be psyched if anyone loved me like that. But I get it. And maybe you need to rethink the politics so they fit you better. Like maybe the theories are like pointers, like general guidelines. Then there's how you practise them. I mean, if you took it all to its logical conclusion you'd be married to a black lesbian who is five foot nine with dreads because the only lover who can ever know what it's like to be you is you. It's crazy, babes.'

She is right again.

Rejecting Simon is mainly about this idea I have in my head of who I am. I'm stubbornly clinging to a political position I arrived at in the absence of love – when I was in college and charged with a righteousness that was deeply powerful and naively abstract – instead of deciding that it's more complex than I want it to be. I'm not powerless in the face of love, but, simplistic and naive as they sounded, I can't ignore the two core tenets of my upbringing, the big ideas that guided my life until college. The first is that race is fiction, a myth the Boers and the slavers in America made up to oppress us. Growing up, families like the Jeles and the Mfenes – where the mothers were white and the fathers were African – were testament to the absurdity of race. The second was that kindness and fairness were important. Objections to interracial love in a racist world make sense to me. I can't reject them. In the end, though, it boils down to this: I prefer having Simon in my life to not having him. I would rather work through our disagreements and fight until we are exhausted than walk away from this man I love – who loves me more completely than any man ever has. This knowledge is more powerful than any intellectual debate. I have to learn to accept the contradictions. This is one that I will wrestle with over and over across the years; some questions are never resolved. Clichéd as it sounds, we live the questions and it is in the joy and the pain of asking them – of being asked the questions in sometimes sharp and hard ways – that we find meaning.

So, still half-drunk and vomity, I listen to my sister. Then I text him: 'Come see me in Cape Town?' He says yes.

◆ ◆ ◆

Simon and I married in 2003. We have two children. Over the years, we have made our way and the making of our way has become our way – our path and our progress. We have learnt that it is not us against the world; that sometimes our fights are precisely about us and how we are in the world. His love and patience have taught me that love is a grappling, and ours is like every other love on the planet: often too hard and sometimes bitter but always available in abundance. In our hardest moments, we have still loved one another. Simon does not talk about -isms in the same way I do. He understands them and tries his best. His views are sensible and smart and sometimes profound. He believes in God and I am sceptical about God. I have learnt not to be bothered by his faith just as he is unperturbed by the lack of mine. I have learnt to respect and admire his belief, to respect the fact that he goes to church when he wants to and that when he doesn't feel like it, he doesn't. He is freer of dogma than anyone I have met, yet he has an unshakeable sense of himself and I have come to understand that he owes a large part of his emotional stability to his belief in God.

I have learnt to appreciate his commitment to and love for the ocean. It enriches me and gives me a sense of wonder. I admire his feeling for the seas because I know that it carried him through a childhood that was sometimes lonelier than it ought to have been.

He has taught me that love is not based on sameness or difference. Through him I have discovered that love lives in its own dimension and whereas it is connected to real life – to objects and systems and elements that are solid – it is also mysterious.

I love his children. When I meet her, Gabi is coltish and scared. She is only eleven and has her father's uncertain smile and she carries in her the same hurt in her eyes, the same determination to be okay even when she is not. Nick is laid back. He is eight when I first set eyes on him and he is wearing a necklace with a shark's tooth on the end. He loves the sea. He is naturally cool. He wants his father to love him so he laughs at my jokes.

In time, we all grow to love one another because we decide that we will love one another. They are part of him but my love for them must be worked on. They have a mother and I am only a young woman – someone who knows nothing about children in Australia.

But I love him so I decide to love them. They make it easy. Their mother is good and honest and kind and she makes it easier still. We live our way into our life. I don't know how else to say this: our life is our life and we learn not to explain or apologise. We learn only to give in to what it is that life and love are asking of us.

Mummy and Baba love Simon. They are too kind themselves, too human and filled with the morality of their generation, to ignore the kindness in his eyes. Mummy makes him her son, and his gratitude for her love and acceptance is a joy to observe.

In the early days I have moments where I wonder whether this was the right thing to do. Sometimes, for long stretches I lose my patience because, when you are young and there is much to do, even love seems expendable. During these times I pepper him with questions and expect him to give textbook answers. He fails all my tests. Even when he sees them coming, he fails my quizzes. In time we both realise he will never pass any test designed as a trap.

He has his doubts too. His fears are about my capacity to be better behaved than I often am. He will wonder whether he should believe in me or whether he should just accept me as I am. He will wonder if he should leave and sometimes the answer is not clear because I give him so little to hold onto.

He is kinder, gentler, more thoughtful and more steadfast than anyone I know. He is my patience and in time I learn to be his temper. When he encounters meanness I take his side. I am loyal to who he is at his best and even when he is at his lowest I know who he can be and when he doesn't remember, I do. If he is wrong we figure it out together but because so often he is too quick to blame himself I learn that he is seldom wrong in matters of the heart. Still, we have our complications.

Simon teaches me how to *be* in love. He teaches me that living in love means existing, over long and sometimes painful periods, as no one but yourself in the presence of another. To be yourself alone is one thing. To be yourself in a partnership is a gift.

I let him love me. I love him and my love grows fiercer and less liable to fall apart when it is tested.

Anyone who has ever loved and been loved will know what I mean when I say that I resigned myself to loving Simon. I have learnt to hold us close and that means shrugging at attempts to define us in ways that diminish what we have gone through and who we are to each other simply because others are curious about my blackness and his whiteness, as if that could ever be the most definitive thing there is to say about us.

Aids

THE TRANSITION – WHICH has been fluid and exciting in these early years – is suddenly turning into something hard and unyielding. Aids is everywhere. Every newspaper headline, every billboard. Suddenly it seems everyone is dying at once. Aunties are dying quietly and uncles are slipping away. No one wants to say what it is, even though we all know. At work, people begin to disappear slowly into their clothes, their mouths drying out and their tongues turning to cotton wool.

Aids oozes and seeps and leaks across the country, winding its way into every community, into even the hardest hearts. Everybody it seems is sick or sad or both.

The only person in the country who seems not to be grieving is the president. Instead, he seems outraged that our glorious story is turning to shit because of this Aids nonsense. He seems convinced the media is over-reporting it. Worse, he begins to flirt with denial-ists, spending time reading up on the subject and com-municating, in imperious and confusing ways, about an epidemic he says is about poverty rather than dis-ease. The points he makes are academic. He pontificates and his words get bigger and bigger and he sounds more and more pompous until I think to myself one day he might fly away like a balloon full of self-generated heli-um. He skirts around what he wants to say but his ac-tions are clear. He does nothing. This slows down the machinery of the state.

As the denial deepens and his stubbornness and in-ability to accept he is wrong deepen into a crisis, there comes a point where I cannot bear to look at him any more. But he does not fly away and I cannot ignore the president of the country that has gradually become mine.

President Mbeki stays firmly tethered to the ground, kept in place by a political party that is growing more and more cowardly in the face of his outrageous con-duct. Because his tone is never fiery, and because he is known for his erudition, his denialism wears the robes of reasonableness. He sounds statesmanlike, even when the implications of his 'reasoning' are so bleak.

His Aids dissidence is met with increasing outrage. Journalists write and editors editorialise but nothing happens. Instead, those who question the weird science he endorses are accused of racism and of undermining the president. We are all told we want to see an uppity black man fail.

The more Mbeki is pushed to change his approach,

and the more loudly he is told to hurry up and help the sick and the dying by providing the medicines they need, the more obstinate he becomes. These years are difficult for me because Aids is not simply an issue in the headlines. I am now working for the United Nations, and the focus of my work is sexual and reproductive health. Aids sits firmly in the middle of my portfolio. I live and breathe statistics. I work with a team of activists who believe Aids is the struggle of our generation. Whereas our parents were called upon to fight racism, our job will be to address socioeconomic rights, to ensure the Constitution isn't simply an empty document that lets South Africa's people down.

So, Aids arrives as a painful syndrome that strips the best and brightest of our generation of energy and, in too many cases, of life itself. When the president begins to deny it, many of us are shocked. At first, we try to engage him. We listen respectfully as he pronounces on the matter. But it becomes clear very quickly that the fight we must take on is as much about the right to health as it is about the rights we have to question, to protest and to influence government policy.

President Mbeki's dismissiveness jolts us out of complacency and reminds us that democracy will have to be defended.

The president's official spokesman – a man who has issued statements on his behalf for years, a man who has sat beside him in aeroplanes as he has crisscrossed the globe, a man who has fielded media requests and honed his speeches over a period of years, a man the president may be tempted to call a brother – begins to shrink. He is not-so-slowly dying of Aids even as the president insists the illness exists as a function of poverty rather than being a virus that can be directly identified.

The public shakes its head, disbelieving of the spectacle that is unfolding in the most awful way possible. The president is naked and the man who said he wears the finest clothes in the land is now dead – killed by the very virus they refute.

The spokesperson is a man named Parks Mankahlana. He has been one of Mbeki's faithful, which means that he was struck by the same peculiar strain of madness that afflicted his boss. Mbeki seems to be embarrassed to admit that an STD is ruining our economy and diminishing our human development indicators. It seems somehow beneath us.

Mbeki can't see that apartheid has written this virus into our landscape, that it is evident that the virus spread because of the infrastructure of apartheid, because of the social dynamics created by that system. Instead, Mbeki looks for bogeymen – Western aid agencies over-inflating the statistics and pharmaceutical companies looking to find cheap markets in Africa.

I attend National AIDS Council meetings. There are many updates about who is doing what. There are announcements about comrades who have passed away. There are resolutions about letters that need to be written. But as the crisis deepens, the meetings become bigger, more impassioned. The comrades from the Treatment Action Campaign (TAC) swell our ranks. There are marches. Zackie Achmat stops taking his ARVs until all South Africans have access to them and Nelson Mandela is sent to tell him to resume treatment – for the sake of the country, the old man says, we need you alive.

We begin to wear T-shirts that proclaim 'HIV Positive'. We are all HIV-positive as an act of solidarity, as a statement about justice. Finally, when the nation is on its knees, when the ANC has been torn apart by the obstinacy of a president who is increasingly aloof and disdainful; after our rulers have spent far too long squabbling among themselves, and the trust they once had is beginning to fray; when Mbeki has been begged and begged to stop; after there have been marches and sit-ins and die-ins; after South Africa has become a virtual pariah and media around the world have puzzled about the land of Mandela and its strange new president – it is only after all this, and the deaths of hundreds of thousands of black people, when the government itself has been sued for letting people live with the virus without giving them the medicines that would ease their suffering, the government begins to supply ARVs.

The activists win. The media wins. The state is forced to pay for drugs to prevent HIV transmission in pregnancy and to purchase ARVs to prevent deaths among those already infected. The victory is significant.

Mbeki never fully backs down – but the state is compelled to deliver and so it does. He remains a glowering presence in our politics. The ANC government concedes that it was reckless – that it should have acted earlier. But it is too late. By this time, I have stopped believing that the leaders of the ANC are somehow special. I should never have believed it in the first place; that sort of thinking is dangerous. But I did because I grew up in a magical bubble, in a time and place in which the worst excesses of the liberation struggle were invisible to me and the best of what we could be had been laid out in front of me, painted like a picture with words of strength and struggle and dangled before me by the uncles and aunties who danced in our living room.

It has taken some time to see the truth, which is that the leaders of the ANC are no better and no worse than anyone else. It has taken the loss of needless lives for me finally to understand this. I find it hard to believe that the authors of the wretchedness that ruined a generation were the same magical comrades who made Lusaka feel like home, but I have little choice. Denial is a privilege we can't afford.

During that long and painful season of denial and paranoia, I begin to see that the pride of the ANC – the very thing that kept us strong in the long years before freedom – will be this country's undoing.

I know, as I watch this scene play out, that Mbeki and his acolytes are drunk on pride. And I know, too, from having watched President Kaunda on television in Zambia and having chased President Moi's motorcade in Kenya, that it was the combination of power and pride that made these men so callous.

The pain of ordinary people is less important than Mbeki's need to be right. Mbeki is willing to sacrifice the country over his ego. In the end it is this, more than anything else, that makes me lose my religion.

As a child I had adored them. I had soaked in their pride and basked in it and grown strong in it. As a young woman, finally home and trying to be something new and without burdens, I had discovered that they were not simply proud – they were excessively opinionated. I saw that what had felt like dignity in the dark days was actually haughtiness. They reeked of grandeur and it made me nauseous.

It has been tempting, sometimes, for me to want to read into all this a sense of inevitability; a feeling that, no matter how courageous Africans have been, once they are in charge they succumb to corruption and paranoia. The truth is, of course, that Frederick Douglass was right:

Power concedes nothing without a demand. It never did and it never will. Find out just what any people will quietly submit to and you have found out the exact measure of injustice and wrong which will be imposed upon them, and these will continue till they are resisted with either words or blows, or with both. The limits of tyrants are prescribed by the endurance of those whom they oppress.

Our leaders do what they do because we allow it and we allow it because we remember the sins of the past and that past was awful. So we find ourselves trapped – the callousness of the present is excused by the horror of the past. Some people in South Africa want us to accept this. In the early years of our new dispensation – when democracy is still new and we are still naive and young – we refuse to accept this. We learn the most important rules for a healthy democracy. First you fight. Then you win. Repeat.

Amakwerekwere

OUR FRIEND ALAIN confesses that, until he met us, he had never been invited to a meal at the homes of any of his South African friends. We are sitting outside in the little grassy area set aside for Mandla's use in the small townhouse complex where she lives. She bought the place when she got her first job, working for a parastatal in Sandton. Her neighbours are all young professionals – mainly white. None of them bother us. Even when there is a small get-together like this one, they are unperturbed.

Until now, we have been relaxed and laughing. It is a perfect summer afternoon. Alain is an integral part of a group of friends we all loosely call The Guys. The Guys are from Congo and they have been regaling us with stories about their early days in South Africa; the talk has revolved around the 'liberated' women of South Africa, and their jealous boyfriends. We love these stories. Their descriptions of South Africa are like a Zouk version of Sting's 'Englishman in New York'. You could not find two more different groups of Africans than South Africans and Congolese.

South Africans are totally uninterested in chic. The township aesthetic that is in fashion in the late 1990s and early 2000s includes wide-leg shortened pants, shiny Carvela shoes and striped casual shirts for men. The Guys can't get their heads around the look. They wear linen shirts of the finest French fabric, and pressed jeans or Lacoste shirts and Italian moccasins.

Like so many of the Congolese men I know, Alain – who has just devastated me with his statement – is lean and well groomed. He is also outrageously funny, and incredibly gracious. You want Alain in the room when you are having a party because he will talk to everyone and make them feel at home.

I immediately understand the reason why no one has invited The Guys to their homes. I am hit by a wave of shame. I stand up and take my plate inside, pretending I want more food. I stand over the sink – out of sight for a moment – and brush away tears.

The Guys are a brotherhood to match our sisterhood. It is impossible to be friends with only one of The Guys, just as it is impossible to be friends with only one of the Msimang sisters. We are all a package deal.

Alain is in marketing. He works at Cadbury but his dreams are bigger than advertising accounts and marketing budgets. He is a genius – as he is fond of telling anyone who will listen. He manages to be a ladies' man and a sweetheart all at once. When we first met I often wondered how he broke their hearts – if he just went quiet, or if they knew from the minute they met him how it would end.

Willie is Alain's brother. He is married to Simone and they have two beautiful daughters, Ntita and Taifa. Willie's personality is so large we don't need to see him a lot to feel that he is with us. He fills up any room. He's a rooster – compact and self-assured. He specialises in a bit of this and a bit of that. He makes us all laugh, often until we are crying, with his stories about ending up in places he should not have been and surviving by the skin of his teeth.

Paul is quiet and brooding (he rarely smiles but he has a big heart) and Jean-Pierre (whom everyone calls JP) is a talented architect whose smile is beatific and who can moonwalk like Michael Jackson.

The Guys arrived in South Africa just as the Mobutu regime was falling, in 1990. In those days they wore turned-up pink shirts and sharp shoes and expensive linen trousers. They have the flair of the famously flamboyant Les Sapeurs, but are too level-headed to plunge headlong into an obsession that has eaten at the pockets of so many of their country folk.

They came to South Africa because the schools in Lubumbashi were closed. Zaire was on the verge of obsolescence, a relic of a bygone era that was replaced by a new country with old borders and habits that would not die: Congo. The Guys made it out just in time. As they left, the country was becoming nothing more than a series of territories no longer connected by Mobutu's strong hand. They came to South Africa in search of a future and found a country that seemed calm and ordinary, even as it was in the throes of political turmoil and uncertainty. South Africa was conflicted but stable.

When they arrived, everything about the country was on the verge of being new. The Guys would marvel at the buildings and the roads and the sheer weight of South Africa's history – the imprint white people and black labour have left here. Johannesburg was not just old, it had been built to last. It was there to stay.

The boys enrolled at the University of the Witwatersrand. Their parents were middle class and Congo was not yet in flames so they could afford the tuition. It was easier here than in Belgium or France – where so many Congolese men their age were going. The ones who went to Europe often never returned. They got lost there in suburbs where they were despised, in a country that would refuse to let them forget they were the children of King Leopold's chattel. So, they chose South Africa where at least, they thought, they may have the protection of Nelson Mandela. It was a country where their dreams could be as large as their healthy egos, where the limits of their grandeur would not be prescribed by stereotypes about the continent on which they were born. Or so they thought.

They met girls and flirted. They got part-time jobs, supplementing the small allowances their parents sent by cutting hair and modelling. The modelling was possible because of the emergence of a new market of black people with access to credit. With freedom came an increasing number of Africans with accounts at Joshua Doore and Truworths. They had grown up with a francophone aesthetic. They were happy to make a bit of extra cash just by being who they were.

The Guys settled well. By the time we met them, they

knew the city far better than we did. This included the most fun parts of Hillbrow, where the other Congolese gathered. They knew the drug dealers and the businessmen, the politicians and their children. The Guys always moved around together – not in a group that was too big, but seldom alone. They smiled and made the right jokes and were careful not to make enemies. They knew all the spots: nightclubs and wine bars, rooftop hangouts and salsa parties.

I got to know them through Mandla. They met at a house party. She was quiet and kind and one of them took a liking to her. And so they became her friends and soon Zeng and Simon and I were in the mix, too, spending almost every weekend with them. They fitted well into our broader social network: Gael and Richard, who were French and South African; Micheline, who was Ugandan via America; Lauren, an African-American woman who had come to work and never gone back. There was Nana from Rwanda, who had grown up with The Guys in Lubumbashi, and her husband Craig, a white boy from Johannesburg's northern suburbs.

We explored South Africa together – the lot of us. The Guys were at our wedding in 2003. We booked weekends away. We went to Dullstroom and Warmbaths and Cape Town and Durban. We hiked Thaba Nchu and swam in freezing-cold springs and lay in the sun to warm up again. We ate well – *uphutu* and yams and cassava and the finest terrines and hot crusty bread. We were everything the new South Africa was supposed to be – cosmopolitan and successful and free.

Except the ugly truth was that our friends from Europe and America had a far easier time of it in South Africa than The Guys. Although they were upwardly mobile and had good jobs and a wide circle of friends,

The Guys had a harder time with work permits and visas than our European friends. They also struggled more with black South Africans, who were hostile when they encountered black people who did not speak local African languages. The Guys knew from too many angry or dismissive interactions that, in the eyes of many, they were merely *amakwerekwere*: people 'from Africa'.

Alain's admission reminds me of how often I had flinched when I had come home, when I was still adjusting to life in South Africa. I was often struck by the odd way in which the term 'Africa' was deployed by South Africans – irrespective of race. People would ask me where I was from because I speak with an American/British/Kenyan accent – the result of our family's wanderings. I would explain that I was born to South African parents outside the country and that I had lived in Zambia and Kenya and Canada and that my family also lived in Ethiopia. Invariably, the listener would nod sympathetically until the meaning of what I was saying sank in.

The conversation always followed the same lines, like a dance people had been taught in school. 'So you grew up in Africa.' The word 'Africa' was enunciated carefully, the last syllable drawn out and slightly raised as though the statement were actually a question. Then the inevitable, softly sighed, 'Shame.' Sympathy and muted horror playing at their lips.

It took me some time to figure out how to respond to the idea that Africa began beyond South Africa's borders but did not include our very own country, which sits firmly on the African continent. I was surprised to learn that the countries where I had lived – the ones that had nurtured my soul in the long years of exile – were actually no places at all in the minds of some of my compatriots.

They weren't geographies with their own histories and cultures and complexities. Instead, they were dark landscapes, Conradian and densely forested. Zambia and Kenya might as well have been Venus and Jupiter. They were undefined and not easily definable. They were snake-filled thickets, impenetrable brush and war and famine and ever-present tribal danger.

Although they thought themselves to be very different, whites and blacks in South Africa were disappointingly similar when it came to their views on 'Africa'. At first I blamed apartheid: South Africa had been both isolated and insular. Its very survival had depended on scare tactics.

I thought that, over time, with exposure and the new openness that followed the fall of apartheid, South Africans would stop fearing the continent and begin to understand that their place in the world was bound up in their place on the continent.

I couldn't see that this flattened and stereotypical view of Africa was at the very heart of the idea of South Africa itself. Just as whiteness means nothing until it is contrasted with blackness as savagery, South Africanness relies heavily on the construction of Africa as a place of dysfunction, chaos and violence to define itself as functional, orderly, efficient and civilised.

The apartheid state kept its borders firmly closed to ensure that the African savages at its doorstep would not get in. 'Africa' was a bogeyman, of course, used to set up the paranoia that would keep the National Party in power. But whites were not the only targets of the bogeyman. Black people were told that the Africans beyond South Africa's borders lived like animals; they were ruled by despots and governed by black magic. In a society that taught black people to hate themselves, the message was easily assimilated.

There have been periodic outbreaks of violence aimed at foreigners since I returned. These are the vicious evidence of the noninvitations The Guys talk about when we first meet. They flare up then die down. The government is reactive but it seems that, in the times between flare-ups, little is done to address the economic competition and isolation that lie at the heart of the conflicts.

Then quite quickly a new season of violence is upon us. For two weeks in May 2008, South Africa burns with rage as community after community attacks foreigners from the rest of the African continent. The violence begins on the edge of Johannesburg, in Alexandra township, and spreads through the province. Within a few weeks, parts of Durban and Cape Town are also in flames as are townships in places like Limpopo.

People from Mozambique and Zimbabwe bear the brunt of the 2008 attacks but a number of South Africans who are assumed to be 'illegals' are also killed. Nationalist rage is often imprecise. Over three hundred shops are looted and over two hundred burned down. Hundreds of people are injured, thousands forced to flee. At the end of it all there are sixty-two dead bodies.

During those horrifying weeks, Ernesto Nhamuave is attacked and set alight in an informal settlement on the eastern flank of Johannesburg. A crowd watches as he burns to death. His dying moments are immortalised when a photographer captures them. In spite of the media attention, Nhamuave's family never receives justice. The case is closed in 2010 after police conclude that the suspects are unknown and there are no witnesses. Yet the murder happened in public, in front of cameras.

Everyone knows who the killers are but no one is prepared to speak up.

In a newspaper article I read at the time, the following lines hit me in the solar plexus: 'The woman sees the killers at least once a week. Her recounting of details surrounding Nhamuave's death has remained consistent for nearly seven years, when she first revealed details of the murder. At the time she was willing to speak to police. "But the police never came here. Now, I don't trust the police here," she said.'

None of the attacks on foreigners involves Europeans or Americans. White foreigners are never the targets of mass mobilisations of outrage. In daily life whites may fall victim to crime but they are seldom deliberately targeted for the sorts of political and economic anger that inspires xenophobia. It is black foreigners – deemed to be taking jobs and women from locals and bringing crime and drugs and filthy habits here – who are the problem in the minds of many South Africans in 2008.

◆ ◆ ◆

When the violence sweeps through Johannesburg's inner-city areas in 2008 The Guys are never at risk. In addition, by this time they have been living and working in South Africa for many years, and have little to fear from police or immigration officials other than the arbitrary cruelty of personnel in uniform. Still, the violence has a chilling effect. It is intended to remind all African 'foreigners' that they are not welcome. The message to The Guys is that they will forever be from Congo and will always be strangers, no matter how many houses JP designs and builds and how many advertising campaigns Alain manages. Their citizenship is only a technicality.

In 2008 South Africa returns to its roots – reminding Alain and JP and Willie and their families that they will never really be South African. Home will always be another country.

Congo Road

A SMALL COVERED walkway leads directly to the kitchen door from the front entrance facing the road. The walkway – which smells like jasmine – is flanked on one side by a small garden and on the other by a mirror that reflects the garden back to the visitor coming in from the street. Ivy creepers and white roses and a few slender olive trees are planted delicately along the side of the house. Water burbles somewhere in the back. A small brown canary hops about on the immaculately placed pavers that plot a path around the house. We enter through the kitchen door, which is painted a subtle green. There is a lovely soft grey marble on the floors and the walls of the kitchen and beyond it lies a large living area filled with casual but expensive furniture. In the distance, through the living room windows, a generous veranda runs the length of the house. I catch my breath. This is it. This is the house we will grow old in. But before that, it is the house in which my children will be born. I imagine a baby crawling through the sliding doors. Then I picture another little one steadying himself in the archway that leads into the bedrooms.

I smile at Simon across the long passage that connects the front of the house to its hindquarters, where the bedrooms are. We see a future for ourselves here. The year before was difficult, and we are delicate but mending. The house will be yet another step in our process of reconnecting. We make an offer. We are acting impulsively but we don't mind. We trust our instincts. Within hours, the owner has accepted and we are the proud owners of a new house. In some ways, this house represents the new South African dream. Set in a gorgeous neighbourhood, close to public amenities and a public school that is walking distance away, it had once been off limits and now we have just bought it. Where once we would have been locked up for breaking the immorality laws, now we simply signed on the dotted line. Where once the neighbourhood would never have allowed black residents – other than the women who lived in the servants' quarters to enable the lifestyles of the occupants of the beautiful and large homes on the street – now we have neighbours of all races.

We say goodbye to the Melville house with its ultra-cool cement floors and its steep stairs. We will miss the glass doors and watching the electrical storms from our bedroom. Still, I am pregnant and if there were ever a time to nest, this seems to be it.

The February day we set for the move is sunny and warm. I have just passed the seven-month mark. The baby inside my belly feels as though she is filling up every available inch. She moves frequently and I wince a lot but I am active and strong. I have never been healthier or happier.

While Simon organises the movers in Melville, I drive myself to the new house early in the morning and survey it one last time before it is filled with our things. I take a short walk down the street to figure out which entrance the truck will need to use. The house stands on a large corner block, set a street away from a busy road. Large jacarandas line either side of the road. Their branches meet overhead, vine-covered and lovely against the Johannesburg summer sky. I decide we should use the main gate at the back of the house – close to the veranda. I push it open and it is heavier than I had estimated. I walk back to the veranda and sit on the stone step. The baby gives me a swift kick as if to say, 'Take it easy, mama,' and I smile. We've made a great decision.

◆ ◆ ◆

Until we moved into Congo Road we were living in Johannesburg, but our life in Melville had not been typical. We had travelled so much – both inside the country and outside it for work – that we had only been skimming the surface. The purchase of the Congo Road house, which is surrounded by properties whose manicured lawns and immaculately painted facades are clearly a point of pride and identity for their owners, forces us to reckon with a part of South Africa we have not yet encountered in any meaningful way. It is not until we move into this neighbourhood that I begin to understand that suburban South Africa is more than a geography. It is a place as haunting as it is manicured; a place lacking in soul and propelled by fear even as it is splashed in sunlight by day and bathed in streetlights by night.

◆ ◆ ◆

The Monday morning after the move we lie in bed and listen to traffic stream by. The road that runs past the house on one side is a shortcut, used by cars and taxis avoiding the main road. We might have discovered this had we waited a few weeks before making the offer. We would have known it had we driven past the house on a weekday, rather than allowing ourselves to be fooled by the Sunday afternoon peace. Simon counts over five hundred cars in an hour.

An hour later, I get up to go to the office. The traffic has not slowed. I wait at the corner for fifteen minutes – unable to turn into the road that will eventually take me to work. I am fuming. That afternoon at five I sit in a long queue of cars, stuck in traffic only a few metres from our front gate. I feel myself stiffen with rage. We have moved into the right house on the wrong street, which means, actually, that we have moved into the wrong house. This is a big problem. Having fallen in love with the house because it promised a calm and peaceful life, one in which there was no traffic, only canaries and sunshine, I feel as though I've been duped. By the end of the first week I am no longer prepared to give it a chance. I am unequivocal about it: I hate the house.

I dream up ways in which the previous owner has lied. I despise the agent. It is baseless, of course, but I can't shake the sense of betrayal.

Within months of our moving in, the housing bubble bursts. Not only have we bought a house that didn't live up to our expectations, we have massively overpaid for it. It seems we are doomed to stay in the house, no matter how we feel about it.

Simon is less disappointed than I am. He hasn't fallen for it quite as hard. For him, it's just a house. For me, of course, the house on Congo Road is supposed to be the final stop in a life spent wandering. The house where the children are born, where they will grow up, leave to go to university and come back for holidays. It's supposed to be the nest my sisters and I never had.

For middle-class black families like mine, the transition to democracy has proceeded in the most orderly way possible. There have been few hitches for our kind of new South African. The children of the elite families who were prepared for the transition have landed firmly on their feet. I don't want to admit it but I am used to things falling into place for me. I grew up in a warm and loving family. I was educated at elite schools. I attended a well-respected university in America. I married a great guy and I've had a successful career. Finding the 'perfect' house and then discovering it is flawed – albeit in ways that only matter to people who are privileged enough to worry about issues like traffic and noise – is a First World problem. I should be able to get over it but I can't. I find myself stuck – spiralling into worry and anxiety about the fact that this house is not going to work for us.

In the weeks before the baby is born, the feeling of being trapped deepens.

In the lush green suburbs the obviousness of our privilege begins to eat at us. The daily chores required to ensure that our home is well maintained put us in treacherous terrain. The system we have bought into is set up to convince us we can't do it on our own. Living in this house, and on this street, smacks of domination. It requires hedges clipped like so, and roofing tiled to a certain standard. It forces us to ask Baba Petros – the man who gardens and fixes – to redo his work. I am ashamed of the narcissism involved in maintaining the facade of the house. I had not realised that, in falling in love with the aesthetic and in buying the house, I was also pledging to oversee the labour that would be necessary to maintain it.

In exile we only thought about the Boers. We never imagined the houses – what they were like inside and how it felt to live in one. We lived in nice houses ourselves. We had maids and my sisters and I were little madams. Mummy and Baba had always explained that we should respect the aunties who worked in our houses. The difference, of course, was that now I was my own madam. I was no longer an innocent.

The house makes me complicit. Suddenly I hold shares in South Africa Inc., and my participation in a firm whose business I loathe makes me anxious. It takes me a long time to figure out that this is the core of all the troubles we experience in the house on Congo Road: it places us firmly in the heart of whiteness.

◆ ◆ ◆

While my discomfort feels all-consuming, there isn't anything that can be done about it. The baby is due in April and we have much to sort out. Our domestic arrangement has been loose until now. An older woman named Eunice comes in to clean the house twice a week. Simon and I are pretty self-sufficient and we both travel a lot for work so she is seldom busy. We call her Aunty, in the respectful manner that all younger black people call older black women in South Africa, regardless of employer-employee status.

We decide that when the baby arrives Aunty will continue to do the ironing and laundry but she is too old to task with looking after a small baby who will quickly become a toddler.

Simon and I regard Aunty with some degree of awe. Throughout the 1980s she lived – as she tells it – the life of a gangster. By her own account, she is a former drug dealer.

She boasts about wearing a floor-length mink coat on a South African Airways flight from Joburg to Durban in the 1980s before black people were even allowed to travel on planes. Then, she says, in the early 1990s she was arrested and, after her release (she doesn't say how long she was in for but Simon and I suspect it was no more than a few nights), she had a stroke and found Jesus. She got herself straightened out and she has been cleaning houses since then. Aunty splits her time between Mandla's townhouse and our place.

She's a skollie old aunty – enlisting the help of her extensive network of church mates and township pals to clean the houses of other people and taking a cut from each introduction to a new madam who agrees to employ one of her friends.

To supplement her income, she often sells Tupperware and cheap cutlery sets and faux-fancy watches. I am a regular, reluctant and captive customer. My cupboards are overflowing with low-cost Eetrite knives and forks because I can't say no to Aunty.

Beneath her hilarious stories and behind her quirkiness Aunty has her own stories of sadness. She lives with her sister Julia and they have raised Julia's child, Lizzie, together. Lizzie has given them a grandson – a handsome boy named Moeketsi, who is two when we first meet Aunty. Aunty doesn't have any biological children. She has told me that, before she became an independent woman who dealt drugs in order to have her own nice things and support Julia and Lizzy, she was married. He was a handsome Zulu man. He courted her with sweet words and warm smiles.

Soon they were married and, once he had her, he began to beat her. 'Zo,' she would say, with her creased lips twisted in anger, 'that man was cruel. So, so mean.' Things got worse when she failed to produce children. 'He never think to himself, why I never have kids even before this Eunice,' she would say, reasoning it out so many years later. 'For a man it is always the lady's fault.'

After eleven harrowing years, she called it quits.

When I tell her we need someone to help with the new baby, Aunty starts suggesting various friends. On this issue, however, my deference to her age and her street smarts retreats. I am an anxious mother-to-be and nothing feels more important than the decision about who will help to care for our child while we are working.

I even ignore Mummy who, like Aunty, has all sorts of ideas about which distant Swazi relative is best placed to move to Joburg to help raise this long-awaited first grandchild.

At my office, a colleague tells me about a young woman who had cared for twins with a disability for five years. Her name is Nikki and she's currently doing a bit of office admin for his wife in her home office. There isn't enough for her to do there, he says: 'She's lovely and needs work.'

When she arrives I am struck by how thin she is. She

is dressed conservatively, in a loose brown skirt and a white button-down top that is tucked in at the waist. Her hands are rough and dry and when I shake them I am surprised. Her grip is strong, though. Her straightened hair is pulled back severely off her face. Simon and I both say hello and she smiles and says hello back. Her smile changes everything; it is as wide as her cheek bones are high. Her teeth are perfect and, when we tease her in an attempt to ease her obvious nerves, her laugh is rich and genuine. She is both eager to please and open to spontaneity.

She tells us about her last job. She worked for an American lawyer, a single mother who had twins. The girls were premature. There were three of them but one died at birth. The other two lived but had some difficulties in the early months. Nikki started working for the lawyer when the girls were just eight weeks old. She changed the feeding tubes that were attached to their shrivelled navels, helped them stretch their tiny legs in the daily physiotherapy that the doctors recommended and helped nurse their mother back to health.

She says she has dreams of becoming either a nursery school teacher or a psychologist one day. Simon and I don't need much convincing. She is the answer to our prayers.

Whereas Nikki clearly needs the job, she has one non-negotiable, which is that she can only live in if we allow her sister to move in. Of course, we defer.

We set up a time for Nikki and her sister Dipuo to come see the accommodation we have prepared for them. It's a pretty and spacious apartment above the garage of our new house. It has a large bedroom big enough for two queen-sized beds. It has a television seating area and a small kitchen and bathroom. The sun is lovely in the daytime and we turn on an electric heater and it warms up quickly at night.

Dipuo is tall and striking. She is a bright yellow-brown colour with ample breasts, an even more ample bum and long lean legs. She is wearing a tank top, a pair of jeans and All Stars. She is an absolute stunner.

We soon discover that Dipuo is as distracted as she is distracting. Her head is always in the clouds, and her earphones are always plugged in. She is a typical teenager. At seventeen, she is finishing her last year of high school. Twelve years younger than Nikki, she could be my child. I am starting this motherhood business late.

The sisters are close but Dipuo is typical of much younger siblings. She seems not to notice the sacrifices Nikki is making for her. But she is sweet. Dipuo is less talkative than her sister, who, once she has settled in and become used to us, turns out to be quite a chatterbox. Dipuo, on the other hand, looks down frequently when she addresses me. She hardly looks at Simon at all. But I like her. And, most importantly, I can see how much the two of them love each other.

It takes a while, but eventually Simon and I will learn just what this bond will do to us.

Mummy insists on meeting the two girls before we hire Nikki. When she sees Dipuo for the first time her eyes first widen, then narrow in suspicion. I know what she is thinking before she has a chance to say a word.

Afterwards, when they are gone and Mummy is giving me her feedback, she says slowly and in that especially low voice she reserved for important conversations, 'This is South Africa. Don't think that any of these girls will leave your husband alone just because you are paying her salary. Be careful my girl. Be very, very careful.'

I tell her Simon only has eyes for me. She laughs a little bit and looks pointedly at my heavily pregnant belly. I smile but she returns quickly to the seriousness of the conversation.

In terms of Nikki herself, 'She seems okay,' she sniffs. No one will ever be good enough for her children. She raised us, but seems forever surprised by how trusting we are. She often says we're not cut out for this society. Mandla and I especially. 'Too soft,' she says when I tell her a work story or recount an anecdote about a friend who I think may be taking advantage of me.

Mummy's view is that Mandla and I inherited from Baba a sort of idealism about how the world should be, and how people should behave. We are often surprised when people show us who they are, whereas she is never surprised when people turn out to be awful. Mummy is always ready to be let down. 'Zeng is lucky,' she often says. 'She knows people, just like me. She won't be fooled. But you two – just like your father.'

I don't know if it was exile that toughened her or whether growing up in Mbuluzi in Swaziland and being the child of a schoolteacher and a pastor had simply instilled in her the practical and hard-nosed sensibility required to survive. Regardless of where it comes from, Mummy knows we need her to protect us from our inherent optimism. But there is also the reality that the South African project requires a toughness we simply haven't been required to demonstrate in our lives thus far.

So Mummy says yes, Nikki seems like a fine choice given that we are ignoring her list of willing Swazi relatives. We offer Nikki the job; she and Dipuo move in two weeks before the baby arrives.

Over the next two years violence clucks around us like a restless chicken sensing a fox in the bushes. We discover that violence is the organising principle of the community in which we now live – that it structures our daily schedule and those of our neighbours, that it pervades our every action. Bruises show up everywhere: dark marks mocking the naivety of my long-held aspiration of living in a peaceful South Africa and getting old on a rocking chair on a wide, polished veranda. Congo Road reveals itself to be a typical white suburban neighbourhood. We are not just proximate to the mundane inequality that made apartheid successful; we are complicit. Worse, we are unprepared to see and accept our complicity. We are multiracial and fair and kind. We are on the right side of history.

But it is another story for the people who rely on our largesse to survive: the women who live in our house and care for our children and feed us. They have trouble treating us as their equals because they know we are the haves and they are the have-nots, no matter how often we may greet them with respect, sit down at the same table to eat with them and fawn over pictures of their children. Simon and I and our friends and my sisters and everyone who comes to stay with us or to visit for a while – my parents, Uncle Stan and Aunty Angela – all of us occupy a South Africa in which there are limitless possibilities. We are new blacks and we live in the South Africa of Mandela and rainbows, the South Africa of the Constitution and progressively realised socioeconomic rights.

They live with us, yes, these women. They laugh and listen and they share. Their bodies are warm and their hands are sturdy, yes, but when they stand in queues at the bank, when they go to the hospital, when they enrol their children in school, they might as well be ghosts. This is no country for poor people. It is a country in which only the wealthy are respected; those without wealth know this best.

It is fitting, then, that the house on Congo Road and the women who live in it – The Help – bring on the existential crisis that forces me to confront my place in South Africa. Were it not for the ghosts who love my children and take them from me when I need rest – the women whose mother has abandoned them and whose children they would leave for their jobs in my house if I willed it – I would not have learnt that, in my heart, I am from this place but not of it.

❖ ❖ ❖

Nikki's cell phone is stolen by a man with a knife as she walks home from the shops. Dipuo is stabbed in the arm on a Sunday evening as she makes her way home after a weekend in Soweto. It is a deep wound requiring stitches. A few months later a man in a car in Pretoria chases Simon as he walks in a quiet parking lot after a meeting with his laptop bag strapped across his chest. When he gets home he is pale and drawn as he recounts how he had to be rescued by a stranger.

We are uneasy, but not alarmed. Funny, that. A decade into our democracy, South Africans have learnt to live with crime and violence. We all know better than to panic about small events. Alarm is for extreme situations.

We tell ourselves nothing extreme has happened – that these are simply the daily reminders that we live in an unequal society. We are the luvers. If this means becoming victims of petty crime, so be it. All this changes in October 2009. In the space of two weeks, Simon and I lose our religion. We realise what others have known all along: that democracy means nothing if you are dead. We become atheists, cast into the wilderness. We discover – very late – that our exceptionalism will not protect us. We finally understand that it is impossible for anyone in South Africa to remain unscathed by brutality. We also finally see that the fault lies with us. We have elected to become part of the system, rather than to challenge it or think outside it. We thought that simply being – black and white and normal – in Congo Road would change Congo Road. This was naive; worse, it was reckless.

The violence jolts us out of our reverie.

Becoming a mother

S IS BORN in Johannesburg on an autumn morning in 2008. Dr Mseleku injects the anaesthetic into my back. I feel rubbery and numb from the waist down. I cry even though it doesn't hurt. Simon is standing next to me in green hospital scrubs. I can feel Dr Mseleku cutting but it still doesn't hurt. I am scared. What if the drugs never wear off and I am paralysed forever? I am frightened and overwhelmed with the lights and the sterility of it all.

Dr M is my stylish doctor who loves me because I am stylish and successful too. We are the same kind of woman, determined and slightly tougher than everyone else we encounter. I have a sense, though, that she is more vulnerable than she lets on – that there are hurts there she might open up about if I weren't sitting across from her with my belly between us, a patient but not a friend. I like her togetherness and her depth.

Over the months of my pregnancy we have sat in Dr M's waiting room looking at the colour-blocked bulletin boards crammed full of images of newborns: red screwed-up bally faces next to exuberant new mothers and fathers.

Each card on the wall is from a grateful mother thanking Dr M for bringing forth a new life. Most of the cards are written in the voices of the newborn infants. They offer glimpses into a life I am not sure I can hack. 'A year later and look how I have grown! Thank you so much, Dr M, for bringing me into this world!!! I will never forget that special day when I was born.'

In the few minutes before S's arrival, Dr M is no longer skinny or sexy or an almost-friend. She is simply a doctor, completely focused on the task at hand. Her dreads are held back off her face and she has no makeup on. This is serious business. The strange assurance I got from the girly discussions we had in her office is gone. I had convinced myself that, if she could indulge in frivolities, if she could be so concerned with shoes and vineyards – which is what our appointments always ended up focusing on – then maybe there wasn't so much life-and-deathness to this birthing business after all.

Now she looks professional and in control, hunched over, pushing my baby into position and then pulling her out of me like a rabbit out of a hat.

She is here: a steaming, squalling, bunched-up, writhing, lifedrenched thing. Purple veins wending a spider's web across her eyelids, blue arteries crisscrossing her thighs and she is as white as white can be.

'She's white.'

I say it in an involuntary gasp, a strange sort of stage whisper. I am half-amused, half-aghast, not so much because of her whiteness, but because of her apartness from me. And I suppose I am also exhausted. Simon is embarrassed. He reddens in his green scrubs. His eyes are disappointed and I am not sure whether it is me or the baby who has let him down.

The medical staff laugh out loud. Back slaps to Simon.

'Well at least you know she's yours!' they brag on his behalf, papering over my post-apartheid postpartum gaffe. I have overstepped. What is happening to this country when a black woman can be disdainful of her half-caste child?

I want to explain that I am not disdainful. I love her.

I expected her to be fair. After all, her father is white. But I didn't anticipate this pallor, this translucence. Yet here she finally is after months of hiccups and pokes and frightening stillnesses that had me bruising myself to jolt her into action. Here she is, lying on the collapsing heap of my belly. Alive. Mine. A long glistening larva, pale against my mud.

Maybe it's the medicine. It's not helping me to express myself.

Later, Simon tells my sisters not to mention the baby's colour to me. He thinks I am traumatised. He has been hoping – for my sake – that she will be darker. He only tells me this after the eightmonth fog of my postpartum depression has lifted. By then I am well enough to cry proper tears, not just the exhausted ones that no longer make water. I sob because he is showing me in the kindest way possible that my idealism and my personal politics can be unrelenting and this has its effects on those around me – on him. He has borne them well but my militancy is a lot to take.

But now, on the day of S's birth, I am not yet depressed – just overwhelmed.

The kids arrive in the ward. Nick is fifteen and sensitive and Gabi is all feelings and mouth. They hold her and Gabi cries. Nick takes pictures. Mummy is there. Baba is afraid of infants. Or has some sort of cultural thing perhaps so he isn't there. He is in Japan. I think he would be too choked up and doesn't want to admit it. Mandla and Zeng come, and then Gael and Richard. The friends pour in. S bites on my breast and my stomach lurches with the pain of it.

There is too much love. So much it hurts. So much that my uterus contracts and blood gushes. I am an animal. I am wounded and tender and sore. Then everyone leaves and I stay awake, guarding her against demons. I listen to her breathe. I wonder if I deserve her trust. She needs me too much and I have never been more scared in my life.

❖ ❖ ❖

Six days later I fill in a job application. The foundation where I have been working for four years is hiring an executive director. I have been encouraged to apply. I have no idea what I am doing.

I get the job.

There are eighty staff members. I am the youngest. I am a woman. We work in ten countries. We are cowboys, flying in and out of Zimbabwe and Congo and Zambia and Lesotho. Human rights champions. I am brave. I stand up to New York when they try to tell us how to behave. I pump milk at lunch. I check my BlackBerry after six every evening to see if there are any messages. I make time for dinner with Simon but only because it's the right thing to do. I do not miss my baby. Work is the only thing I know how to do. I am sailing towards disaster and I do not know it. Everyone watching me is impressed. 'My, how she sails,' they all say. 'What a dynamic young woman.'

Simon is worried. I cannot sleep. I cannot be alone with the baby. I don't know what to do. I don't know how to be good enough for her. I am very tired.

I do not crash because there is too much at stake. I keep sailing. I pretend I am okay. I cry a lot. Sometimes alone. Most often with Simon. Something about the way he looks at me, as though he is worried I might drown, makes me cry harder. Only he knows I am not sailing. Only he knows I barely know how to swim. It is our secret.

He forces me to go to the doctor. Dr Mseleku sashays in, as well put together as ever. Then she looks at me – her almost-friend who is also a patient – and I cannot hold it together any more. I weep. She frowns in empathy. She sends me to a psychiatrist. I take the medicine and I feel better but I need to understand why.

Simon steers me to Linda, whom we saw for a few months during our worst years when we thought we might fall apart. Her office is still sunny. Her couch is as old and worn as I remember. There is a dachshund at her feet curled into a ball. When we are not talking I can hear the dog snore. Linda does not smile with her mouth, only with her eyes. She makes me feel safe.

She says, 'Of course you are falling apart.' She reminds me of what I have been through and says I have looked for this precise meaning for a very long time. Can't I see that this is the most important way that one person can belong to another? I am standing upright, but a child requires you to bend towards her. I am the soil and she is the seed and words will not do. Need is the only language her love understands. I will get there but I have to bend. I cannot stand still and strong and be a vision for everyone to behold. I cannot move too fast, the way they expect me to at work. I have to learn how to bend – to be someone I have never been before.

One day, when she is old enough, I will tell her the truth, which is that my love was never in question. I was afraid. I only wanted to be enough.

The violence

NIKKI IS STANDING outside our house. S – now eighteen months old – is in her pram. Nikki is wearing walking shoes and a hat. S wears a bonnet and a pink dress. A man gets out of a car and approaches them. He pretends that he is asking for directions and Nikki obliges. Then suddenly he is standing too close to Nikki. He is pointing a gun at them and saying that he wants her phone or he will shoot them both.

The jacarandas kiss overhead. The sky is a spring blue.

Nikki pushes the pram into the street, away from the sidewalk where he is standing with the weapon leering at them. On our pretty street, she screams and tries to flag down a passing car. The car swerves to avoid her, the driver's mouth a shocked O. She persists, scared that she is going to be hit by oncoming traffic, but even more fearful of the young man with the gun in the shadows. The next car she flags down stops. The driver opens the door, sees the guy on the sidewalk, and threatens him with his own gun. The assailant disappears. The Good Samaritan makes sure that they are okay and quickly gets back in his car.

I am in the office. Just before lunch, the phone rings. 'Come home now,' Simon says. He is trying to sound calm, which panics me. 'Everything is okay,' he says to reassure me. And then there is a catch, a sharp intake of breath. 'But you should get here.' I arrive and the story rushes out in a pallid tumble.

As she watches us and hears the story retold, as she looks at our worried faces miming what has just happened, the baby vomits. I mark the moment in my heart. She is too small to know what has happened but she is old enough to understand. I want to fall to my knees and weep, but I cannot do that because I am a mother now and this is not the moment for weeping. In the face of this, my tears will not protect her.

Compared to other tales of crime and gore in South Africa, this is not really a story at all. It falls into the category of 'it could have been worse'. A glinting gun pointed at the soft skull of a baby girl on a warm day in a quiet Johannesburg neighbourhood only makes the headlines if someone pulls the trigger.

The sun filters into the room, a deceptively soft yellow. We hold the baby tighter and we wonder how we will live in this strange place we love, this place that seems not to know how to be loved in return.

◆ ◆ ◆

A week later my colleague and friend Alpheus Molefe is found at 4 a.m., dead in his car. He is the victim of a botched hijacking. He leaves a wife and a daughter, thirteen-year-old Princess. She is beautiful, soft-spoken, bewildered.

Her mother sits stoic in their Katlehong house as mourners pour in. Alpheus was a people's man – always busy, always making connections. The president of the American philanthropic foundation for which I work sends his condolences when he hears the news. He remembers him personally. Alpheus was our driver, but he was also our ambassador: earning a diploma in tourism, getting a certificate in tour guiding, spending weekends regaling our visitors from the US and Europe with his stories of life under apartheid. He stood for many of the things we tried to instil in our staff in the Johannesburg office.

I do not know what to do with myself. I am the boss of the organisation. There are eighty of us in shock and all eyes on me. I sit in my office and cry. I go home and look at my baby, and cry.

In a quiet moment at the house, in the days before the funeral, one of my colleagues looks at Princess and asks, 'How are you?' She responds wisely: 'Outside I am okay, but inside I am broken.'

It is a refrain that comes back repeatedly in the months that follow as Simon and I begin the slow dance of deciding.

Alpheus's death is senseless and tragic and of course entirely logical within the context of inequality and need and the legacy of brutality that South Africa hasn't managed to confront directly. I want to give up. I feel like the whites who whinge about crime on the radio. I become obsessed with everything that is failing and yet I find it impossible to walk away.

◆ ◆ ◆

Mummy stops by constantly. She phones the nanny several times a day to check on her. For months after the near-miss, she cannot stop thinking about what happened. She orders us to buy a new house, preferably one that is inside the gated community where she and my father live. This is an instruction we cannot obey.

Baba is equally worried but his prescription is worse. 'If I were your age,' he says to Simon in the way that men sometimes do when they must take charge, 'I would pack up my bags, take my family and leave this place.'

For a while there is a ban on walking in the neighbourhood but this is absurd and everyone is miserable. Mummy is the originator and primary enforcer of this rule. She does drop-ins to ensure Nikki isn't outside with S. She often whisks S away to her house on weekends as though the bigger gates and complicated security system will keep her only grandchild safe. After a few months we begin to defy her. Staying inside is making us all bad-tempered. The child likes the street and the neighbours and the barking dogs.

'We can't live in a cage,' we say to each other resentfully when Mummy is not around, angry at each other although none of this is either one's fault. Still, we are not brave enough to say anything to my mother's face. After all, her fears are well founded and her vigilance is necessary.

The incident forces us to retreat into our privilege. The house becomes unbearable. We talk feverishly every night. We are convinced we must leave. But then we laugh at ourselves, hysteria tingeing our conversations. Why would we leave this house and where would we go? We can't afford to sell and we hate the idea of living in a gated community. We are stuck.

We are careful not to say anything aloud but my interior monologue is bleak. I feel like all those whites we have been mocking for years – the ones who have fled to Australia and Canada and the UK and who Facebook obsessively about South Africa's horrors. Except we are still here.

We talk through how we would live with ourselves if anything were to happen to S. We remind ourselves that something already has, but that we were just lucky. The questions we ask ourselves are real and shameful and life-changing.

A year passes. We recover. Somewhat. We accept that the pretty little home we joyously imagined we would settle into like bricks will not be our last home. We stay.

The house no longer feels like home but the stoicism of Johannesburg has settled itself into our bones and we ignore the fact that we have been betrayed by our dreams. We don't trust ourselves any longer. We are not sure who we can trust. We cleave closer together. We turn our backs against the outside. We question not just the country but the entire enterprise. South Africa has failed us. Our sense of who and where we are is in flux.

The violence creates despondency. We blame it for everything. It is the fault of the violence that Dipuo failed her final year and cannot matriculate. We pay for her to go to a special college where she will be coached for the rewrite. She fails more dismally the second time: 4 per cent in maths, 19 per cent in English, despite her born-free fluency.

Then Aunty's Lizzie dies of Aids. Aunty and Julia double down, grannies becoming mothers again. Moeketsi, their eight-year-old grandson, is devastated. His mother is gone and he is too young to reject the old women. Still, he is old enough to remember his mother's love and to know that he is angry with her for dying.

The longer we live with Nikki and Dipuo, the more their lives seem to unravel. We find ourselves mired in a patronising relationship that is both of our own doing and of theirs. We have still not fully understood that we are enmeshed, that we are in the belly of the beast.

Within a few months of Alpheus's death and the incident, Nikki tells us she is pregnant.

A few months after that I am pregnant too. As winter approaches, our bellies grow. Nikki is excited about having her first baby. Dipuo is thrilled she will be an aunt. S will have two babies to play with. I am worried. Will I have postpartum depression again? How will I survive a second child and S with Nikki having just become a new mother? She will just be returning from maternity leave and will have to face nursing her own child as well as caring for mine once I go back to the office. I am concerned she might be distracted by her own baby.

Yes, I think these thoughts – African feminist madam that I am. I worry about myself far more than I worry about Nikki, who, in any other circumstances, I would call a sister. She has, after all, provided a warm pair of hands into which S has leapt every morning. She has given S love and laughter. She has worried about her when she was sick, as though she were her own child. She darted into the street, risking her own life, for this child of mine. And I am concerned about the inconvenience I might be caused by her decision to exercise one of her most fundamental rights – that of having a child.

I am betraying my class status and I don't like myself

this way. I am the girl on the bike again, angry with the boy who has the audacity to take what he needs.

So, I focus on the joy. I acknowledge that I feel strong and capable. I focus on fortifying myself because using Nikki as a crutch is not a sustainable way to live my life anyway, let alone the fact that it places an undue burden on her.

I fortify myself and think it would be nice for me to be there for Nikki the way she has been there for me. This logic is twisted, of course, shot through with paternalism and condescension and liberal soppiness. I am ignoring the financial relationship that exists between us – the fact that she loves S in the context of a job. It is hard to know what to do with this sometimes.

◆ ◆ ◆

Nikki goes into labour at home. At first none of us is sure but, as night falls, it becomes clear what is happening. She packs her bag and Simon drives her to the hospital. The baby is born after too many hours of labour. Nikki does it alone. My pregnancy is advanced by now and I can't be there. Dipuo can't handle it. Nikki is strong and healthy, though, and the boy is beautiful. She names him Ofense.

A few days after delivering, Nikki is not feeling well. She is having difficulty breathing so she has to go back to hospital. Again, Simon takes her. This time it is complicated. Simon walks with her into the overcrowded emergency room at Johannesburg General. The nurses are harried and the doctors are busy. There is no feeling of concern here. There are bodies – most of them black – in various states of disease and pain. Except for Simon's there are no white faces in the room. After waiting an eternity Simon stands up. Nikki and the baby are distraught, the pain in her chest is getting worse, her breathing is laboured.

He strides to the front of the line like a white saviour and miraculously help appears. 'How can I help, sir?' asks a junior doctor. He is black. Simon points to Nikki. 'She needs help. We have been here for hours. What is going on here? She has a baby, she can't breathe, no one is telling us how long it will be until we might see a doctor.'

The doctor defers. 'Of course, sir.' They usher Nikki in. She has the protection of a white man so she is no longer simply a ghost.

They treat and discharge her quickly. They give her a Panadol and tell her if the pain persists she should come back. Simon tries but they have reached the limits of their patience with him too.

Unsurprisingly in the coming few days the symptoms persist. This time we call our family doctor and she makes a few calls so that we do not need to take her back to Johannesburg General. She tells us to go to Rahima Moosa Mother and Child Hospital. She gives us the name of a consulting doctor there so that we aren't turned away. Here, they are kinder. They tend to her. They admit her because it is clear she has a clot in her lung – likely caused by the trauma of the delivery. They monitor her and give her medicine to dissolve the clot.

They let the baby stay in hospital with her, which is a relief. Still, when she returns she needs care. We talk about how important it will be for her to have medical aid – especially with a baby. I investigate the options, my guilt propelling me to get organised. I can't believe we didn't think of this. All that time we were busy with driving lessons and spending money on Dipuo's bridging course, but we hadn't even covered the basics. I don't say what is really on my mind, though, and what is on hers. That life is not fair, that I would never have found myself in that hospital, waiting and waiting. That the birth of my boy in a few months' time will be luxurious in comparison. I don't say that my forgetting about her medical aid was an act of complicity rather than a simple mistake. I forgot because it is easy to forget about ghosts, even when they wash your clothes and bathe your child and live in your house.

◆ ◆ ◆

Nikki stays upstairs for most of her maternity leave. We have a temporary nanny – Sandra – who comes daily. When Nikki comes back from maternity leave, though, she is different. She is distracted – obviously by motherhood, but also by a romantic relationship with the baby's father that seems to be going off the rails. She has been seeing him in an on-again, off-again way for many years.

He has also simultaneously been in other relationships. She worries constantly about what his straying will mean for her. What it might mean for the baby. She can't trust him but she loves him.

'It's the lying that I don't like, Sonke.' Time and again she says this to me. Time and again she cries. I have been here before and I tell her this.

'It's not about him, it's about what you will tolerate, Nikki.' She nods each time I say this, but she does not seem prepared to leave him yet. We are close – as we have always been. The banter is light. The excitement of this baby – and the new one coming, also a boy – fills our little house with a hum it has not had before. I feel closer to Nikki than ever. When she first arrived, I needed her desperately. Knowing S was with her made me feel safe. She reassured me. That feeling is raw and powerful. Now I feel as though we know each other, as though we are ready to share this next phase of our lives together.

I forget about reality. I immerse myself in fantasy. I forget that I am living in a neighbourhood defined by ancient boundaries. I forget Nikki grew up in Soweto, defined as much by those boundaries as if she had been born on Congo Road. I forget that the heart of whiteness beats as strongly as ever in our little house – regardless of what I want to think. It is fitting then that in the end it is a lie that unravels us. Everything comes crashing down because of a stupid little lie.

◆ ◆ ◆

Mummy is home. She is clutching S and her face is drawn. Something is wrong.

She shows me a small burn mark on S's leg. It is about the size of a coin. 'Look at this,' she says.

'What happened?' I ask both her and S at the same time.

'I burned,' says S in her little lispy voice. I want to smile even though I am worried.

'How?' I ask.

'The iron,' she says. 'Where?'

'In Nikki's room.'

'Sorry,' I say, 'did it hurt?' 'A lot,' she says tearing up.

I take her in my arms. 'That's okay, I'm sure Nikki made it feel better.'

'She wasn't here,' says S. 'Where was she?'

She shakes her head. She doesn't know where Nikki was. 'So were you with Puo?' I ask, surprised.

She nods yes.

Mummy stage whispers to me, ostensibly so S can't hear. 'Something fishy is going on. When I arrived Nikki was here. The first thing S did was tell me this same story. Then Nikki says the child is lying. How can a two-year-old know how to lie? Not about something so detailed like this?'

I'm puzzled but not alarmed. Accidents happen all the time. So S accidentally brushed her leg against an iron that may have been on the carpet upstairs in Nikki's room. Not a huge deal. The girls would need to be more careful. Mummy tells me to call Nikki so we can get to the bottom of this. Her Gogo antennae are out, feeling for danger.

I call Nikki downstairs. I am not angry, only puzzled. 'What happened?' I ask.

'I don't know,' she says.

'S says you weren't here and she walked into an iron.'

'No, I've been here all afternoon. She was upstairs while I was preparing her.' Now I'm really confused.

Mummy pipes up.

'*Yey wena*, Nikki. Are you sure about this story, because it doesn't sound right? Why would a child lie?'

Nikki looks at us both and doesn't skip a beat. She is equally confused and I believe her. This is a strange mystery, one of those things where a child simply can't tell you for sure what has transpired because she is too little to articulate it fully.

'Okay,' I say. 'Anyway, it's just a small thing, no real damage.'

Mummy is livid. After Nikki leaves she says to me, 'You are too soft. You can't go through life with this mentality that you're going to save everyone and listen to all their stories. This girl is lying and your child is going to pay the price.'

'Mummy, you don't have to be so suspicious of every-one,' I retort. 'I'm tired. There's no big deal. S is okay. Please let's just leave it.'

Mummy is not impressed. She had popped in just to see the baby. But now she decides to stay until bedtime. She puts S to sleep. Tonight, her actions are not animated by her usual grandmotherly bustling. Tonight, she is taking charge. Clearly I'm not capable.

In the bedroom Mummy goes over the story with S again. 'What happened with your leg today, Beanie?'

S repeats the story. She is remarkably consistent. She doesn't seem to be confused. It is only me and her Gogo who have doubts. I go to sleep confused. Nothing about this story makes sense.

Where was Nikki? If she wasn't home and had run quickly to the shops, so what?

The following day I can't stop thinking about it. I sit in meeting after meeting, but I am distracted.

Mummy calls me three times to ask what I am going to do. I snap at her. Then Aunty Eunice messages me. She wasn't working yesterday but Lala's mother from next door – who gossips with Aunty all the time – told her Nikki was gone most of the afternoon. She took the small car we had bought for her to take S to playdates, and had only been in the house for a few minutes when Mummy had come home. I was grateful to Aunty for her intel but irritated at Mummy's meddling. Mummy must have called Aunty to tell her the story and to find out what else she knew.

The old women are clearly worried. Their mission is to protect the innocent S from these two young women who don't seem to know what they are doing. This in-cludes protecting her from me, her mother – who be-lieves everything she's told because of her soft exile heart.

Driving home, I decide I will go straight upstairs to the flat and ask Nikki and Dipuo what happened. I want to hear Nikki tell the truth herself. I pull into the garage and Nikki runs down the stairs. She meets me as I get out of the car. Her face is taut.

I am pregnant and heavy so I get out of the car slowly.

I am barely out when she starts. The story rushes out. She tells me she wasn't gone for only a few minutes. She says she was downstairs cleaning S's room so she decided to leave S with Dipuo for forty minutes. Ofense was on her back. She didn't want me and Simon to get angry with Dipuo. She says because we have been so upset about Dipuo's poor school results, she thought maybe this would be the final straw.

My heart sinks. She is lying. 'Let's go inside,' I say.

We go to the TV room and I close the door.

I force myself to be tough. I tell myself Nikki is a person, an adult, not a project requiring my bleeding-heart, do-gooder sympathy.

She is not telling the truth and if I am going to trust her with S again, and with this new child who is due in less than a week, I will need to know what she is hiding.

I tell Nikki I know she wasn't at home when S burned herself. I tell her I know she took the car out and was gone for hours. I hate saying this because I now look as though I have been snooping, checking up and asking the neighbours. Still, I am grateful to Mummy and Aunty for their own lack of trust, for their ability to do the dirty work my liberal principles will not let me undertake.

I tell her I wish she knew she could be honest. I tell her the burn on S's leg means nothing – it will heal and it was an accident, of that I am sure. But the lie. The lie is devastating.

She looks at me for a long time. She looks as though she is thinking, trying to find a way out, an angle to push.

'Where were you?' I ask.

She refuses to answer. Even now, given the chance, she won't tell me the truth. I finally see that she has never trusted us enough simply to say, 'I need to go to town. Is it okay if I leave the baby with Dipuo?' It is this that defeats me in the end. I feel as though Simon and I were marks; we were gullible and silly and now I see that we were never the big brother and sister we thought we were.

She says sorry. She looks down. It doesn't sound genuine. The words bounce off the walls and land at my feet. I want to kick them away, to pretend they are stones on the road I can simply ignore. She is not saying sorry about the many times she has left S for hours on end with her distracted sister. She is not saying sorry for anything because she really isn't sorry. I see it there, shining through as I have so many times before: she resents me and she is sorry she got caught but she is not sorry she left work time and again. She is saying sorry because it's the right thing to do and perhaps she still hopes there is some way out.

There isn't. She still thinks I will be soft – the way I always am – but something in me has been crushed.

I say to her, 'You need to leave. I can't trust you any more. I don't understand why you are still not telling me the truth.' She cries but the next day they pack up. They are gone. Just. Like. That.

◆ ◆ ◆

Nikki was the walking wounded. Her survival depended on both her capacity to love and her capacity to play the system. As much as she had given us – stability and nurturing and the joy of not worrying about our child's emotional safety in those precious early years – she had also taken advantage of us. She had seen our kindness as a sort of sweet foolishness, as something that could be exploited when necessary because it was born of our horror at our own complicity in inequality.

Many of her manipulations were understandable, given the world that she had had to navigate. Still, her lies shattered the tenuous peace in our home. After Nikki and Dipuo left, Simon – with his kind heart – kept in touch with them on our behalf.

Even now, with so much time behind us, I am still hurt. Simon shows me their pictures on Facebook and they all look well. I rarely say anything. I just look. I am happy for them but it still hurts. I am not proud of myself but this is how I feel. I am not over it because it was a betrayal that cut to the core of everything I thought I was – fair and kind and generous and not like the other madams in Emmarentia. But in her actions, and in my response to those actions, I proved that I was just like the other madams. I was self-involved and blind to what I did not want to see.

Nikki held S through the worst days of my depression. I leaned on her emotionally, even though I never told her. She could see, though, how badly I was doing and how much I needed her. And she stood firm. She was there in the morning, with her hands warm and ready to take the baby so I could catch up on the sleep I had not been able to get the night before. She cradled her when I was exhausted and despondent.

So, there should be no issue. She lied, yes, but in the

grand scheme of things, was her offence – which she never admitted, but which others were happy to fill in the details about – so bad? She left work to see her boyfriend. She left to try to work things out. She left S in the care of her dizzy, but ultimately reliable, little sister.

I can't forgive her, though. I feel like a fool. I am disappointed in Nikki because she saw through me. I hate her for it for a while – for seeing me as I have not wanted to see myself, as a rich woman, as an employer. I have seen myself as Alice in Wonderland, a naïf, innocent and pure, discovering a land in which nothing is as it seems. It turns out I am also not what I seem to be. I'm disappointed in myself because I could not even see my own avarice.

Our falling out is a proxy, of course – a stand-in for a greater battle. I have gradually fallen out of love with the ANC and now my doubts spread. It is not simply the politicians I can't get my head around. I am doubtful of the whole enterprise. I trust no one, least of all myself and my instincts. Apartheid's legacies seem to have woven themselves into the most intimate of spaces. Dysfunction pulses at every street light and violence seeps under every door. I am suspicious of everyone. The momentum of freedom has carried me just past a decade but I am beginning to wonder if it can take me any further. I am out of step; more an exile than I thought.

◆ ◆ ◆

We scramble and find a full-time nanny. We interview a woman named Pinah. She is from Zimbabwe, like so many of the women who now care for the children of the elite. She is a former schoolteacher. This time Mummy and I appraise her with the eyes of seasoned upper-class women. She is older than Nikki. Stable. No demands. She has a son who is thirteen but we want her to stay with us. She says she has just shipped him home to Bulawayo. She wants him to have a good education but she is fearful for his safety in Hillbrow. We nod and agree. Self-servingly, I don't offer to take him on – to educate him at the school down the road.

We pay her well to massage our guilt. We offer her medical aid. We give her a thirteenth cheque. We pay her overtime far above the minimum wage. We are good people. She seems grateful but now I am wise enough to know that unfairness is built into the system so her gratitude does not change the fact of our complicity.

Unless one of us is prepared to resign from our job and radically alter our lifestyle – unless we are prepared to refuse any sort of domestic help and do it ourselves – we are consigned to this system and to this feeling. So, we learn to live with the guilt and keep a slight emotional distance even as we breathe one another's air, live under the same roof, talk about *Scandal* and *Generations*, and eat together once a week.

Congo Road is not what I had hoped, yet what I had hoped was never going to be possible. That sort of fairy tale isn't real anywhere, and was certainly not real in the South African neighbourhoods that new blacks like me began to occupy after apartheid.

The children I imagined when I first walked into this house were born, but biology has a different momentum from sociology. The security I had imagined, the idyllic quiet, the kind of emotional tranquillity that is implicit in the scene I sketched as I stood on the threshold the afternoon we put the offer in – that never materialised. I discovered, over five years in that beautiful haunted house, that nothing in South Africa is safe – especially not your dreams.

And yet, the paradox of South Africa is that every morning we rose. In spite of the underlying dread, in spite of the fear, we put on our clothes and we left our children at home. We left them in the hands of black women whose presence in our homes we owed to apartheid. We trusted the women. We abhorred the system. And so, on some level – when we muttered under our breaths about the laundry or the food – it was evident that we abhorred the women too, because they were living, breathing monuments to everything we had left behind when Nelson Mandela put his hand on the Constitution and took his oath of office as the first president of democratic South Africa.

So, like all our friends from exile, and those who had stayed and endured and fought, we lived in this fancy neighbourhood. We lived with the unasked questions and a churning in our guts that was worse on some days than on others. We did this because the whole system was rotten and we knew that, by moving in, and by choosing to buy beautiful old houses in Emmarentia and Sandton and Melrose, the beautiful tree-lined neighbourhoods from which people like us were barred only a decade before, we were killing certain parts of ourselves.

We killed the questions and tried to still the noise that came when we moved into these quiet places where we were meant to find peace and evade nosy neighbours and township dramas. We silenced our own questions and pretended the alienation was simply a passing phase because we wanted to deepen and extend and preserve our new-found privileges.

We told ourselves that this is what our parents had fought for. This was not true, of course. Our parents had fought for equality,

but we were not occupying spaces of equality – we

were simply ascending to places higher up on a ladder that we knew provided unfair leverage to a tiny group. We were now part of that group.

This is middle-class South Africa: hoping for the best. Bringing home the bacon. Buying new cars. Planting hedges. Hoping for the best, but creating the worst. We pretend we don't know this, and it is this pretence that is most abhorrent. Because, as James Baldwin says, 'it is not permissible that the authors of devastation should also be innocent. It is the innocence which constitutes the crime.'

Failure

I AM OFFERED a fellowship at Yale University. It is an opportunity to get out of South Africa without committing to leaving South Africa. Simon has been ready to quit the country since that October day in Congo Road. In spite of it, I have not been able to contemplate a move. South Africa is the home towards which I travelled from the moment of my birth. For Simon, though, this is a test run: a chance to see whether his wife could tear herself away from the country of her heart.

Simon and the kids join me. The fellowship is generous so we have a two-bedroom place – a townhouse that is part of a larger complex in which there are dozens of postgraduate students with their families. We are from all over the world. The playground looks like a mini United Nations.

The office continues to pay my salary. This is a gift. I see it as a reward for the seven years I have put into the organisation. The recommendation that probably got me into the programme came from the president of the organisation himself. He is widely respected – some might say iconic. His blessing means a lot. He is not easily impressed.

Yale gives me the space and the freedom to think: no expectations. I do not get involved with local politics. My activist self stays well hidden: resting. I stay on the perimeter: cloistered, privileged, safe.

Suddenly I can relax.

The last five years have been intense. Juggling the career and having children hasn't been easy, and the looming crisis in terms of my relationship with the country has been both exhilarating and destabilising.

By the time I decide on my sabbatical I feel confident that I can leave the office for a while. I am wrong. All hell breaks loose in a story that is long and complicated and still makes me upset, mainly because I still can't believe I didn't see it coming. But at the time I thought I had earned the respect of my colleagues. In spite of being a woman and young and a new mother when I started, in spite of the depression and the fear, I found a way.

I learnt to be tough but kind. I remembered that I was smart. I decided to stand up for my team and be loyal to their instincts, rather than to worry about small details. I used Mummy and Baba as sounding boards and hustled to attract resources so that, on my watch, we became bigger and brawnier than any other foundation in the network to which we belonged. We shook off the deadwood and marched forward – together. Or so I thought.

There were some people whose ire I raised and in some instances they were right. I learnt how to be the boss lady in a way that worked and sometimes that meant making hard decisions.

I am confident that I have done a good job as CEO. I am ready to move on and I want to use this time to prepare my successor. I am so confident that I overreach. I begin an elaborate restructuring process a few months before my departure. It is overdue and necessary but I under-estimate what it means to people to have a secure job. I think the best and the brightest will take packages. I am convinced that, if we award generous cheques and put in place proper performance management systems, people will buy into the plan. I am wrong, of course. Horri-bly naively wrong.

So I leave. This break affords me an opportunity to let my brilliant and funny deputy manage the office with-out me by his side – a test run. He is a smart and kind-hearted man – he has been a wonderful deputy.

Then, all hell breaks loose. There is a disgruntled em-ployee. She was there when I left. She was unreasonable so we began proceedings to get her dismissed. My depu-ty and I are *ad idem* about how to deal with her, but her case turns into a nightmare. It drags on, and as it does the office rumour mill goes wild.

I begin to get frantic messages. 'Come back to Joburg. Can you fly back?'

I am resentful. I do not realise this is now officially a big deal, not something I can delegate. It does not dawn on me, until it is too late, that this is no longer simply about a disgruntled employee and her gripes. The situa-tion has morphed into a referendum about the restructuring. We are in deep, deep trouble.

I get a call. 'Come to New York.' The new boss wants to see me. I call a colleague. 'It's bad,' he says. My stomach turns. I go to New York. The boss is new. He doesn't know me. He knows nothing about what I have done, how hard I have worked, how much I have cared. I have met him before and he came across as crisp, but warm. We sit and my feeling is the same. He is crisp and warm.

Then he suggests the crisis has become toxic. It is too big to fix. There are too many people who feel burned, who are worried about their future in the organisation. I am stunned. I thought that people who assured me they were okay were telling the truth. I thought I could rely on the goodwill I had built up over so many years. It turns out this was a rookie mistake. It is one thing to be a good manager. It is quite another to take people through a painful and difficult process that involves the possibility of their losing their livelihoods. Even if they are highly educated and you assume they are mobile and you give them years of advance notice. There are some processes you can't short-circuit.

There have been complaints about me. Some members of staff say I was a bully. I know they say this. It is part of life as a woman leader – and a young one who is having babies – to be called either a pushover or a bully. Some say I tried to ram the process through without enough consultation. Maybe.

It is clear that the new boss has made up his mind. There is no point talking about details. The fact that the words have come out of his mouth not as a question, but as a statement of fact – that there is concern about me and that it is best I leave amicably – means it is done. I have far too much pride to argue with him.

I listen. I will myself not to cry and miraculously I

do not. He is suggesting I write a letter, announcing my resignation. He will make sure it is all handled amicably. I wince and smile at the same time. This is not happening to me. There is nothing amicable about being asked to leave a place you have loved, a place where you have felt valued and respected. There is nothing amicable about a putsch.

I leave, somehow – it is a blur. I am on the streets and so, like everyone around me, I walk. I walk for what seems like hours on end but can't be. Eventually I call Simon and when I hear his voice, the tears begin. I cry in big gulps, struggling to hold myself up. I lean against a window then I step back, afraid someone will tell me to move away – I am still a black girl on the streets of New York, conscious of how she occupies space. I look at myself in the window crying. Nobody so much as turns. This is New York – everyone just keeps walking.

I sob into the phone. 'I could just go to Joburg and sort this all out,' I say. I want to fight back. To clear my name. I want to say I trusted everyone so I thought they were fine because they said they were fine. Simon tells me not to do that. He says, 'Just come home,' and I am grateful to hear him say these words.

I get on the train and I go home. I ride the two hours sitting on the edge of my seat looking out of the window, lifted on my haunches like a bushbuck, ready to spring forward. I am in a strange country. Failure is new to me so the terrain is unfamiliar. I could leave tomorrow and be back in Joburg the following day. The fight in me is back. How dare they? They knew I was planning on leaving. I told them I would hand over – why go for blood when I am not even there? It feels cruel and ugly in ways I can't understand.

I don't take my eyes off the landscape. Disused American cities whiz past. This is a country of graffiti and broken windows. And in the wide-open spaces between cities, there are leafless trees and still water. There are bridges painted white and boats perfect against the grey sky. At each station there are scowling black men who wait in uniforms and, standing at some distance, there are perfectly turned-out white women. As we pull into station after station, I feel more and more adrift. This is America and I am a stranger. On an Amtrak train, I slice through space and time, lost but moving towards a place I know. I am going home, to Simon.

The train pulls into New Haven and he is there, waiting.

◆ ◆ ◆

For months I am raw. This is not the sort of thing that happens to people like me. Smart, likeable, fourth-generation, middle-class African women like me don't fail. I have a plan for myself and it does not include setbacks like this.

I have always had my way and this has bred in me a kind of confidence that may be mistaken – in an African woman – for arrogance. Indeed, in some ways the sort of confidence that I carry is a close cousin of entitlement. Having succeeded in everything by virtue of class allows for a certain blindness. I have always assumed people had my best interests at heart simply because I thought they should.

My generation of children were the main characters in the postcolonial narrative. We embodied Africa's positive trajectory. We were told we would drive independent Africa's economic liberation. With our shiny skins, we were well-nourished, bright-eyed achievers who recited their times tables with ease and gained entry to the best universities on the strength of their native intelligence.

This burden, combined with the specifics of my particular upbringing, created an entitled sort of innocence about me – a naivety born of access rather than lack of exposure to the world, and this perhaps was why I found myself blind-sided by organisational matters I had not thought were important.

I saw myself as an exception. I believed I was above petty politics and office gutter talk. I took for granted that I had backing when I didn't. The arrogance of class is that you can be blind to what others see because the world looks upon you kindly. I was blindsided because leaving – taking a package – was not frightening to me and so I could not imagine that it would be to others in a similar position.

No leader can make this mistake and, no matter what else I may have done, I failed in that regard.

◆ ◆ ◆

I have been fine, of course. I have gone on to forge a new career for myself – to make the pivot I had been wanting to make. There was enough goodwill towards me from before those wretched few months that I remained well regarded in the institution. My networks carried me; my access and privilege kept me afloat.

I would like to pretend that my subsequent trajectory has simply been due to my innate talents and my ability to learn and grow. The truth is far less flattering: I had options that most women and black people don't. Those networks – that social capital – were a massive asset. There were people in positions of power who liked and trusted me and who continued to do so, in spite of my mistakes. This is as it should be for everyone. The mistake I made was assuming that my exceptionalism was the norm. It is one thing to understand feminism as a concept and it is quite another to practise it in a real and authentic manner. It doesn't come naturally, even when you are marked by your blackness or your womanness; even when you try to be thoughtful. Sometimes it is only cold, hard experience, it is only fucking up, that opens your eyes to your own privilege.

My mending was a function of having a supportive family. I was able to heal because my education and my crisp clean English guaranteed I would be okay in the end. My networks and the glowing words littered across my cv – Yale, World Economic Forum, America – were shiny baubles denoting access and progress. My pain was tempered by my potential, and my potential was infinite because I had been favoured by circumstance. I wasn't Nikki or Aunty Pinah. I wasn't even Mummy. I was freer.

It sounds clichéd to say that leaving that job under a strange light-grey cloud was the best thing I ever did, but it is true. It would be nice to think the lesson was about life throwing me lemons and me making lemonade, but it was bigger than this.

The lesson was that I needed to learn how to manage my privilege. I was born into a family that – for generations – valued education. Like all the exempted natives who had come before me, I thought of myself as special. My social status as a great-granddaughter of these Christians who had converted early and had reaped the educational benefits of selling out to the missionaries was a blessing. But I hadn't yet learnt to manage my elitism, how to tame it and use it, and how to see in spite of it.

Women have known how to walk the tightrope between autonomy and geniality since Mary gave birth to Jesus. Women learn early that, to protect our brilliance, sometimes we have to hide it. We learn that if we will not or cannot hide our shine, we will need some sort of strategy to deflect the attention that will come our way. Women know a quiet demeanour or an accomplished husband or a respected father are powerful tools with which to face the world because they allow us entry into polite society.

As a woman, you can't always resist being made invisible. So, you learn to be legible; to be understood not simply as a woman standing on your own two feet, but as a woman whose worth derives from those who can vouch for her. The colleague who can say, 'Oh, she's really nice.' The relatives who can provide assurances: 'She's very humble. She doesn't use her education to act as though she's better than others.'

Women who have no such ties, and who refuse to kowtow to convention, are worse than dangerous: they are disposable. I had never accepted that I was playing any sort of game of legibility, so I did not know my position was precarious until I stumbled.

Still, this is not a story about being overpowered by colleagues who may or may not have had it in for me because I was a woman and I was young. I certainly felt battered and bruised for these reasons at different points in my tenure there, and have no doubt that things may have gone down slightly differently had I been a man, but that is not the most important part of this story, if only because that is a story we all know too well. It is also a story that allows me to hide from my own errors – to point outwards without looking at myself. It is a story that says privilege is flat and black women are only ever victims – never themselves holders of power. It is a story that denies the ways in which power intersects and operates in ways that can simultaneously advantage and disadvantage all of us.

This story is more complicated, because it reminds us that, when you have the safety net of class in a world that is largely poor, you get to lose your innocence without losing your life. You get to fall forward because there are many strong and powerful arms waiting to pick you up and set you right again.

◆ ◆ ◆

We spend the rest of our time in New Haven regrouping. Simon picks up my pieces and sticks them back on where they fit. He holds me together. Our closest friends from Johannesburg come to visit: Gael with her beautiful black hair into which I cry and cry and cry as we walk around Mystic, and Richard with his sturdy arms around me in a tight hug that says he still believes in me.

The four of us spend a weekend together drinking too much. It does wonders for me. It is an affirmation, a reminder that work is not everything, even if I have always staked my self-esteem on it. As they leave, already I am feeling better. I am still tender, yes, but gradually feel less and less raw.

A few weeks later, Simon and I go out to dinner without the kids. It is a cool October evening and we walk hand in hand, talking about nothing in particular and everything that matters, bumping shoulders and feeling as though we are a single organism. The recent turmoil has made us closer.

It is dark and the street is empty and someone walks up behind us. We hear the footsteps and we don't even turn. He hurries past us and we are not afraid. We both note the ordinariness of that moment and the act of not flinching at the approach of a stranger in the dark. Simon says this is our cue. It's time to leave South Africa. I agree with him. From a distance, far away in a safe little Ivy League town where the rough side of town never penetrates the perimeter of the campus, it feels like the right thing to do. I say yes immediately this time.

Our decision is helped along by a set of circumstances that are particular to us: Simon's parents getting older, Gabi and Nick soon finishing their studies and us wanting to be more flexible for them, and my no longer having a job that holds me down.

Until now, the hardwiring of a childhood spent in a nomadic trek from one country to the next has kept asserting itself, preventing me from committing. I have hated the idea of giving up on South Africa. Simon scoffs at the idea.

'You're not giving up, you're following your husband. Why does everything have to be cast as a political discussion in South Africa? Why does this have to be about some grand statement? We can try something new, in my patch of the world, without loading all this meaning onto things.'

He is right of course. He is speaking without being shackled by history; I didn't think I had that luxury. So, despite what he says, my heart reneges on my promise to him. In the weeks after that conversation I don't tell him about my doubts, even as they multiply.

I feel torn between the man I love and the country I can't bear to leave. I know he wants to go – to be closer to Gabi and Nick and his parents, to stop the gnawing feeling in the pit of his stomach every time he pulls into the driveway. I know I should feel the same. The violence that threatened to take S should have shaken me to the core, certainly enough to make me want to leave – to make me want to save her.

And so I am stuck between the guilt of a mother whose instinct for her child's survival seems faulty, and the pain of a child whose most prized possession is about to be snatched out of her hands.

Finally, after weeks of acting like I am still there in the grips of that moment of clarity we hit upon as we walked home from our date, I tell him the truth. The ambivalence is back. We whisper so the kids don't hear us argue. 'I am not prevaricating,' I say. 'I'm just reconsidering.' He smiles at my wordsmanship, but he is not amused. I can see that my love affair with South Africa is tiring. When he fell in love with me, he had not seen that I would feel the pull towards what was in essence an abstract idea, a geography that could not hold me or touch me or kiss me and yet somehow managed to fulfil me. He had not yet seen the hold it had on me, how I would cry at the idea of not living there, how I would pine for it, how I would go back even when it made no sense to do so.

It doesn't matter, though. He sees now. And so, with every ounce of the kindness that made me fall in love with him, he says, 'Okay.'

In the coming weeks I realise Simon's okay doesn't really signal a yes. There is a little patch of land we bought a few years ago in Mozambique and suddenly it is all he will talk about. Simon is a man of action. So, as we prepare to settle back in South Africa, he begins to put a plan in place for us to leave again. He knows that, if it is left to me, we will never leave.

Why I write

ON 16 AUGUST 2012, in a small town called Marikana in South Africa's dry, rusty platinum belt, the South African Police Service opened fire on a crowd of striking mineworkers. We were in America when this happened. I watched the video footage online in horror. Thirty-four mineworkers were killed and seventy-eight were wounded.

In the aftermath, once the bodies had been counted and the relatives had been informed, the police claimed their officers had been under attack. The fact that the miners were armed only with handheld traditional weapons while the police had assault rifles didn't seem to matter much.

In the months after the massacre, the government offered no apology. The massacre represented the most serious incident of police brutality since the fall of apartheid. Still, our leaders said the police had done what was necessary. Our president had looked hapless.

No one was fired. Nobody said sorry.

Instead, the ANC leaders blamed the miners. The party even boycotted the funerals. It turned its back on the mourning widows of dead men from distant rural villages and, in so doing, turned its back on its own history and that of the most important and vulnerable of its constituents.

The nation's clergy prayed in earnest. They prayed for the dead but they prayed for the living as well. They asked God to forgive those who had perpetrated the crimes. It seems these intercessions were insufficient.

The government continued to deny responsibility for its murders. A commission of inquiry, the Farlam Commission, was set up, but it was a sham. It was established to quash the questions of outraged citizens, and was never about accountability. At times, it appeared to be a satire, just like the TRC: everyone knows the truth but the only people prepared to tell it are the victims.

The South Africa to which we return in early 2013 is different from the one we left. Marikana hangs like a spectre over our politics. It feels eerily similar to the Mbeki years. Once again, the bitterness and the meanness and the arrogance of the ANC are on full display.

This time, the ANC doesn't only have the blood of the sick and the dying on its hands, but also of the healthy and strong. There were the bullets and bodies, beamed across the world. There was the devastating vulnerability of the black bodies for all to see. They lay strewn – arms and legs akimbo in heartbreaking stillness – and if you didn't see them it was because you chose to look away.

The bond of trust between citizen and leader – what was left of it, anyway, after the brutalising Mbeki years – is broken.

In the wake of Marikana, living in South Africa is like living in a haunted house. There are ghosts everywhere and they seem to be gathering force. They are no longer mournful either. No, this time the dead are angry and their spirits are shrieking. It is as though they are preparing to send a war party to those who authored their destruction. Those of us left standing can only wait to see what forces will be unleashed.

It is tempting to see Julius Malema – the fiery young politician who is filled with rage – as the product of their fury. For years, the young man from Seshego has been in the public eye. A badly behaved misogynist, a tiny tyrant, his rise seems to represent everything that is rotten in the ANC: the flaunting of wealth from questionable sources, the culture of moral impunity and a growing intolerance for debate and dialogue.

If I were more spiritually inclined, I might put forward the idea that Malema's turning, his decision to leave the ANC and become a man of the people again, was the work of the spirits.

In the months after Marikana, no one is as blistering and as articulate about the damage that has been done to us collectively, to the psyche of the nation and to the soul of South Africa, as Julius Malema. I watch and I listen as he channels the rage many of us feel. He says many of the things that have needed to be said about the leadership of the ANC.

I admire Malema in spite of myself. While I am vocal at home about my disgust for the ANC, I have not yet nailed my colours to the mast. The ANC is not just a party, it is home. I have not attended an ANC meeting for years, and I stopped paying my monthly dues a long time ago, but still, I consider the ANC to be in my blood. My great-granduncles Richard and Selby were founding members. My father was in MK. I was born in exile. I am ANC through and through. This is the story I have told myself about my obligation and commitment to the party. But as its politics worsens, I begin to understand that I must stop this language. The ANC is not in my blood, it is in my memory. There is a paternalism built into the way I talk about the ANC that is designed to silence me. There is no genetic code that makes me more or less ANC than others. There is nothing inheritable about ANC membership: I am not a princess.

I realise the claim of being a child of the ANC is one that is bursting with prestige; it is a profound form of entitlement. Buying into it at any level makes the views of others less important. I am guilty of the very cronyism I abhor in the leadership of the ANC. This insight does not come to me at once. Yet in the aftermath of Marikana, as my revulsion towards the ANC grows, I begin to see that stepping away from the 'child of' language is allowing me to accept the truth. I am a grown woman and I am not beholden to the ANC. I am a citizen of a country I love – and that perhaps is a function of having been raised by people who believe in the principles of equity and justice. The fact of my citizenship, the security that comes with my legal status, which guarantees me a place in this country, obliges me to take my responsibility to democracy seriously. If Julius – who said he would kill and die for Zuma – can break ranks and leave home, then, I realise, so can I. In fact, I *must*.

◆ ◆ ◆

Leaving – breaking ranks, saying goodbye to the ANC, moving away from my need to be in South Africa as a geographic space – is a process. It begins with writing. Leaving begins when I pick up my pen.

A few weeks after our return from Yale, I meet up for a coffee with Branko Brkic. Branko is the editor of a start-up, upstart publication called the *Daily Maverick*; an online newspaper that does real analysis. Too much analysis, sometimes. Still, it is on the pulse of the politics of the new South Africa. It has a small but influential readership, and is growing every day.

Branko is a gruff-looking Serbian who has seen the ugly side of politics in the Eastern bloc. We are introduced by Richard, who insists that I write now that I no longer have the excuse of my job holding me back from sharing my opinions. Branko agrees. He has no idea whether I'll be any good, but he is running an operation that needs content, particularly from black writers.

'Can I have your first column by Wednesday?' he asks. Welcome to the family.

And just like that, I have a gig. It doesn't pay, but that's okay. I'm just looking for a platform.

I have no employer, so the only agenda I want to push is my own. I am an African feminist, a meddlesome social justice type – in spite of the ways I have fallen short in my own home. I see very few other women on the opinion pages of our major papers, and even fewer writing about civil society, about the issues that affect people's daily lives: violence and water and sanitation. Very few writers tell stories about people rather than politics. So, I tell myself, this is why I am writing: to fill a gap. I say to myself, there aren't enough women's voices in the media, so I am writing, in a sense, for the sisterhood.

This isn't the whole truth. I am also doing it for my

ego, for the thrill of seeing my name in print. I am doing it to stake out a distinct space for myself in the public arena. And yes, I want to do something with that space. I'm interested in it not for its own sake, but for the sake of elevating certain ideas, talking about issues I think matter. In the last decade I have come to believe politics is dirty. Somehow, though, the media seems less sullied – more suited to the life of the mind and to mapping out a future – than politics seemed to be.

I make many mistakes at first – awful grammatical errors and misspellings because I don't realise I am on my own and, short of a quick sub edit, there will be no support team. I am not a journalist. My experience has been in the civic sector, not in the newsroom. I have this fantasy of what a newsroom looks like and the sorts of resources available to writers. The reality is far less glamorous.

It doesn't matter, though. The Maverick team gives me carte blanche to write what I want and they give me no pointers or tips about how to do that – it's my business. They don't interfere or give me orders. I write what I like.

Neither Branko nor Styli (his trusty sidekick) ever rejects anything I submit. Indeed, when I am threatened with defamation by RW Johnson – who takes offence to a satirical piece in which I imply that he is a racist (because I believe him to be one) – Branko and Styli get their lawyers out and defend me as part of the fold.

I write about feminism and race and the faultlines of South Africa. At first, I find this difficult to manage. The trolls upset me. After a while, getting upset seems like a waste of time. Then I figure out the game and realise the trolls help me. Their arguments are sometimes useful they provide me with handles, with layers of discussion worth having.

Beyond this, I begin to recognise that their venom has little to do with my ideas and everything to do with the very idea of me – with my opinionated, middle-class persona. It becomes clear that, no matter what I write and how well I express myself, I will not be beyond reproach. I am writing in an era in which reproach is the entire point of the game – without it, the writer loses currency. So, I begin to write into the hostility and outrage of readers who don't want me to have opinions, the ones who look at my picture and are angered by it, the ones who patronise me.

This sort of writing is satisfying on one level, but ultimately hollow. It's like a sugar hit. There is a rush, but the hunger pangs don't go away. Then I begin to understand that the real well, for me, is a place of deep anger; that my best and most thoughtful columns are those that navigate the contours of betrayal. I am writing to manage my hurt.

I have been hurt by the betrayals of the ANC. I am writing because I don't know what to do with how I feel about myself and South Africa and the political movement I once loved. I write because the longer I live in South Africa, the more evident it is that my country is a father who can never return my love. I love this place so deeply yet I am not of it so there is always a level of superficiality in what I can know in my bones about this place. I am the observer – the outsider who can see precisely because she stands apart.

Understanding this helps me to write my way into being stronger and clearer and kinder to myself for my distance. I write my way into forgiving myself for not being able to become the ultimate insider. I write from where I am, rather than where I want to be. So my columns become essays. I write from a place of questioning and heartbreak. Everyone says to watch the word count, but when you don't care any more about sounding authoritative, rules like that matter less. I write the way I am. I write as a woman who has travelled and is confident and sometimes vulnerable and disappointed and often unapologetic and angry because, really, this is the stuff of life. I write into an embrace of the criticism I get every week online. I lean into the troll hate and I begin to write against being called a bitch and a cunt and I refuse to let any of it cut me down. I write because of who I am and I write in spite of everything that makes me afraid.

When you write in this modern age for the public, when you write and you look like me and believe – as I do – that you are as good as anyone else, then you draw all the venom and all the hatred and you can either let it poison you or can drink it as the goddesses drank ambrosia.

At first I wrote for the clicks and the attention but that soon passed. I began to write for posterity. So that S might know me differently. So that E might boast to his friends one day and say about his mother, 'She was a writer.'

At first I wrote to make Mummy and Baba proud, so I also wrote, I guess, out of a certain sentimental yes-we-canness.

I write, now, for slightly different reasons.

I write because I am an African woman who is literate and there is no diminishing what this means in a context in which so many others cannot.

I write to escape my children and to find my peace with them. I write, sometimes, just to hear them say, 'Are you still writing a book? How many pages in it, Mama?'

I write because Africans and women and humans

who have been considered less than others have always had stories and imaginations to take us out of the impossibility of the situations in which we have found ourselves stranded.

I write because Simphiwe Dana sings and because Brenda Fassie is dead. In the face of the certainty of death, what else can I do? Where else can I go but the page when I am overcome by the knowledge that yesterday's songs were sung by women who died because they worked too much and lived in a world that was too hard and yet their melodies were so soft?

What else can I do but write when I know life is not just breath, it is also voice? I write because I cannot paint and I cannot sing. Words are my brush and my warbled song. I have written in the margins of every book I have ever loved, so I write because I read. I write because I am black – that peculiar word that is more than the brown of my skin. Black is a solid mass of many shades that stand together facing the future; it is a hole. Black is an equation defying even Einstein's brilliance, even as it is nothing, not a thing at all.

I write for myself because women seldom have spaces for themselves and writing is space; it takes up space, it creates space, it gives me space. I write because writing is solitary and women are seldom alone with just their thoughts – their responsibilities intrude. There is this to be done and that to be paid for and those moments when it is just you and your words are rare and all the more beautiful because of it.

I write because South Africa was liberated and she is not yet free. I write because I have been let down and sometimes I write because I do not know the answer and I am hoping someone might search with me.

I write because when I was in high school Baba marked

up my essays with a red pen.

I write because Mummy taught me how to spell, just like she taught me the only true thing that counts, which is that you are always only one breath away from death.

I write because – as Nikki Giovanni said about love – there is nothing for me, but to write.

Mothers and daughters

MUMMY DOESN'T ALWAYS agree with everything I write. She is pragmatic and unsure how all this public rabble-rousing will do anything but provoke retribution. I am as idealistic as ever. I believe it makes a difference. It is absurd to think my speaking out will have any negative consequences but I have always been an idealist and Mummy has always been correct about most things. We spar gently. We rarely fight directly. It is not in the nature of our dynamic to do this. Mummy has a strong sense of decorum. She thinks it is unbecoming to argue and fight. Yet she believes in telling the truth. So, we work out a system. Now that we are all grown, we revisit the rules.

As the ANC falls apart, and as South Africa becomes politically unsettling, we find our stride as a family of adults.

Mummy and Baba are still part of our daily lives. We are like five fingers on a hand – separate but deeply connected. Mummy and Baba have moved out from under the shadows of the Menlyn Park mall. Their house sits on a big plot of land halfway between Pretoria and Johannesburg. The property used to be owned by a vet. The vet and his family emigrated and Mummy and Baba bought the place.

It has stables and a long driveway and the whole neighbourhood is full of horses and quiet privilege.

We are all doing well. Mandla is working – making her mark in telecommunications. Zeng has finished university and is making a go of events management and conferencing. Simon and I are married and the kids have been born and we are busy with our travels. We see each other on most weekends. Mummy and I speak on the phone every day. Mandla and Zeng and I speak on the phone every day. Mummy talks to the Mandla and Zeng every day. The three of us talk to Baba every few days. Mummy of course talks to him all day, every day – phoning him to remind him of this or that.

It's as though cell phones were invented for our family.

If I am angry at Mummy, I call Mandla to tell her. Mandla calls Mummy to tell her, 'Sonke is upset. You better call her.'

If Mandla is angry with Zeng she lets me know. She says something like, 'Your sister is so wack.' (We love the word 'wack' because somehow in our teens it found its way into Mummy's vocabulary and the incongruence of it – the hip-hop-infected slang of it – coming out of her mouth is hilarious. After a while it just becomes habit. We use it well past its sell-by date.)

'Why is she wack?' I ask, putting on Mummy's voice to lighten the mood.

'She always does this. I'm sick of her always coming to me at the last minute with this stuff.'

I call Zeng.

'Your sister is mad at you. She said you're wack. You better call her.'

This system works. We aren't simply a telephone exchange, though. We are one another's intermediaries and sounding boards. Our conversations sometimes require that we take sides. The one who gets the call can always push back.

'Yes, she is last-minute, but you also never take her into account.

You know this is going to happen. Why not plan for it?'

Or: 'But aren't you the one who told her to call you if she needed a ride? Don't say it if you don't mean it, babes. Stop offering if you know it bugs you.'

We are a web of conversations, an intricate pattern of strings held together by love and loyalty. Mummy has opted to pick up a new instrument as she gets older. She is no longer the conductor. She has taken her place alongside us. We do not notice at first, that she is no longer at the front. That she is sitting beside us.

We are an imperfect quartet.

We love Baba very much. He is not like us though, because he is a man. Our allegiance tilts slightly, so that we hold her more closely and let him go a little bit. He is the best man we know but we no longer need to adore him. Now we are women and not simply daughters so we have begun to see the ways in which Mummy needs us now. It has been hard for her to be strong for so long without knowing when she might be loved back rather than simply needed. It is her time to need. She needs our eyes to shine when we look at her. She needs to know we see her for who she has always been. She does not tell us any of this but somehow we begin to know it quietly and without discussion.

The end

'Lost really has two disparate meanings. Losing things is about the familiar falling away, getting lost is about the unfamiliar appearing. There are objects and people that disappear from your sight or knowledge or possession; you lose a bracelet, a friend, the key. You still know where you are. Everything is familiar except that there is one item less, one missing element. Or you get lost, in which case the world has become larger than your knowledge of it.'
– Rebecca Solnit, *A Field Guide to Getting Lost*

ON A HOLIDAY in 2011, just after E was born, we decided to buy a small piece of land in Mozambique. We thought we'd build a vacation house on it, and use it for family holidays. It is in Inhambane, which is either a short flight or a long drive from Joburg.

After our return from the US, Simon begins to put in place a plan for swapping our hectic lives in Joburg for more and better time together. The kids are growing up quickly. Joburg has him spooked and I no longer have the job to hide behind. We can work from anywhere.

So, in January of 2014, after months of planning, we move to Inhambane. Inhambane is a small town in southern Mozambique. Mozambique is not without its complications. With its long independence struggle and a bitter civil war that was prolonged and exacerbated by the apartheid government's support for Renamo, Mozambique is a complex place. Still, it is somewhere else, a place where we can feel that the problems – the poverty and hunger, the political dramas – aren't ours.

For South Africans Mozambique is easy. In Mozambique there are easy smiles and there is the appearance of a *que sera, sera* attitude towards race relations. As a consequence, many white South Africans think of it as a paradise where the black people aren't aggressive and angry about racism. At the same time, a small but growing number of black South Africans of means see it as a warm getaway. In Mozambique the rand takes you far. During school holidays and over the festive season, cars with Gauteng licence plates overwhelm the town. There are quad bikes and loud voices and bad South African beer everywhere. In the off-season, though, Inhambane is quiet and simple. The boats go out at five in the morning and the catch of the day is spread out on sandy market tables by nine.

I have lined up a few consultancy contracts and we have found a sweet school for the kids, and a builder to begin to put up the house. We have enlisted JP to design something for us. We don't know how long we will stay but Mozambique represents a happy compromise. Simon has the beach and a chance to be free of the pace and jitters of Joburg. I ostensibly have enough distance from South Africa and its politics to focus on him and the kids. To say I have been a distracted mother since becoming a writer is an understatement. I am on the computer, writing, or on the phone, talking about politics, or on the radio, being interviewed, or at seminars, talking about what I think about the state of the nation.

The Daily Maverick column has led to more columns. One of those columns leads to an invitation to a television show and on social media the comment goes viral. Suddenly I am seen as a writer. People read my words and think about what I am saying – even if it is only to dismiss or contradict me. My love affair with South Africa has deepened. The country feels toxic, yet I'm obsessed with it. I swing between depression and euphoria.

So, by the time we escape to paradise, Simon is at his wits' end with me. I understand at an intellectual level that I need to unplug, to focus on the kids and Simon and not on the state of the nation. But in my heart I am just grateful Inhambane is so close. It's a fortyfive-minute plane ride and there is a daily flight.

Mummy is not happy about the move. She understands our need to be together as a family on a beach in a far-flung place. She also sees my ambivalence about leaving South Africa and Simon's lack of equivocation and she worries about the rift this might cause. We want such different things.

She knows too that the only way to resolve it is to test it out – to step away from the city that is pushing Simon away, the city I love. She doesn't say it, but I can see the wheels turning. She has always been our biggest supporter. In part this is because she has become the respectable mother who wants her enviably married daughter to be happy. But it is also because she loves Simon. She loves him for his kindness, for the moderating influence he has on me. Mummy knows that leaving will prove to both of us that I love him more than the country of my heart.

On the day we leave, Mummy is emotional. She does not cry but her eyes are full of feeling. As Simon loads the last items into the car, she is already talking about her and Baba's first visit. As we get in the car she says, 'Take care of my children.'

'Of course, Mummy,' I say.

We both pretend that she's not sad.

The kids will miss her. They have become used to her unannounced arrivals and her insistence on swooping in on Friday afternoons and taking them from us for the weekend. I will miss her too: especially her hawkishness. Who will cast a stern eye on everyone who comes into contact with S and E? Who will be suspicious on my behalf, allowing me to be the big-hearted naive madam? I will even miss her unsolicited advice.

I know she will be there to visit in a few weeks. She'll never leave us alone. Still, I mark the moment, knowing what we must look like. We are mirror images of one another: mother and daughter with the same face, holding their heads in the same way, both pretending to be fine.

To know your mother as an adult is to finally see that she has lived many more years as a woman than you have been alive. To be a grown woman who loves her mother is to understand that it is no easy thing to raise children so beautifully that they don't worry about you until they are grown up and ready to carry the complex burden of that anxiety.

I was not a child who took care of her mother, although I have realised that some do, from a very young age. Some children learn to worry about their mother's health and they know how to soothe their tempers and gauge their moods, because their mothers are volatile or inconsistent or not fully ready to be mothers even though their children have arrived. I had the good fortune not to have to worry about Mummy until I was a fully grown woman and even then it was only for short periods. She was never sick, never broke, never heartbroken enough to warrant needing me. She was her own even as she was fully mine.

As a girl I sometimes had an inkling of this other being when I watched her with her friends. I got this sense that she was a full human and would have been one with or without me. That feeling was fleeting, though. I would get a sense of it sometimes as I stood at the kitchen door waiting for her to notice me so I could ask her permission to let some girls come upstairs to our bedroom, or to get more cool drinks for the kids in the back, or whatever it was I needed. In those moments before she noticed me I would see her – just briefly – as a woman who was someone else as well, someone who was more than simply my mother.

Or she would be drinking wine and laughing until tears ran, making jokes I couldn't understand, and she would look like somebody free, someone who wasn't tied down to three little hearts bound in skinny ribcages. She didn't look at all like a woman who had planted three umbilical cords beneath the forests of Mbuluzi. You couldn't tell she was a woman who had once slipped on ice on an Ottawa street and picked herself up and kept walking. Still, you'd sense she was the sort of woman who loved herself enough to turn her back on everything known and safe.

◆ ◆ ◆

Five months later Mummy died. Her departure was abrupt – too sudden to comprehend, even now.

We happened to be in Johannesburg visiting when she died. We were staying at home with her and Baba in the house where we married and where Mandla was married too. The house where S and E had walked with her too many times to count – down the long path to the chicken coop to fetch eggs for breakfast in the morning with the dogs wagging their tails and the neighbours waving. We were all in that house when it happened. We were all there yet she left us as if we didn't even exist, as if we weren't there, visiting her.

It was school holidays and even though Mummy and Baba were with us in Inhambane just a week before, we were with them again. The babies were asleep in one bedroom and Simon and I were in another. All of us were upstairs behind the security gate at the top of the stairs and behind the burglar bars on the windows – safe from harm.

Baba came into our bedroom tentatively and woke me. He told me he was worried that Mummy was not rousing and she had been in the tub too long.

I padded over to the bathtub and then got Simon because surely he could do something but it was too late. The night was a blur of emergency calls and Simon on his knees in the bathroom giving her CPR and the sound of his breath pumping into and out of her mouth. The paramedics arrived and they tried too, even though they could tell that it was too late.

They noted the time. The zipper bag went down the stairs. Zeng arrived as they left and she kissed her. I had no such courage. I stayed upstairs clutching the over-night bag I had packed when we thought the CPR might work. I called Mandla. She was in Cairo on a work trip. She screamed at me and told me to stop talking – she didn't want to listen any more so she just kept saying stop. I repeated it. 'Mummy's gone.' She screamed again. 'What do you mean? Sonk? Sonk?' She kept saying my name like that and I stopped talking. I couldn't talk. Then I found my voice again and I told her to come home.

Afterwards – for weeks – I couldn't stop the blood from pounding in my belly. There was a pinpoint in my navel and it was there for weeks and then months and even now. I smiled so that the kids wouldn't fall apart. They were so confused. S was a little rag doll and some-times I wondered if she could ever be right again. Simon held us all in his arms even though he loved her so very much and his heart was also broken.

In her goneness the choices before us were even stark-er. She was our children's biggest advocate, morbidly ob-sessed with their survival. Suddenly, 'Go!' was scrawled across every wall in my parents' house; it hissed at me in every room she occupied. 'Go.' And so we did.

Simon was ready and I finally accepted that, given everything that had happened – the betrayal and the sadness and Mummy's no-longerness – I would rather be homesick than home. Without her, I was free to be-long wherever it was that I happened to be and so, finally – finally – we left.

◆ ◆ ◆

When Mummy died I felt a profound sense of loss. I also became profoundly lost. I was – as Rebecca Solnit describes it – both 'missing [an] element' and in entirely new terrain. I was suddenly aware that the world was 'larger than [my] knowledge of it'. In many ways perhaps more than lost, I felt homeless. I did not know where to go to feel at home. Our house felt haunted, no longer there for any particular purpose except as a meeting place for the grieving. There was nowhere on Earth I could go where I might find her so I felt that, quite abruptly, I had gone from knowing who I was and where I was going to belonging to no one and knowing nothing. When she died I lost the surest home I ever had. Her death helped me to understand I had always had a home, even as I was searching for a country.

Mummy was the best kind of role model for how to be a partner who is both in love and able to love herself. The three of us girls often teased her about her 'boyfriend,' Baba. They loved each other deeply over a span of forty-two years. They had their troubles but they drew close when it was necessary and they knew how to let each other be. The enduring memory of my childhood is of hearing them waking up in the morning and turning on the old Grundig radio. Three short sharp beeps. Then: 'This is the BBC World Service.' Then I would hear their voices murmuring, the sounds of them running the bath and talking and laughing. It seemed they never ran out of words for each other. They were making plans and talking and laughing until the very end.

I still had Mandla and Zeng and Baba and Simon and the kids, so I had love. But it was not that I felt unloved – it was that I was suddenly unmothered. I felt strangely homesick. I was lonely without Mummy. I had no one to ask, 'What should I do?'

I am still that way. I miss her most when things are hard. I miss her too when I have done something wonderful and I know she would be proud. I miss her when I am bored. I miss her all the time and the missing will not stop.

Until her death I believed that geography and belonging were intertwined. I had this idea that who you were was tied to where you came from. I envied people who had grown up in a particular house on a certain street in a single town. I wanted to be anchored like those who only leave a place when they are old enough to go of their own volition. I was jealous.

I thought that where people were from inevitably wound its way into who they ultimately became, and so, because I had never had a spatial connection to the place I called home, I always longed for a physical address. Instead, I grew up with a succession of PO boxes, staying for long enough to know my way around but never long enough to know any place with depth.

Mummy suffered no such worries about her sense of place. She was always able to make herself at home. Wherever she was, she made things work. Somewhere along the way she figured out that, for her freedom-fighter husband and the girls she had borne in exile, freedom wasn't simply about the end goal. She knew that the journey itself was freedom.

In her own quiet and steady way, Mummy spent her whole life teaching us that it was having a map, rather than belonging to a country, that would make us free; that it was those we loved, and not where we lived, that would make us belong, and that it was open hearts, rather than closed fists, that would help us navigate the world.

For this I owe her everything. She – and Baba who found her because he left South Africa in search of freedom – bequeathed to me everything in me that is restless and questing and that wants to go further than someone like me ought to want to go. They were, perhaps, the wisest cartographers who ever lived: they managed to circumnavigate the globe without once losing sight of home.

Acknowledgements

THANK YOU TO all those who read various drafts, especially Richard Lee who got me believing I could make a go of writing. Thank you to Zeng, Panashe, Richard Pithouse, Gabi and Eusebius for your generous and extensive comments. Thank you to Bibi and Zukiswa for giving me inspiration and courage. Thank you to Howard Willis, without whom this version of the book would not have been possible, and to Tim for being a steady voice when I was feeling shaky. Thanks to Caroline and John Wood for giving me a (flexible) space and place where I feel welcome and valued at the Centre for Stories. To Ester, thank you for believing in this book before there was even a manuscript. Isobel, your demure badassness constitutes a life goal for me. Thank you for everything. Thank you Branko and Styli for giving me a start. Thanks Gen for accompanying me, for making me think harder and be smarter.

Thank you Gael for your strength and wisdom and accompaniment. Thank you to everyone who animates these pages – the friends and cousins and aunties and uncles and colleagues without whom there would be no stories at all.

A special thank you to Mummy and Daddy. Your contribution to my life and my values is immeasurable. I could not do it justice here and perhaps I will have to write another book about your lives and your wonderful journey. Lindi and Dumi, my big sister and brother who taught me to see the world through bigger eyes, you are in me and with me all the time and your presence through everything has been everything.

Mandla and Zeng, you are my world. You inspire me and make me work harder to impress you. This book is also for you and for your brood of girls and their father Siya.

A special thank you to Baba for instilling in me the discipline and rigour required not simply to write, but to revise and to edit. And whose belief in and respect for me has allowed me to soar. This book is for you too.

Lastly, and most importantly, I owe my biggest debt to you, Simon. This book would not exist were it not for you; were it not for your faith, your love and your determination. You make me a better version of myself than I would have been had we not met. You are the best and daggiest mate I could ever want. Most of all, thank you for bringing me Gabi and Nick and S and E, whom I love with all my heart.

Photo Credits

All photographs except those listed below are from the author's personal collection and are used with permission.

The photographs on pages 13, 140 and 232 were taken by Max Bastard.

The photograph on page 165 is from "Macalester Today" Paper 33 http://digitalcommons.macalester.edu/macalestertoday/33 © Jean Pieri/Pioneer Press.

The photograph on page 193 © Ulli Michel/Reuters.

The photograph on page 206 © Peter Turnley/Corbis/VCG via Getty Images.

The photograph on page 270 © Kerry Cullinan/Health-e.

Lyrics on page 144 from the song 'Mona Lisa' by Ray Evans and Jay Livingston reprinted with the permission of Sony/ATV Music Publishing.

The chapter 'Amakwerekwere' in part draws on an essay titled 'Belonging – Why South Africans refuse to let Africa in', originally published by Africa is a Country, http://africasacountry.com/2014/04/belonging-why-south-africans-refuse-to-let-africa-in/.

Excerpts on pages 352 and 359 from *A Field Guide to Getting Lost* copyright © 2010 by Rebecca Solnit, reprinted with the permission of Penguin Random House/Viking as well as Canongate.

On the Design

As book design is an integral part of the reading experience, we would like to acknowledge the work of those who shaped the form in which the story is housed.

Tessa van der Waals (Netherlands) is responsible for the cover design, cover typography and art direction of all World Editions books. She works in the internationally renowned tradition of Dutch Design. Her bright and powerful visual aesthetic maintains a harmony between image and typography and captures the unique atmosphere of each book. She works closely with internationally celebrated photographers, artists, and letter designers. Her work has frequently been awarded prizes for Best Dutch Book Design.

The author pictures both on the cover and inside were taken by photographer Nick White (Australia).

The photograph on the cover has been edited by lithographer Bert van der Horst of BFC Graphics (Netherlands) to give it a colorful and bright character that brings out the lively feel of the narrative.

Suzan Beijer (Netherlands) is responsible for the typography and careful interior book design of all World Editions titles.

The text on the inside covers and the press quotes are set in Circular, designed by Laurenz Brunner (Switzerland) and published by Swiss type foundry Lineto.

All World Editions books are set in the typeface Dolly, specifically designed for book typography. Dolly creates a warm page image perfect for an enjoyable reading experience. This typeface is designed by Underware, a European collective formed by Bas Jacobs (Netherlands), Akiem Helmling (Germany), and Sami Kortemäki (Finland). Underware are also the creators of the World Editions logo, which meets the design requirement that 'a strong shape can always be drawn with a toe in the sand.'